TWO FACES OF PROTEST

TWO FACES OF PROTEST

Contrasting Modes of Women's Activism in India

AMRITA BASU

UNIVERSITY OF CALIFORNIA PRESS
BERKELEY LOS ANGELES OXFORD

University of California Press
Berkeley and Los Angeles, California

University of California Press, Ltd.
Oxford, England

Library of Congress Cataloging-in-Publication Data

Basu, Amrita.
Two faces of protest : contrasting modes of women's activism in India / Amrita Basu.
p. cm.
Revision of thesis (Ph.D.)—Columbia University.
Includes bibliographical references (p.) and index.
ISBN 0-520-06506-9 (cloth : alk. paper)
1. Women in politics—India. 2. Women political activists—India. 3. India—Politics and government—1947– 4. Right and left (Political science) I. Title.
HG1236.5.I4B37 1992
320.954'082—dc20 91-44884
CIP

Printed in the United States of America

9 8 7 6 5 4 3 2 1

The paper used in this publication meets the minimum requirements of American National Standard for Information Sciences—Permanence of Paper for Printed Library Materials, ANSI Z39.48-1984. ♾

For Rasil, Romen, Rekha, and Patwant

Contents

Acknowledgments

It is difficult to part with a book that bears the affection, support, and guidance of so many people. This book had its origins as a dissertation at Columbia University. My two principal advisors, Philip Oldenburg and Howard Wriggins, and the other members of my doctoral committee, Dennis Dalton, Ainslie Embree, and Joan Vincent, carefully read the manuscript and offered incisive advice and criticism. Bela and Nripendra Bandhopadhyaya, Dipankar and Dora Dasgupta, and Tarashish Mukhopadhyaya taught me much of what I know about Midnapur district and a great deal about West Bengal. Chaya Dattar, Nirmala Sathe, Vijay Kanhare, and above all Dinanath Manohar and Gail Omvedt not only helped me understand the Shramik Sangathana but also the larger theoretical issues that are central to this study. Several people provided research assistance, including Bela Bandhopadhyaya, Shreemati Chakrabarti, Manisha Desai, Sujata Gotaskar, and Hira Shinde.

For their instructive comments on this and other work, I am grateful to Radhika Coomaraswamy, Mary Katzenstein, and Atul Kohli. Colleagues in the departments of Political Science and Women's and Gender Studies at Amherst College, and my former colleagues George Kateb and Doris Sommer, have made teaching the most challenging form of learning. Lurline Dowell, who typed the original dissertation, has seen this project through to completion without ever losing her good cheer. Naomi Schneider and Pamela MacFarland Holway at the University of California Press skillfully supervised the book's publication.

In the course of my research I received support from the American

Institute of Indian Studies and the Karl Loewenstein fellowship at Amherst College. Pradip Mehndiratta could always be relied upon to smooth the way for my research in India. The Southern Asian Institute at Columbia University provided research facilities while I was on leave in New York in 1987. Thanks are also due to Sonia Kruks, Rayna Rapp, and Marilyn Young, the editors of *Promissory Notes: Women in the Transition to Socialism*, in which a portion of this book earlier appeared.

My family has contributed in rich and diverse ways. Rasil, Romen, Rekha, and Patwant, to whom this book is dedicated, have always provided encouragement, love, and understanding. Ann Kesselman's unquestioning acceptance continues to sustain me in her absence and provides a model to emulate. My children, Ishan and Javed, have increased my understanding of both the dilemmas and the rewards surrounding women's activism.

My gratitude to Mark is difficult to record. If (as I suspect) in a rare attempt to clean out his study Mark threw out my field notes from the second phase of my research in India, he added in exchange what no amount of research could: trenchant criticism, enthusiastic praise, and loving support. The book is incomparably better for his influence.

In the course of researching this book, I experienced the extraordinary generosity of women and men in Dhulia and Midnapur districts, who fed me, housed me, and spoke to me at length. Their questions about the purpose of my work and their comments about their own provided the most demanding of standards. Their struggles not only inform this book substantively but inspired me to write it.

A. B.
New Delhi
January 1992

Abbreviations

AIDWA	All-India Democratic Women's Association
AIKS	All-India Kisan Sabha (All-India Peasant Organization)
AIWC	All-India Women's Conference
CADP	Comprehensive Area Development Program [later: Corporation]
CITU	Centre for Industrial Trade Unions
CPI	Communist Party of India
CPI(M)	Communist Party of India (Marxist)
CPI(M-L)	Communist Party of India (Marxist-Leninist)
CWDS	Centre for Women's Development Studies
GSS	Gram Swarajya Samiti (Village Self-Government Organization)
IADP	Intensive Area Development Program
IRDP	Indian Rural Development Program
MARS	Mahila Atma Raksha Samiti (Women's Self-Defense League)
NFIW	National Federation of Indian Women
PBGMS	Paschim Bangla Ganatantrik Mahila Samiti (United Democratic Bengali Women's Organization)
PBMS	Paschim Bangla Mahila Samiti (United Bengali Women's Organization)

RDP	Rural Development Program
RSP	Revolutionary Socialist Party
SSMS	Shramik Stri Mukti Sangathana (Laboring Women's Liberation Organization)
SWAB	Social Welfare Advisory Board
SUC	Socialist Unity Centre

Part One

Political Strategy, Social Structure, and Political Economy

Chapter One

Introduction

Dhulia district, Maharashtra, August 1978: 300 women and 150 men have assembled to protest an assault on a female agricultural laborer. Several days earlier a landlord had beaten her until she was almost unconscious because she had reprimanded him for his abusive behavior. The woman's appeals to local police had been fruitless. When she then related the incident to some members of the Shramik Sangathana (Laborers' Organization), they persuaded her to speak with other villagers. On an appointed day a crowd of women gathered in front of the culprit's home, demanding that he justify his actions. When he was unable to do so, the women decided upon an appropriately degrading punishment. They seated him on a donkey, smeared his face with cow dung, garlanded his neck with sandals, and paraded him through the surrounding villages. In the evening they released him and returned to their villages.

Compare this with an incident the following year in Bankura district, West Bengal. During the summer of 1979, West Bengal experienced its worst drought in fifty years.[1] In June the Communist Party of India (Marxist) organized districtwide demonstrations to demand increased allotments of funds and grain from the central government. The CPI(M) women's organization, the Paschim Bangla Ganatantrik Mahila Samiti, sponsored a procession of one thousand women to encircle the offices of the Block Development Organization and the *panchayat* (rural self-governing body) in a subdivision of Bankura district. Lotika Moitra, the local secretary of the PBGMS, addressed the rally:

We demand that the government officially declare this block drought-stricken and release funds for relief rations and employment. We also demand equal wages for men and women; public, interest-free loans; free tiffins [light lunches] in the schools; creches [child care facilities] for working mothers; better irrigation facilities; reduced kerosene prices; and adult education for women.

We do not want any violence to break out. We realize that the Left Front government has been trying to help us. But we will encircle this building and remain here until our demands have been met.

Half an hour later Lotika Moitra emerged and informed the women that the *subapati* (head of the block-level *panchayat*) had agreed to their demands. A series of speeches by male party officials followed. Thc first speaker began:

We congratulate the *mahila samiti* [women's organization] for this gathering of over a thousand women. You women have shown a lot of courage in fighting alongside us. We need your support, for several political parties are spreading rumors about us. They say that we have done nothing to help the rural poor. . . . They have been campaigning for the elections in a situation of drought and scarcity. . . . Congress (I) protects hoarders and is responsible for famine. . . . The Jharkhand movement has been causing divisions between Hindus and tribals. This has not stopped us. We are still pursuing the democratic movement.

Come forward and save the people from the drought! Unite to wage the struggle! Rich, middle, and poor unite. When it comes to the drought, we are all equally affected!

The next speaker continued:

New Delhi controls all the resources of the country, and West Bengal is powerless. You must support our demands for greater autonomy from the center. . . . We were fooled in 1947 but we no longer are. We have learned to stand up.

As the contrasts between the two demonstrations indicate, protest has assumed widely divergent forms in contemporary India. In the first incident, villagers used direct action tactics, while in the second they relied primarily upon negotiation with government officials. After helping the victim communicate her grievances, Shramik Sangathana activists receded into the background. By contrast, CPI(M) leaders orchestrated the women's demonstration in Bankura district. In the Shramik Sangathana demonstration, women challenged sexual exploitation by a man of dominant-class status. By contrast, CPI(M) leaders directed their ire exclusively against the central government, thereby obscuring class and gender differences among their constituents. Although it is true that, as the one speaker remarked, the drought spared none, it did not affect men and women, or rich, middle, and poor peasants, equally. Women suffer more than men from food scarcity; the rural rich have larger food reserves and greater access to irrigation and drinking water than the poor.

However, with the passage of time the story of the Shramik Sangathana and the CPI(M)—as well as the task of its rendition—becomes a good deal more complicated than the straightforward contrast between the two demonstrations implies. Consider the following vignettes to supplement (though not supplant) the earlier anecdotes.

Dhulia district, January 1983: a group of women have congregated to discuss an allegation of sexual harassment. But this time the tone is weary, disillusioned; the accused man is not a Hindu landlord but a full-time Shramik Sangathana activist. Although many of the women doubt that he is in fact guilty, they are deeply disturbed by the way the Shramik Sangathana has handled the incident. Rather than allowing women to determine the course of action, the largely male Shramik Sangathana decided unilaterally to expel the accused activist. Nor does the sense of disillusionment end here: landlord repression of *adivasis* ("tribals") has increased, the Shramik Sangathana has become factionalized, and about half of its activists have joined the CPI(M).[2]

How could these two Shramik Sangathana demonstrations be separated merely by a space of five years? Perhaps one feature of the earlier demonstration should be brought into sharper relief: despite their prominent role in it, the demonstration was neither spontaneous nor directed by women; the influence of male activists was evident throughout. And perhaps the vocabulary of class and gender needs to be supplemented by that of ethnicity, for the women were *adivasis* and the landlord a Hindu.

Calcutta, West Bengal, January 1985: the Left Front returned to office in 1982 with stronger support than it enjoyed when it was first elected in 1977. However, three years later the tone is somber: the CPI(M) has organized a demonstration in a central *maidan* in Calcutta to decry the machinations of Congress (I) in precipitating "communal" violence.[3] Although the calls for unity and emphasis on

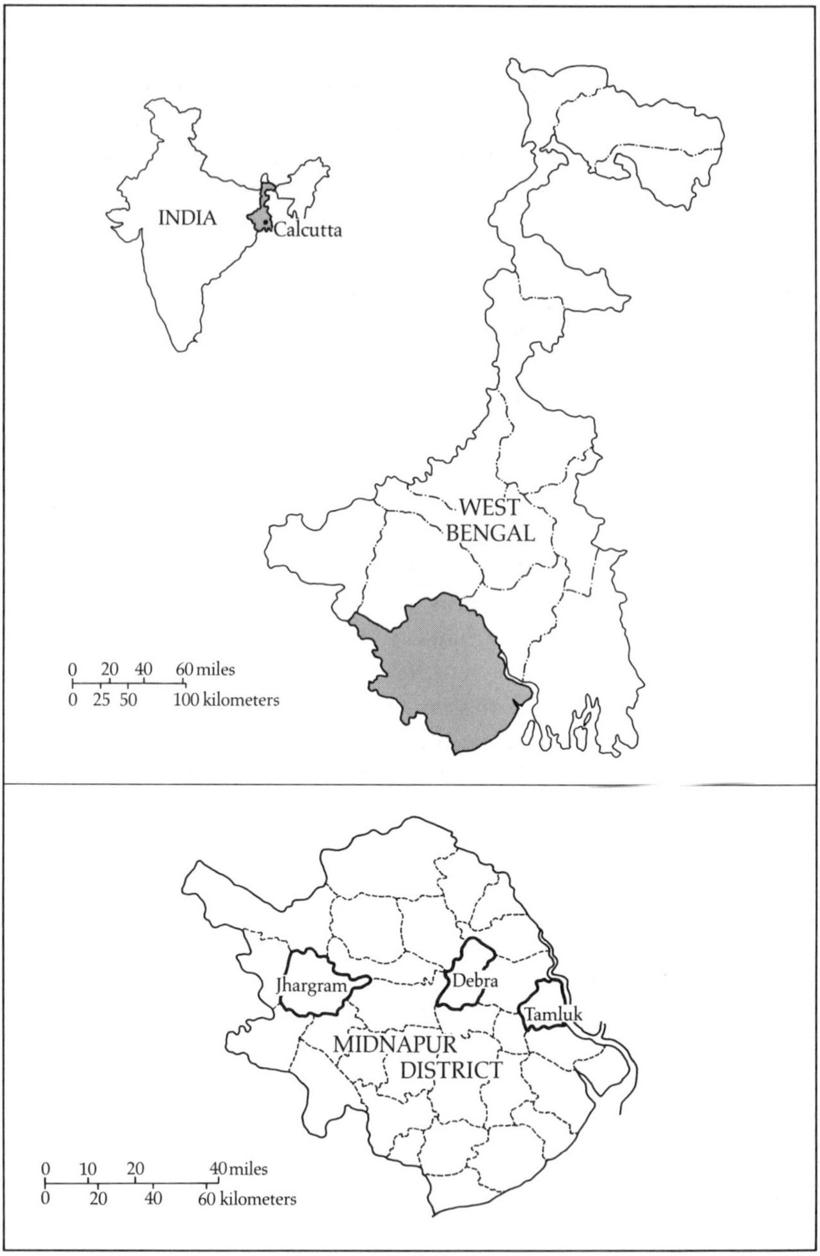

MAP 1. Midnapur District, West Bengal

Source: Census of India (1971). Series 22, West Bengal. Part 10-B. District Census Handbook, Midnapur. Directorate of Census Operations, West Bengal.

stability are familiar, their appeal is greater than in the past: in New Delhi, Kanpur, and elsewhere, Hindus have butchered thousands of Sikhs to avenge Indira Gandhi's assassination in 1984 by her Sikh bodyguards. But Sikhs are relatively safe in Calcutta. Perhaps even six years earlier, the CPI(M)'s admonitions against the Congress party in Bankura district were more than empty rhetoric.

This study compares two of the principal forms of leftist political activity in contemporary India: parliamentary communism, under CPI(M) leadership in West Bengal, particularly in Midnapur district; and grass-roots activism, exemplified well by the Shramik Sangathana in Dhulia district, Maharashtra. (See maps 1 and 2.) Other leftist alternatives have paled: the Socialist party abdicated its autonomous identity when it joined the Janata party, the Communist Party of India lost credibility when it supported the Congress government during the Emergency (1975–77), and the Communist Party of India (Marxist-Leninist) is highly factionalized and generally discredited. By contrast, the recent past marks a watershed in CPI(M) history: since 1977 it has dominated three consecutive left coalition governments in West Bengal. It has thereby outlived other elected opposition governments at state and national levels in India and communist governments in other parliamentary regimes. The Shramik Sangathana is one of the oldest among thousands of grass-roots organizations in India today; until recently it was among the strongest.

In the case of the CPI(M), I focus on the period since the Left Front government's election in 1977 so as to assess its approach to achieving social change both on the streets and through the corridors of power. With respect to the Shramik Sangathana, I focus on the period between 1972 and the mid 1980s, from its creation as a radical alternative to parliamentary communism to its fragmentation over the very question of its relationship to the CPI(M).

In 1979, when I began research for this study, the two organizations appeared to embrace wholly opposing strategies. The CPI(M) was committed to parliamentary reform, whereas the Shramik Sangathana disdained such reformism and instead engaged in grass-roots activism. The CPI(M) was active at the state and national levels, whereas the Shramik Sangathana confined itself to Dhulia's villages. The CPI(M)'s major base of constituents was small and medium landowners, whereas the Shramik Sangathana's was landless laborers.

Differences between women's consciousness and activism in the

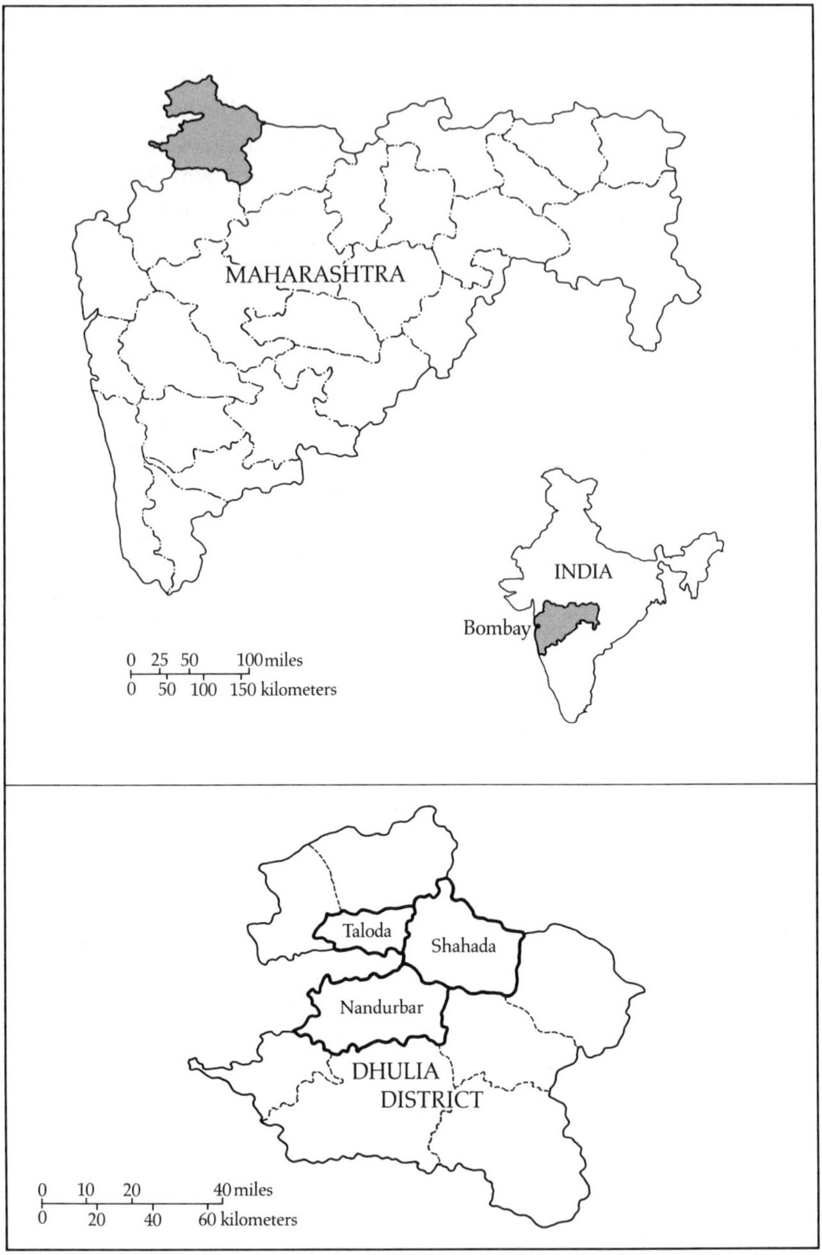

MAP 2. Dhulia District, Maharashtra

Source: District Census Handbook: Dhulia. Directorate of Census Operations, Census 1971. Series 11, Maharashtra.

two movements were especially striking. The PBGMS possessed little autonomy in relation to the CPI(M) and mainly involved women in so-called constructive activities. *Adivasi* women in Dhulia district, by contrast, were enlightening male Shramik Sangathana activists about the limits of their own emancipation and organizing struggles against male domination, initially independently and, after 1980, through their women's organization, the Shramik Stri Mukti Sangathana (SSMS), which was affiliated to the Shramik Sangathana. However, the crisis that later engulfed the Shramik Sangathana also laid bare the limits of the SSMS's autonomy. Today the comparison between the CPI(M) and Shramik Sangathana and their affiliated women's organizations reveals neither stark contrasts nor convergence. Rather it reveals the similar dilemmas that the most dissimilar leftist organizations encounter in widely divergent contexts.

What explains the greater militancy of the Shramik Sangathana? In particular, which aspects of their ideology, organization, and leadership are associated with their different understandings of class and gender inequality? To what extent are these strategies the products of different social and economic conditions in Maharashtra and West Bengal? By observing these strategies over time, what conclusions can be drawn about the relative merits of each approach, especially from the vantage point of women?

Before spelling out my argument, note the place of women and gender within this study. (The awkwardness of this caveat is itself symptomatic of the problem.) This study would certainly have been more coherent if it had focused exclusively either on women or on generic peasant movements. However, by shifting back and forth between women and (male-dominated) peasant movements I can best explore the tensions between what have traditionally been discrete areas both of enquiry and of activism.

In other words, I examine the CPI(M) and the Shramik Sangathana through the lens of women's experience. This vantage point not only grounds my judgments in some referent outside those employed by the activists themselves but also elucidates certain tensions within these movements. Thus the question of what constitutes a "progressive" measure becomes a good deal more complicated when gender is given serious consideration. To take an example, although land redistribution doubtless advances the interests of the male peasantry, it may actually widen gender inequalities if women do not receive land titles.

Contrasting Political Approaches

Which features of Shramik Sangathana and CPI(M) strategy help explain both the striking differences between them as well as the similar dilemmas they later experience?[4] Two among the many differences between them appear particularly significant: their organization and their stance on electoral participation. Despite the CPI(M)'s social democratic approach, it remains committed to the vanguard party and the tenets of democratic centralism. If cohesion is one benefit, a serious cost is the *bhadralok* (urban, educated, upper-caste) character of the Party. The PBGMS has no more autonomy vis-à-vis the CPI(M) than women have vis-à-vis the PBGMS.

By contrast, born of a critique of the "old Left," the Shramik Sangathana favored a nonparty, decentralized, democratic structure. Rejecting a largely middle-class leadership, the activists included significant numbers of *adivasis*, landless laborers, and some women. Yet the Shramik Sangathana's decentralized character made it susceptible to the kind of factionalism the CPI(M) was able to avoid.

With respect to the other key facet of their differing political approaches, from 1977 on the CPI(M) devoted greater priority to attaining and maintaining power than to extraparliamentary methods. This in turn meant that numbers—judged by votes, party membership, and the strength of mass organizations—increasingly became ends in themselves. Moreover, the need to reconcile the differing class, gender, and ethnic interests of the CPI(M)'s constituency all inevitably increased. By contrast, the Shramik Sangathana's initial rejection of electoral participation signified and confirmed its ideological purity but so marginalized it from the formal political arena as ultimately to precipitate a backlash against its grass-roots radicalism.

Strategic differences between the CPI(M) and the Shramik Sangathana do not emerge in a socioeconomic vacuum. A clue to recognizing the different conditions associated with parliamentary communism and independent grass-roots movements is that each is strong among groups and in regions where the other is weak; hence the weakness of the CPI(M) in Maharashtra and of nonparty formations in West Bengal. If one reason is that independent groups have found the space in which to emerge where the "old Left" is not hegemonic, another is that structural conditions of class and caste in Maharashtra and West Bengal substantially differ.

Class Structure and Capitalist Development

There have been intense debates among scholars and political activists about the relationship between the mode of agricultural production and the extent of agrarian radicalism in India. A major source of disagreement concerns the extent to which the introduction of capitalism has generated peasant protest. My research suggests that peasant movements occur in regions characterized by varying levels of economic development. However, the extent of capitalist development may influence their constituencies, methods, and objectives.

West Bengal's weak capitalist impulse has strengthened the communist movement by reducing the political power of the rural and urban bourgeoisie.[5] Although large landowners support the Congress party, they are not directly active in either agricultural production or political life. At the lower level of the class structure, a pauperized mass of peasants has brought the CPI(M) to power. Yet West Bengal's retarded capitalist development and the concomitant absence of class polarization help explain the CPI(M)'s reformist orientation. By contrast, capitalist growth in Dhulia district, Maharashtra, spawned the Shramik Sangathana. With lavish state support in the form of credit, transportation, and irrigation facilities, the dominant classes engaged in extensive cash-crop production from the 1950s. Increased demands for their labor, alongside transformed working conditions, were critical sources of agricultural laborers' militancy.

A comparison between the two states reveals that at the upper end of the class hierarchy the dominant classes are weaker in West Bengal than in Maharashtra. Most Bengali employers are middle peasants who, in the face of immiseration, have intensified the exploitation of wage laborers. At the lower end of the class hierarchy, whereas agricultural laborers are sharply differentiated both economically and politically in Dhulia district, the Bengali rural poor are an agglomerate of sharecroppers and agricultural laborers whose interests often conflict. The likelihood of agrarian conflict is therefore much greater in Dhulia district than in West Bengal.

The consequences of capitalist development, mediated by complex social structures, differ significantly for women in Maharashtra and West Bengal. While women's performance of paid labor has been consistently high among Maharashtrian Bhil *adivasis*, Bengali Hindus' disdain for manual labor has contributed to the marginalization of

Bengali women from the labor force. Whereas in West Bengal women constituted 14 percent of the work force in 1977–78 and 11 percent in 1983, in Maharashtra they constituted 48 percent and 47 percent during those same periods.[6]

However, there does appear to be a link between women's economic independence and their politicization. Economic independence in turn necessitates not only women's wage labor but also their control over their income, which *adivasis,* unlike caste Hindus, permit. Thus women's participation in the labor force is not only more extensive but also more empowering in Maharashtra than in West Bengal.

Caste Systems and Social Structures

The CPI(M) and Shramik Sangathana are similarly products of divergent caste systems and social structures. Given its peripheral location, West Bengal was never subject to the Brahminic Hindu influences that Maharashtra experienced. Mass conversions to Islam, coupled with the rise of Hindu reform movements, further weakened the caste system in West Bengal. The fluidity of caste barriers encouraged the assimilation of *adivasis* and *dalits* ("scheduled castes") into Hindu society.

As a result of West Bengal's malleable caste structure, the Bengali communist movement could draw its leadership from among the intermediary castes and thereby deprive the Congress party of potential support. Furthermore, an intermediary-caste leadership, coupled with upward caste mobility, eroded caste barriers between communists and their constituents. However, assimilation into caste Hindu society may have lessened *dalit* and *adivasi* militancy.

By contrast, a critical impediment to the growth of Maharashtrian communism was the strength of caste barriers. The Communist party's Brahminical leadership failed to gain the support of Marathas, who constitute over 40 percent of the state's population. Instead Congress co-opted leadership of the Non-Brahmin party and became hegemonic in Bombay province through Maratha support.[7] Today, party politics in Maharashtra are deeply influenced by caste considerations.

Caste and social structural differences between the two states have important implications for women's activism. Paradoxically, although the Bengali caste system permits social mobility for men, it rigidly circumscribes women's roles. Perhaps because it considers women repositories of tradition, Bengali culture emphasizes a sharp dichotomy between the private world of women and the public world of men. Women's centrality to the construction and maintenance of lineages, kinship networks, and caste boundaries has further confined Bengali women to the family and limited opportunities for autonomous political action.

Unlike Bengali Hindus, Bhils permit marriage by choice, and at a relatively older age, as well as divorce and widow remarriage. Not only are sexual norms more egalitarian but the public-private distinction is less marked among Maharashtrian *adivasis*. Thus, in challenging the unequal sexual division of labor or domestic violence, Bhil women find support in indigenous traditions that acknowledge the public relevance of what are generally deemed personal concerns.

If one objective of this study is to differentiate the social, economic, and political sources of agrarian mobilization in West Bengal and Maharashtra, another is to emphasize their interconnectedness. By way of example: in the agrarian context, peasants' use of their labor and relationship to their land are generally thought to be determined by their class position. What becomes apparent by analyzing women's participation in the labor force, however, is the extent to which these relationships are profoundly mediated by caste, ethnicity, and gender.

Similarly, it is often impossible to differentiate the economic from the political logic that informs the actions of leftist organizations. Take, for example, the CPI(M)'s tacit support for agrarian capitalist development signified by its inclusion of rich peasants (capitalist farmers) within its peasant organization—a position that can convincingly be attributed either to economic or to electoral considerations. Likewise, the Shramik Sangathana's anticapitalist stance can be explained both by the successes (and ravages) of capitalist development in Dhulia district and/or by the Shramik Sangathana's nonelectoral stance.

However, political organizations may develop their social bases in a way that defies economic logic. Thus, for example, although West Bengal's large population of agricultural laborers may be an important element in the communists' strength, the CPI(M) has subordinated their interests to those of landowning peasants. Evidence for the significant element of choice in the CPM(M)'s approach is that in Kerala, where the proportion of agricultural laborers is smaller than in West Bengal, the CPI(M) has better represented their interests.[8]

But the absence of socioeconomic constraints does not signify that political organizations are thereby unencumbered; certain political constraints are implicit in the conditions of liberal democracy. Although these constraints may be most apparent in the case of the CPI(M) because it has chosen to play by the rules of the game, the Shramik Sangathana could not escape these rules by opting against electoral participation.

The Indian Context

One reading of this work thus far might be: however accurate my findings concerning Maharashtra and West Bengal, their relevance is limited both geographically, to two rather exceptional regions, and in time, to an eclipsed period of leftist mobilization. For today, the argument might continue, the most militant struggles are not class based but "communal," not for women's empowerment but for their seclusion and subordination, not leftist but right-wing and fundamentalist.

However, I suggest that this conventional logic errs in part by viewing class and ethnic identifications as polar opposites when in fact they are often complementary. As I elaborate below, although Marxist vocabulary is misleading here, class politics were premised upon and fueled by passionate ethnic identifications in Maharashtra and by regional identifications in West Bengal. Just as the Shramik Sangathana has sought to strengthen *adivasi* identity in order to achieve radical change, the CPI(M) has embraced Bengalis' proud and distinctive cultural identity to mobilize opposition to the Congress party. Seen in this light, the leftist movements that I studied have more in common with "communal" movements than is initially apparent.[9]

Furthermore, by emphasizing the dilemmas that both the CPI(M) and Shramik Sangathana experience in two states in which conditions are relatively propitious for leftist movements, this study helps explain the greater weaknesses of leftist organizations in other regions of India. To explore this question further, the next section considers the caste, class, and political influences that help explain the modalities of protest at the national level.

Class structure and capitalist development. For many scholars, one pillar of Indian democracy is the relatively advanced, autonomous character of India's capitalist development relative to that of other postcolonial nations.[10] The size and strength of the national bourgeoisie, coupled with its nationalist orientation, were traditionally thought to have saved India from both the military-authoritarian and the revolutionary-socialist scenarios of dependent capitalist states. This is corroborated by the experience of West Bengal, where a weak capitalist impulse has facilitated the growth of parliamentary communism.

Within the rural context, comparative analysis suggests the difficulty of establishing clear linkages between agrarian capitalism and agrarian radicalism. While some accounts suggest that "feudal" forms of oppression have sparked peasant resistance, others associate agrarian radicalism with the so-called green revolution in agriculture.[11] In particular, scholars have pointed to the proletarianization of the labor force, increased class disparities, and state support for dominant classes, all factors associated with the Shramik Sangathana's emergence. Similarly, assessments of whether middle peasants or agricultural laborers have played the leading roles in peasant movements diverge widely.[12]

However, more pertinent than the question of which class is more militant is the question of how the demands of various classes may differ. In West Bengal, where the role of middle peasants has been preeminent, the peasant movement is more durable but less militant than in Dhulia district, Maharashtra, where agricultural laborers have been at the forefront. Similarly, in the broader Indian context, once the myth of peasant passivity is rejected, the question is no longer one of identifying exceptional regions in which a particular class configuration has enabled agrarian mobilization but of identifying the conditions associated with different forms of mobilization.

Caste systems and social structures. India's regional cultures are so diverse that one way to identify the social dimensions of protest is simply to describe the social structures and cultural systems of regions in which mobilization has occurred. Although this approach is useful in explaining why, when protest occurs, it has remained regionally encapsulated, it is unable to identify the common features of regions that have experienced agrarian radicalism but differ in critical respects in their ethnic, religious, and caste compositions.

At a less comprehensive level of generalization, one might identify deviations from Brahminic Hinduism in both Dhulia district, Maharashtra, and West Bengal. In part because of their strategic locations, both of these frontier regions experienced successive waves of migration, which weakened caste orthodoxy and prevented domination by castes that became hegemonic elsewhere. In several other regions as well, of which Kerala is a prime example, deviations from Brahminic Hinduism appear to have facilitated communist mobilization. More specifically, *adivasi* men and women have often been militant participants in protest. Throughout India—Naxalbari and Gopiballavpur in West Bengal, Srikakulam in Andhra Pradesh, Dhulia and Thana districts in Maharashtra—agrarian peasant movements have in fact been *adivasi* struggles against class and caste domination.

Contrasting political approaches. To understand the sources of stability in India in the first decades after independence, one might return to some of the seminal works on Indian politics.[13] Although they tended to underestimate the instability associated with class, ethnic, and gender inequality, they correctly emphasized the Congress party's role in creating a relatively secular democratic state in the aftermath of Independence. The particular skill of Congress, many scholars observed, was its ability to construct a political machine that respected and preserved the diversity of Indian society. Although the costs of this approach were an acceptance of glaring inequalities, Congress thereby embodied and articulated a transcendent sense of national identity.

Conversely, the Communist Party of India was hindered in most regions by its urban, upper-caste composition. With respect to the "nationalities question," the CPI was doubly negligent: on the one hand it was unresponsive to India's regional and ethnic diversity, while on the other hand it divorced itself from nationalist forces, at times by dissociating itself from Congress (recall the CPI's refusal to challenge the Allied powers when Congress was heightening its offensive against British imperialism) and at other times by associating itself with Congress (as in the CPI's support for Congress during the national Emergency).

The period of the national Emergency marked a critical turning point for the Congress party; in its aftermath, religious and caste considerations increasingly figured into Indira Gandhi's electoral calculations. In response to its defeat in the parliamentary elections of 1977, partly as a result of middle-caste and Muslim support for the Janata party, Congress (I) began to cultivate a Hindu constituency. It included both the upper castes and rising middle castes who displayed a powerful sense of caste superiority. Conflicts grew between the lower castes, *adivasis*, and Muslims on the one hand, and the upper and middle castes on the other.[14] Congress's appeals to the Hindu majority also unleashed a spiraling cycle of ethnic conflict with well-known consequences in the Punjab, Assam, and Kashmir, among other places.

The national Emergency also precipitated a crisis of Indian federalism. In a desperate attempt to preserve dynastic rule and Congress hegemony, Indira Gandhi set in motion long-term trends toward personalistic rule, centralization of state power, and deinstitutionalization of the political system. The already top-heavy federal system became even more overbearing, dismissing opposition governments at the state level and declaring president's rule in states where it felt threatened.

The period after 1975 represented a critical test and turning point for the two parliamentary communist parties. While the CPI clung tenaciously to its earlier line of supporting Congress (I), the CPI(M) consistently opposed the Congress party. The CPI(M) thereby became increasingly "responsible" in a dual sense—on the one hand by defending secular principles and on the other hand by moderating its radical stance in favor of a more social democratic orientation. Upon its election to office as the leading member of the Left Front government in 1977, the CPI(M) resolved to display greater moderation than it had under preceding United Front governments (1967–69, 1969–70). Its reformist stance in West Bengal was also reinforced by its growing national aspirations. Thus its attempt to heighten Bengalis' distinctive cultural and political identity complemented demands for the devolution of political power and transfer of economic resources from the center to the states.

The emergence of grass-roots political movements, of which the Shramik Sangathana is an important example, is also closely related to these developments.[15] As a result of the national Emergency, many new organizations were formed while older organizations gained ground. The movement for "partyless democracy" led by J. P. Narayan in Bihar set the tone for the surge that followed in its mix of

Gandhian and socialist principles, distrust of political parties and institutional mechanisms, grass-roots approach, emphasis on direct action tactics, and infusion of moral concerns into political life.

Two major kinds of grass-roots movements can be distinguished: first, urban-based, single-issue organizations that center around questions concerning ecology, civil liberties, and women's liberation; and second, rural-based, multi-issue organizations that have worked among oppressed groups.[16] Although grass-roots organizations are highly decentralized and dispersed, urban middle-class activists of broadly similar orientation have played key roles in most of these movements.

The growth of grass-roots movements, like that of the CPI(M), is closely linked to the transformation of the state. Consider, for example, the state's responsibility for politicizing issues that were earlier deemed personal concerns, particularly with respect to religion and gender. In response, the women's movement has publicized private atrocities within the family, as in its opposition to "dowry deaths," by demonstrating outside the homes of the guilty party.[17] The women's movement has also pointed to the state's responsibility by demanding legislation pertaining to rape and dowry and the banning of clinics that perform amniocentesis merely to determine the baby's sex. Another aspect of state policy that has energized grass-roots movements is its increasing support for upper and middle castes who subject *dalit* and *adivasi* laborers to extreme class and caste exploitation. The dual struggles that these movements have launched against class and caste domination represent a direct response to both the electoral and the economic logic that guides the modern Indian state.

If on the one hand, the Shramik Sangathana and the CPI(M) in its post-1977 incarnation are in some critical respects born of the crisis of Indian democracy, their ability to respond to this crisis is shaped by their regional and ethnic moorings. Not only are their strengths explained by their close affinity for the cultural contexts in which they are active, but their response to the crisis affirms both indigenous and secular principles.

Methodology

What, one might ask, is the possible justification for comparing movements that differ as radically in size and scale as the CPI(M) and

Shramik Sangathana? Whereas the CPI(M) claims a million members in West Bengal and governs a state of over fifty million people, the Shramik Sangathana never exercised state power and at its height had fourteen full-time activists and fifteen thousand members in a district with a population of less than two million. Moreover, are a leftist governing coalition and an extraparliamentary political movement directly comparable?

The more cautious research strategy might have been to compare the CPI(M) in West Bengal with several grass-roots movements in Maharashtra rather than with the Shramik Sangathana alone. However, studying a single organization allowed me to focus on its internal dynamics. More important, differences in the size and scale of the two movements are relevant to this study: indeed a central question concerns the linkages between organizations' deradicalization and expansion, occasioned in turn by electoral success. The very differences in the size and scale of the CPI(M) and the Shramik Sangathana permit me to ask what happens to social movements as they become older, larger, and more institutionalized.[18]

One disadvantage of this approach, however, might have been the tendency to equate the district level, at which the Shramik Sangathana functions, with the state level, at which the CPI(M) functions, thereby disregarding differences in scale. To address this problem, on the one hand I study the CPI(M)'s activities within a single district, Midnapur, while on the other hand I frequently compare Dhulia district to Maharashtra as a whole.

If my focus on Dhulia district within Maharashtra simply followed the lines of Shramik Sangathana activity, my choice of a district in West Bengal presented greater difficulties, for the CPI(M) is active throughout the state. In order to analyze the CPI(M)'s approach to organizing women from poor rural backgrounds, I wanted to select a district in which women's participation had been relatively extensive. Burdwan, the so-called red district of West Bengal, which might otherwise have been a good choice, had no tradition of women's participation. By contrast, women had been active in a range of political movements in Midnapur district, from movements organized by the so-called terrorists in the first decades of this century to the nationalists and communists, of which Tebhaga (1946–48) was the most important example.

The relatively recent origins of CPI(M) strength in Midnapur district, which initially appeared to be a liability, later proved advantageous. Given the fact that Midnapur has the largest number of Legislative Assembly seats of any district in West Bengal, Midnapur plays a pivotal role in determining electoral outcomes in this state. Thus, the CPI(M)'s attempt to improve its standing in Midnapur provided an excellent illustration of its approach to mobilizing the rural poor in a district where it had a good likelihood of success in organizing women.

One additional advantage of studying Midnapur district is that as the second largest and second most populous district within West Bengal, it mirrors the socioeconomic diversity of the state as a whole. Thus by studying villages that differed in their socioeconomic characteristics, it was possible to assess the CPI(M)'s response to divergent structural conditions, a comparative approach that I also pursued in Dhulia district. (At the beginning of chapter 7 I describe my criteria for selecting particular villages and my fieldwork techniques within these villages.)

Aside from the attempt to make my analysis of the CPI(M) and Shramik Sangathana as comparable as possible, there is also a theoretical rationale for studying mobilization at state, district, and village levels. These different levels of scholarly analysis correspond to what might be designated the CPI(M)'s "view from above" and the Shramik Sangathana's "view from below." Both these terms have a dual meaning: the view from above refers on the one hand to the CPI(M)'s focus on the international, national, and state levels, as well as on political institutions, parties, and state policy, and on the other hand to the vantage point of the largely *bhadralok* party leadership. The Shramik Sangathana's view from below, by contrast, refers at once to its focus on informal political arenas, including the family, community, and village, and to the vantage point of the most oppressed rural groups. Whereas the "view from above" is often a male vantage point, for it focuses on traditionally male-dominated arenas of political activity, the view from below embraces the political dimensions of women's "personal" lives.

Adopting both these vantage points enabled me to do greater justice to both these movements than I could if I had viewed them exclusively from either above or below. For example, it would have done the CPI(M) a disservice simply to study its activities at the village level by interviewing *adivasi* landless laborers about agrarian mobilization; this would have neglected both its use of state power to legislate reform and its attempts to organize peasants across class lines. Conversely, to focus simply on the Shramik Sangathana's contribution to electoral realignments or movement politics at the state level would neglect its success in empowering the most oppressed groups within particular villages.

In rejecting one exclusive vantage point, I attempt to explore, through the dilemmas and errors of the CPI(M) and Shramik Sangathana, how these perspectives might best be synthesized. However, this does not mean positioning myself either above these two organizations or halfway between them. While my own perspective has changed, along with that of the Shramik Sangathana, so as to include an awareness of the pitfalls of both approaches, the Shramik Sangathana's view from below, for all its failings, gives voice to those who rarely enter either political or scholarly accounts.

The organization of this study reflects the distinction elaborated above between the view from above and the view from below. Part one provides an aerial view of distinct social, economic, and political influences upon political mobilization in West Bengal and Maharashtra. The focus in chapters 2 through 4 is on political approaches: the CPI(M) as a party of mobilization and governance (chapter 2) and its approach to organizing women (chapter 3), and the Shramik Sangathana (chapter 4). These three chapters highlight the political dilemmas and choices entailed in the strategies of each organization. Chapter 5 compares social structures, particularly caste systems, and chapter 6 the political economies, particularly the class structures, of Maharashtra and West Bengal.

In part two my focus shifts to the village level: chapter 7 discusses three villages in Midnapur district and chapter 8 three villages in Dhulia district that display contrasting patterns of resistance and quiescence among women and men. Whereas each of the chapters in the first part highlights the primacy of the economic, political, and social influences that they respectively examine, chapters 7 through 9 explore relationships between these influences.

The Theoretical Context

This study engages three discrete subjects of scholarly concern: peasant movements, women's resistance, and leftist political strategies.

With respect to the first topic, my study questions the tendency among students of peasant movements to underestimate the influences of ethnicity and gender. Although the gender and ethnic character of peasants find due emphasis in some of the recent literature on peasant society, most studies of peasant movements give preeminence to economic forces. Thus, in the scholarly literature, the social composition of peasant movements becomes equated with their class base while the conditions of their emergence are identified with long-term economic conditions and short-term economic precipitants; one finds only passing reference to "mediating" political influences.

A further contribution of this study to the literature on peasant movements pertains to its interdisciplinary approach. Although anthropologists of India, recently joined by "subaltern historians," have often provided a "view from below," political scientists rarely do so. Indeed one might argue that the very orientation of the discipline mitigates against a focus on peasant rebellion because it occurs outside the formal arenas of power.[19] However, there is no easy resolution to this dilemma, for anthropologists and historians have often been uninterested in relations between the local and the national.

My approach may appear unconventional to both political scientists and anthropologists. I neither focus exclusively on the state, the national arena, or political institutions, as in the tradition of political science, nor, as in the anthropological tradition, study a single village in all its nuances and complexities. Rather, I combine a discussion of political institutions, parties, and movements at the state level with an analysis of six villages. The differences between these two levels of analysis are reflected in the disjunction between the first and second parts of this study. Furthermore, because I have studied a relatively large number of villages, I am unable to provide the fine-grained description that would ideally have been desirable. However, I believe that the advantages of my approach concern the interdisciplinary character of this study, my ability to gain both a view from above and a view from below, and the insights that emerge from a comparative perspective at both the village and state levels.

Surprisingly, given the explosion of women's studies in India, rather little has been written about the conditions surrounding rural women's consciousness and resistance.[20] There is vast documentation of the urban women's movement and rural women's work within the home and in the fields. But why so few studies of rural women's protest? A key is that the study of urban women has followed the burgeoning of the urban women's movement; comparable forms of women's resistance and scholarship about it have been absent in the rural context. Additionally, however, scholarship in women's studies has suffered from an overemphasis on successful forms of organizing and inadequate attention to the partial, contradictory consequences of most political movements for women.

My work can also be situated in the broader context of socialist/feminist scholarship.[21] Over the past few years, rather abstract and sterile theoretical debates about patriarchy and class inequality have been energized by historically grounded accounts of women's struggles in the Third World.[22] Addressing a wide range of contexts, they grapple with dilemmas that are at the heart of this study: to what extent are there conflicts between preserving indigenous cultural traditions and achieving women's rights? Why have communist parties so often subsumed women's liberation within anti-imperialist and socialist struggles? To what extent do land reforms and other redistributive measures entail conflicts between the interests of women and men?

A third relevant area of theoretical enquiry concerns the sources, dilemmas, and consequences of leftist movements. There are striking resemblances between the CPI(M) and social democratic parties in Western Europe. A debate about the extent to which social democratic parties are impelled by the logic of liberal democracy in either an increasingly conservative or radical direction is fruitfully addressed by exploring the trajectory of the Left Front government. Conversely, this debate helps illuminate the close relationship between the CPI(M)'s growing strength and deradicalization.

At first glance it might seem more appropriate to analyze the CPI(M) exclusively within the context of literature on agrarian communism, which focuses on the influences of class and social structure. However, literature on European social democracy is illuminating because of India's unusually durable tradition of liberal democracy.[23] An exploration of the dilemmas of parliamentary communism in West Bengal suggests the importance of dismantling theoretical boundaries between the First and Third Worlds and between Leninism and social democracy.

Despite scholars' tendency to characterize them as post-Marxist, "new social movements" in the West and in India bear a striking resemblance. Such characterizations contain teleological inferences that new social movements in the West are more advanced than Marxist movements in the Third World.[24] However, movements like the Shramik Sangathana in India are characterized by some traits of new social movements in the Western context that scholars consider crucial: their decentralized democratic character, highly sophisticated use of popular cultural symbols, and location within an intermediary space between public and private arenas.

Conversely, situating the Shramik Sangathana within a comparative context reveals the source of some of its problems and dilemmas. For example, the factionalism that the Shramik Sangathana experienced is reminiscent of the "tyranny of structurelessness" that Jo Freeman associates with the women's movement in the United States.[25] Thus the very organizational innovations that are responsible for the success of grass-roots movements are also a major source of their weakness.

Chapter Two

Parliamentary Communism as a Historical Phenomenon: The CPI(M) in West Bengal

The Left Front government's dilemmas concerning the use of parliamentary means to achieve radical reform strikingly resemble those of northern European social democracies. Analyzing theoretical debates about parliamentary socialism in Europe thus helps elucidate the CPI(M)'s approach in West Bengal. How successfully has parliamentary communism achieved radical reform? To what extent do structural conditions determine political parties' strategic choices? Might other strategies have produced more progressive outcomes?[1]

At the risk of oversimplifying a rich theoretical and historical literature, one can discern two major positions concerning the relationship of European social democracies to radical change. One approach emphasizes the progressive dynamic of social democracy. Gosta Esping-Andersen and John Stephens argue that, under certain conditions, the dynamics of electoral competition may impel social democratic governments to widen their policy agenda from political to social to economic democracy.[2] The cumulative character of these changes ultimately collides with the structural limits of capitalism and makes possible socialist transition.

By contrast, a second approach finds that liberal democratic forms exert conservatizing pressures. Adam Przeworski and Claus Offe emphasize the electoral necessity to produce pluralities and thereby downplay class appeals, the tendency for bureaucratic and representative forms to supplant direct participation, and the need for leftist parties to appear politically "responsible" as well as capable of delivering immediate material benefits.[3] Inevitably, social democratic movements have abandoned radical goals in favor of a reformist approach.

Within this second approach, explanations for the conservatizing consequences of social democracy differ. Unlike Przeworski and Offe, who emphasize structural constraints, Leo Panitch highlights leaders' strategic choices.[4] Panitch argues that social democratic parties need not accept the structure of the state, promulgate class harmony, orient mobilization toward electoral ends, and reinforce the division between industrial and political organization. Workers have been abandoning social democratic parties because of their moderation, not militancy.

What light does the Left Front government's experience shed on this debate? To what extent has the CPI(M)'s reform agenda progressively broadened, as in the dynamic described by Esping-Andersen, or diminished, as Panitch and Przeworski suggest? To the extent that the CPI(M) has been deradicalized, does the explanation lie more in structural constraints or strategic choices? How might a radical strategy differ from the CPI(M)'s approach?

If the comparison between West Bengal and Western Europe seems surprising, the CPI(M)'s trajectory has much in common with that of Eurocommunist and social democratic parties. Indeed, there is a certain ethnocentrism in assuming that the Left Front government's experience should be assessed exclusively in light of debates about "peasant societies." Certain structural constraints—such as the imperatives of capitalist development and electoral competition—are the same in West Bengal and in European social democracies. The organization, ideologies, and strategies of social democratic and communist parties are also quite similar. Although the reforms in each context differ in substance, they are formulated through a similar process: by the state, in incremental fashion, on the basis of multiclass coalitions that include elements of capital.

The factors that complicate a comparison between West Bengal and Western Europe are double-edged. On the one hand, a subnational government clearly has more limited autonomy than nation states. On the other hand, while Indian state governments possess considerable latitude, small northern European states are far from autonomous vis-à-vis the international economic and political system. Furthermore, West Bengal's revolutionary tradition, coupled with its underdeveloped political economy, exerts greater pressures toward radical reform than exist in Western Europe. Far from the differences between West Bengal and Western Europe constituting a liability for comparative purposes, they make the similarities in the policy outcomes of social democratic rule particularly striking.

But clearly the first step is to explore the extent to which the conditions that these approaches specify exist in West Bengal. For example, can progressive radicalization of social democratic regimes occur in the absence of economic expansion, transformation of the class structure, and government control over the business cycle, which Esping-Andersen stipulates are necessary? Could the CPI(M) pursue a radical strategy in the absence of a large, cohesive industrial working class, which Panitch considers essential to capitalist transformation?

Dilemmas Confronting the CPI(M)

There are close parallels in the literature on the Left Front government to debates on European social democracy. In a provocative article, "One Step Forward, Two Steps Backward," Ashok Rudra argues that the government's major reforms neither challenge the dominant classes nor benefit oppressed groups. Echoing Przeworski and Offe, Rudra argues, "If a political party aims at majority support among the agricultural population, it cannot but in the ultimate analysis betray the most exploited and oppressed sections of the rural masses."[5] By contrast, Atul Kohli suggests that the CPI(M)'s abandonment of revolutionary aspirations has enhanced its ability to represent the poor.[6] Consistent with Esping-Andersen and Stephens, Kohli argues that the CPI(M)'s coherent leadership, populist ideology, and centralized organization have enabled it to penetrate the countryside without being captured by propertied groups.

Rudra and Kohli agree that the Left Front government's political reforms do not redistribute economic power. However, while Rudra believes that this prevents political power from being democratically redistributed, Kohli assumes that the Left Front government could not alter prevailing class relations and credits it nonetheless for depriving landlords of political power.

Both analyses oversimplify the relationship between economic constraints and political reforms. On the one hand, Rudra is overly pessimistic about the possibility of far-reaching reform through elected bodies. At the same time he seems oblivious to structural constraints when he criticizes the CPI(M)'s reformism. Kohli, on the other hand, disregards the manner in which party organization and leadership have impeded effective reform.

In contrast to Rudra, I do not believe that the only criterion by which to judge the CPI(M) is revolutionary change. Such a position disregards the substantial reforms that the CPI(M) sponsored in its first years in office. However, unlike Kohli, I emphasize the CPI(M)'s failure to achieve even modest reformist gains since 1980. Nor do I believe that Kohli is sufficiently attentive to the CPI(M)'s failure to stretch existing limits. For the CPI(M) to succeed would require combining an effective electoral strategy with creative grass-roots organizing. This approach would require audacity and imagination, which the CPI(M) wholly lacks.

The CPI(M)'s reformism is a product both of necessity and choice. Overwhelming economic and political obstacles to radical reform derive from the context of an underdeveloped, class-divided society, the constraints that the center imposes on state governments, and the CPI(M)'s relationship with Left Front coalition partners. However, some sources of the CPI(M)'s deradicalization, such as its pursuit of an electoral strategy, are only partially determined by "external" necessity; party leadership, ideology, and organization bear major responsibility.

Among the major "external constraints" on the CPI(M) are, first, the underdeveloped character of West Bengal's economy. It is as incumbent on communist as on capitalist governments to develop productive forces. Otherwise, socialism is tantamount to the redistribution of poverty—as generations of Marxists have warned. The CPI(M) has adopted the Leninist dual-stage theory of revolution, which postpones the socialist stage until after capitalism is achieved. The familiar price paid is a refusal to challenge capitalist exploitation.[7]

Second, the CPI(M)'s relationship to the national government has subjected it to numerous constraints that have ultimately compromised radical goals. If, as has been frequently noted, communist nations find it difficult to sustain their revolutionary character within a global capitalist system, the problem is magnified for subnational communist governments.[8] The CPI(M)'s credibility partly rests upon its ability to delegitimize the central government and demonstrate the viability of a leftist alternative. Yet the Left Front government's very survival rests precariously upon central government sanction.

Third, the CPI(M) can become a major opposition party at the national and often even at the local level only by forming alliances. Like many other communist parties, it has at times allied with conservative parties to defend democracy against authoritarianism. Indeed, refusal to do so may reflect extreme sectarianism and blindness. (Recall the Communist party in Weimar Germany.) Yet coalitions have spawned tactical, ideological, and personality conflicts that undermine progressive goals.[9] In the West Bengal context, conflicts among coalition partners were partially responsible for the downfall of United Front governments in 1967 and 1969.

However, not even these daunting constraints are totally intractable. The CPI(M) has scarcely explored means of capital accumulation that are compatible with a radical land-reform strategy, although the Indian federal system provides significant autonomy to state governments, particularly in the agrarian sphere. Moreover, the central government seems disinclined to overthrow the Left Front government. Although the CPI(M) is much stronger under the Left Front government than it was under previous United Front governments, it was far more audacious in the early 1970s than it is today.

To understand more fully the sources of CPI(M) reformism we must consider the party's ideology, organization, and leadership. Of particular significance are the CPI(M)'s emphasis on electoral success and its adherence to democratic centralist principles. Moreover, the imperatives described earlier—to represent multiclass interests, stimulate capitalist growth, and cooperate with the central government—have all grown as a result of the CPI(M)'s long tenure in office. As Przeworski notes:

> To win the votes of people other than workers, particularly the petty bourgeoisie, to form alliances and coalitions, to administer the government in the interests of workers, a party cannot appear to be "irresponsible," to give any indication of being less than wholehearted about its commitment to the rules and limits of the parliamentary game.[10]

The following section analyzes the sources of the CPI(M)'s deradicalization, and the next evaluates its performance under the Left Front government. To understand these cumulative tendencies, I analyze the constraints upon the CPI(M)'s actions. The conclusion returns to questions raised above concerning prospects of parliamentary communism.

The Sources of CPI(M) Reformism

The CPI(M) became India's leading communist party largely because it consistently adopted a more oppositional stance to the state, the bourgeoisie, and the Congress party than did the Communist Party of India. Yet it also avoided what it described as the "revolutionary adventurism" of the Communist Party of India (Marxist-Leninist). The CPI(M) has sought to extend its influence by progressively moderating its stance.

Dissident CPI members formed the CPI(M) on 11 April 1964 because they questioned the CPI's sympathetic depiction of the state, its largely parliamentary approach, and its close relationship with the Soviet Union. Although the CPI allied with the national bourgeoisie, the CPI(M) contended that this constituted an alliance with imperialist forces. The CPI relied primarily on parliamentary methods, whereas the CPI(M) considered them tactically useful but unlikely to achieve fundamental change. Although the CPI favored a close relationship with the Soviet Union, the CPI(M) rejected the Communist Party Soviet Union (CPSU) leadership and sought to pursue an independent path. However, today the CPI(M) has largely abandoned extraparliamentary mass mobilization and become preoccupied with the exercise of power. What explains its changed stance?

Given India's durable democratic tradition, it is more difficult for communist parties in India than in most other Third World countries to reject parliamentary means. The strength and legitimacy of the state, the bourgeoisie, and the ruling Congress party have long confounded the Indian communist movement. Having courted repression and unpopularity by pursuing a purely confrontational strategy, the undivided Communist party decided in the mid-1950s to accept the parliamentary route. The CPI(M) emphasized extraparliamentary methods in its infancy because it did not aspire to attain office. With electoral success in West Bengal (1967 and 1969–70), a parliamentary strategy became more feasible.

The Naxalite movement further deradicalized the CPI(M). On 2 March 1967, when the first United Front government took office,

CPI(M) dissidents supported a peasant uprising in the Naxalbari region of northern Bengal. The Naxalite movement gave birth to the underground revolutionary party, the Communist Party of India (Marxist-Leninist). The Left Front government's former finance minister, Ashok Mitra, noted in an interview that the CPI(M-L)'s formation deprived the CPI(M) of its most militant cadres.

The Naxalite movement also exacerbated the contradictions between the CPI(M)'s revolutionary aspirations and its exercise of state power. Suppressing the Naxalbari uprising would have discredited the CPI(M) among radical critics both inside and outside the party. At the same time, if the agitation grew, the center could simply dismiss the United Front government. When negotiations failed, the West Bengal cabinet voted unanimously to quell the uprising. In arriving at this decision and in subsequently justifying it, the CPI(M) affirmed its opposition to radical methods and goals.

Most important, the repression the CPI(M) experienced during its short tenure in office moderated its stance. The CPI(M)-led United Front government that took office in March 1967 planned extensive agrarian reform. Its minister of land and land revenue, Harekrishna Konar, gave priority to vesting and redistributing land that exceeded the legal ceiling and to ensuring sharecroppers' permanent rights to cultivation on a hereditary basis. Because Konar did not believe that land redistribution could be achieved simply through legal or bureaucratic means, he encouraged peasant organizations to seize land and crops from landlords.

After the central government dismissed the first United Front government from office, Konar formulated an even more radical approach. He now regarded parliamentary participation as a means to "wreck the system from within." According to this strategy, which the CPI(M) National Council adopted in 1968, CPI(M)-dominated coalitions would wage a "relentless class struggle against the center."[11]

The second CPI(M)-led United Front government in West Bengal, which took office in February 1969, made peasant mobilization its first priority. The CPI(M) formed voluntary auxiliary groups, each consisting of five to ten cadres, to encourage landless laborers and poor peasants to seize land in excess of legal ceilings and to persuade sharecroppers to demand their full share of the crop. (Landlords' shares often exceeded the legal limit.) The government claimed that it recovered and redistributed 300,000 acres,[12] but the land-seizure movement unleashed class conflict in the countryside. The central government found ample grounds for decrying the breakdown of law and order and dismissing the second United Front government on 19 March 1970. The state government's demise led the CPI(M) to reject large-scale peasant mobilization in favor of peaceful, incremental agrarian reform.

In the seven years that followed the downfall of the second United Front government, the CPI(M) continued to organize among the peasantry. Its efforts bore fruit: in the 1977 Legislative Assembly elections the Left Front won 230 out of 290 seats; the CPI(M)'s 177 seats represented an absolute majority. In the 1982 elections the Left Front coalition won 238 seats and the CPI(M) 174 seats. In the 1987 elections the Left coalition won 251 seats and the CPI(M) 186 seats.

The following sections analyze the government's major reforms in the industrial and particularly the rural areas, where it has concentrated its efforts. The state government has greater constitutional powers to sponsor agrarian than urban reform. Moreover, given the fact that three-fourths of West Bengal's population is rural, the CPI(M) has earned greater dividends by concentrating on the agrarian sphere.

The Urban-Industrial Sphere

The Left Front government inherited a negative industrial growth rate; since 1977–78 it has "achieved" stagnation. The obstacles to industrial growth are formidable. Because there is little demand for West Bengal's major industries, numerous units are either "sick" or closed. Nor have new industries been established in West Bengal since 1964. Private investors fear labor shortages, power scarcity, and labor unrest, which drove away many industries under previous leftist governments. The central government has undertaken little public investment.

Under such dire conditions, the Left Front government has given priority to stimulating investment and curtailing working-class militancy. At its fifteenth state party congress in West Bengal, the CPI(M) declared that there was nothing wrong or "un-Marxian" about seeking participation by the private sector and multinational corporations in industrialization. The report denied that there was any contradiction between the Left Front government's approach and the objective of "weakening and finally destroying domestic and foreign monopoly capital." West Bengal's chief minister, Jyoti Basu, even visited the United States to seek World Bank loans and multinational investments. The government has started a duty-free export and electronics zone. It has revived the Labor Advisory Board to strengthen collective bargaining procedures and dissuaded workers from striking. It has prohibited *gherao*—a workers' tactic of encircling management to apply pressure.

Citing a Reserve Bank of India study, Manoranjan Rai, president of the CPI(M) trade union CITU in West Bengal, boasted in an interview that worker militancy no longer caused capital flight from West Bengal. Nirmal Bose, minister of industry under the second administration and minister of food and supplies under the third administration, asserted that labor unrest was far greater in the state of Maharashtra than in West Bengal, where trade unions were more "responsible." Rai and Bose may well be right. According to a West Bengal government study, in 1977 there were 206 strikes and 191 lockouts; strikes accounted for 52 percent and lockouts for 48 percent of all work stoppages. By contrast, in 1983 there were only 32 strikes and 139 lockouts; strikes accounted for 19 percent and lockouts for 81 percent of all work stoppages. Likewise, of the number of workdays lost in 1977, 12 percent resulted from strikes and 88 percent from lockouts, whereas in 1983 strikes were responsible for 6 percent and lockouts for 94 percent.[13] The government's successful attempts to subdue labor and empower management may also have adversely affected workers' wages.[14]

In the urban sphere, the Left Front government's failure to improve transportation, sanitation, and other civic services has seriously damaged its credibility. The government correctly denies responsibility for the problems caused by Calcutta's population density and points to the vast influx of immigrants from Bangladesh and Assam. Yet the fact remains that it accords low priority to ameliorating appalling urban conditions.

The Agrarian Sphere

Whereas the second United Front government directed peasant organizations to engage in land and crop seizures, the Left Front government directs bureaucrats to maintain law and order during the harvesting season. The extent and duration of political agitations have also declined since the Left Front government assumed office. When interviewed, the land and land reforms minister under the second Left Front ministry, Benoy Chowdhury, argued that political quiescence in the countryside resulted from the government's success in curtailing landlord repression, which had eliminated the need for mass mobilization.

The Left Front government increased the responsibilities of the West Bengal State Planning Advisory Board for overseeing agricultural development in 1983. The board has closely linked efforts to achieve redistribution and growth. According to Asim Dasgupta, who rose from membership on the board to become the finance minister under the third Left Front government administration, small farms (of 2.7 acres) have the highest cropping intensity in West Bengal, since poor peasants compensate for their lack of capital with their labor. Improving the economic conditions of the rural poor is thus likely to increase food grain production.[15]

Another priority is irrigation. The board has emphasized minor irrigation schemes, which are especially useful to small farmers. In western districts, where water is further from the surface than elsewhere in West Bengal, it has sponsored nonconventional, local resource-based production. The government's strategy for agricultural growth has recently achieved some success: the state's index of agricultural production increased by 47 percent, from 103.9 in 1982–83 to a record high of 150.4 in 1983–84.[16] Yet Kanai Bhowmick, minister for minor irrigation in the second Left Front ministry, admitted in an interview that West Bengal still imports over $400 million annually in food grain. Although the state government has focused its efforts on small rather than large landowners and has emphasized redistributive reform over gains in productivity, it has not significantly ameliorated the conditions of the poorest groups.

Shortly after achieving power, the government embarked upon extensive tenancy reforms. It passed legislation curtailing the ability of landowners to evict sharecroppers. In addition, this legislation made the failure of landlords to issue receipts to sharecroppers a criminal offense. Such receipts enable sharecroppers to register their names on land records, thereby ensuring their tenancy rights. The government has made landlords responsible for proving that cultivators cannot remain on the land.

With great fanfare, the Left Front government launched "Operation Barga," a sharecropper registration campaign, in 1978. After identifying regions containing large numbers of sharecroppers, administrators, peasant organizers, and *panchayat* members held meetings at which they informed sharecroppers of their rights. Benoy Chowdhury estimated, in response to my query, that only 275,000 sharecroppers were bold enough to register before 1977; by December 1984, 1.3 million of two million sharecroppers in West Bengal had registered.

The initial mobilizing thrust of "Operation Barga" gave sharecroppers a sense of efficacy that probably diminished as the campaign languished. As Ashok Rudra points out, because even 75 percent of the crop often does not cover their subsistence needs, sharecroppers must retain landowners' goodwill to secure loans during periods of scarcity.[17] The government has attempted to ameliorate this problem by providing subsidized loans. However, by 1984 it had provided such loans to only about 11 percent of newly registered sharecroppers and recipients of vested land.[18] Sharecroppers may fear that landlords will deny them loans for personal expenses such as marriage ceremonies and medical expenses for which institutional loans are not available. Furthermore, a recent study of four villages in West Bengal finds that dependence on landlords prevents the majority of newly registered sharecroppers from obtaining both the share of the produce and the credit to which they are legally entitled.[19]

An even more serious question concerns the overall direction of the government's tenancy reforms. In contrast to many states that have abolished tenancy altogether, West Bengal's reforms are likely to entrench sharecropping arrangements. The consequences are questionable both on grounds of efficiency and equity. Compared to landowners, sharecroppers have fewer incentives to invest in cultivation. Furthermore, as Ajit Ghosh notes, security of tenure and enforcement of the rent law are likely to increase differentiation between newly registered, economically strengthened sharecroppers and landless households.[20]

Alongside sharecropper registration, the government has redistributed land, much of which previous governments had vested. Compared to other Indian states, the extent of land redistribution in West Bengal is impressive. Out of roughly 4.5 million acres of vested land nationwide, West Bengal accounts for 1.2 million acres; the Left Front government has redistributed more than half of this latter amount.[21] When it took office in 1977, 2.5 million households were landless or nearly landless; by the end of 1984 the government had distributed nearly 800,000 acres to about 1.6 million of these families.[22]

In West Bengal, as in other parts of the country, there are formidable obstacles to land redistribution. In addition to the common practice of registering land under fictitious names, landlords have devised various means of profiting from their vested land. By obtaining a court injunction, a landlord can block land redistribution for decades. During this period, he can cultivate it surreptitiously, sell it, or convert it into nonagricultural land that is not covered by the land ceiling laws. An interview with P. C. Bannerjee, secretary for land reforms, revealed that corrupt bureaucrats often collude with landlords to prevent land redistribution.

In 1981, the Left Front government passed the Second Agrarian Land Reform Act. The watered-down version of the act that the central government approved will doubtless prevent the Left Front government from vesting another million acres of land as it had planned.[23] But even the most rigorous enforcement of ceiling laws would not eliminate gross inequalities in landownership. With an average of less than one-third of an acre per person, West Bengal has one of the lowest "land/man" ratios on the subcontinent.[24]

The government has emphasized sharecropper registration over land redistribution partly because the former is more likely to consolidate the support of small and middle peasants and less likely to incur opposition from large landowners. Even its methods of redistributing land are designed to increase the pool of small landowners without effectively redressing the problem of land hunger. Thus it has been extremely reluctant to experiment with collective or cooperative farming, although the average size of holding (0.6 acres for recent recipients of vested land) is not economically viable. Biplab Dasgupta, a CPI(M) official and director of the CADP, West Bengal's largest rural development agency, asserted that peasants gain a far greater sense of security from individual ownership. Nihar Bose, minister of cooperatives under the second Left Front government administration, stated flatly that "full cooperation is only possible under socialism." Consequently, it is misguided to promote cooperatives in the present context.

The experiences of cooperatives in other agrarian contexts have been so mixed that one cannot assume the likelihood of their success in West Bengal. However, rather than exploring alternatives to the standard models of cooperatives, the Left Front government has simply adopted the Congress government's limited conception of cooperatives as distributive mechanisms. The Left Front government has thereby disregarded the possibility that cooperatives might reduce class differentiation, facilitate the adoption of new technology, and challenge the conservatizing consequences of private property ownership.

The government's tendency to underrepresent agricultural laborers relative to middle peasants is also exemplified by its approach to the issue of minimum wages. The Congress government established the minimum wage rate in 1975. Five years later, the Left Front government had still not increased this rate. Nor had it achieved either minimum or equal wages (for men and women) in the dozen villages surveyed in 1982. Three years later, a trip to Midnapur revealed that wages in the harvesting season had increased significantly and the disparity had significantly narrowed between men's and women's wages. Yet in none of the villages that I visited were men or women receiving the legally mandated minimum wage.

The CPI(M)'s efforts to enforce minimum wage laws appear to have been limited. Although in 1979–80 the party organized relatively few wage strikes during the harvesting season, the incidence of strikes had further declined by 1985. Even if the CPI(M) considers strikes disruptive or ineffective, it could better use institutional channels for attaining minimum wages. For example, the Left Front government could increase the number of minimum wage inspectors in the state and thereby reduce their workload.[25]

The *Panchayat* Reforms

If one of the CPI(M)'s primary goals is to redistribute productive assets, another is to decentralize political power. It has attempted to do so through the *panchayats*, which were traditionally controlled by rural vested interests. Despite central government opposition, the Left Front government had political parties contest the *panchayat* elections. In 1978 the CPI(M) won 67 percent of the 55,801 seats in the three-tiered village, block, and district *panchayats*. In the subsequent *panchayat* elections in 1983 the CPI(M) once again secured a majority of votes, although this time it lost seats to the Congress (I) in the block-level *panchayat samitis* and the district-level *zilla parishads*.[26] The CPI(M)'s performance was even more impressive in the 1988 *panchayat* elections: it won 70 percent of seats in the *gram panchayats*, 79 percent in the *panchayat samitis*, and 91 percent in the *zilla parishads*.

The government made the *panchayats* responsible for implementing a variety of rural development schemes and placed substantial resources at their disposal. It ensured them the equivalent of the annual taxes they collected, a portion of land revenue, and control over vested land and water tanks in the area. In 1983–84 the West Bengal government gave the *panchayats* over $300 million, an average of about $50,000 to each *gram panchayat*.[27]

The government placed block-, subdivision-, and district-level bureaucrats at the *panchayats'* service. Civil servants initially resisted abdicating their authority to the newly empowered *panchayats*. Today, relations between higher-ranking bureaucrats and *panchayat* members seem to be relatively harmonious. In fact, a few bureaucrats have demonstrated even greater commitment than CPI(M) functionaries to government reforms. However, conflicts between lower-ranking bureaucrats and *panchayat* members at the block level have persisted.

The *panchayats* have to some extent fulfilled the government's intention of decentralizing and democratizing the administration. Before 1978, Asim Dasgupta recalled, the central government penetrated no further down than the district level, the state government as far down as the block level, where it posted about fifteen staff members. The rural poor thus found official channels blocked. However, the *panchayats* embody many of the undemocratic, inegalitarian features of the larger society. As tables 1 and 2 illustrate, *panchayats* overrepresent landowning cultivators and underrepresent landless laborers and sharecroppers, relative to their proportions in the population.

The government's overrepresentation of the middle class is also manifest in the social backgrounds of *panchayat* members. The underrepresentation of agricultural laborers and sharecroppers may contribute in turn to the *panchayats'* laxity in enforcing minimum wage laws and ensuring sharecropper registration.

The *panchayats* are also unrepresentative in another respect: given

TABLE 1 *Occupational Distribution of Gram Panchayat Members*

Occupation	*Percentage*
Owner-cultivators:	
owning below 2 acres	21.7
owning between 2 and 5 acres	14.3
owning more than 5 acres	14.7
Total	50.7
Sharecroppers	1.8
Landless laborers	4.8
Others (nonagriculturalists)	42.7

Source: Development and Planning Department, West Bengal Government, 1979.

This table is based on a survey of one hundred *gram panchayats* conducted by the government in early 1979. Note that nonagriculturalists and owner-cultivators are likely to be more numerous, while sharecroppers and landless laborers are likely to be fewer in the *panchayat samitis* and the *zilla parishads*.

their inability to formulate policies, they enable the state government to penetrate down to the village level but scarcely enable villagers to communicate their grievances back to Calcutta. The State Planning Advisory Board has recently extended the scope of decentralization reforms by associating the *panchayats* with district- and block-level planning committees. However, these local bodies still lack autonomous decision-making ability. Indeed, the *mandal panchayats* in Karnataka, which have assumed responsibility for local education, health, and development, exercise much greater autonomy than the West Bengal *panchayats*.

The Dilemmas of Radical Reform

The Dual-Stage Strategy

Given the state's impoverishment, Benoy Chowdhury informed me, agrarian capitalist development was essential to increasing the purchasing power of the rural poor and providing capital accumulation for industrialization. Its absence would perpetuate West Bengal's dependence on the central government and international agencies. Although it would be neither possible nor desirable to curb agrarian capitalism, Biplab Dasgupta argued, the government could curtail its

TABLE 2 *Distribution of Landownership, 1970–71*

acres	*Size of household holding* *households (%)*	*area (%)*
0.0	9.78	—
0.01–1.0	46.74	6.83
1.0–2.5	21.10	20.46
2.5–5.0	12.64	25.69
5.0–7.5	5.38	18.38
7.5–10.0	1.92	9.34
Above 10	2.44	19.30
Total	100%	100%

Source: National Sample Survey, 26th round, report no. 215, vol. 1 (West Bengal), p. 66.

exploitative consequences by redistributing land, increasing wages, and providing credit facilities to the rural poor.

The compulsions to foster capitalist development are strong in West Bengal, one of the poorest states in India. The percentage of the rural poor living below the poverty line increased from 40 percent to 66 percent between 1960–61 and 1973–74. In India the increase during the same period was from 42 percent to 48 percent. By the mid-1970s, thanks to industrial and agricultural stagnation, West Bengal contained the largest percentage of the population below the poverty line.[28]

The CPI(M) has pursued a strategy of class conciliation to encourage rural entrepreneurship. Since obtaining power in 1977, it has distinguished between *jotedars*, whom it regards as "class enemies," and rich peasants, whom it regards as allies. Thus, by 1981, Pramode Dasgupta, the former state secretary of the West Bengal CPI(M), could comment: "We do not regard the big farmer as a representative of feudal monopoly interests. Our class struggle is against the landed *jotedars*, not against the big farmer."[29] More recently, the CPI(M) has called for a unified *krishak* movement, which will include sharecroppers, marginal and small peasants, fishermen, artisans, and craftspersons.

To appease rich peasants, the CPI(M) has not levied a centrally sanctioned agricultural income tax. It has demanded higher procurement prices for agricultural commodities that would primarily benefit middle and rich peasants. The CPI(M) has exempted middle peasants from the procurement levy if they own less than four acres of irrigated land or six acres of unirrigated land. Although higher prices might encourage employers to pay higher wages, such an outcome is by no means certain. Moreover, higher procurement prices would increase food costs for the rural poor.

The CPI(M) has compromised the interests of the poorest rural groups by continually appeasing middle and rich peasants. It has shied away from conferring landownership rights on tenants, sponsoring wage strikes, and experimenting with cooperative farming. For years it resisted organizing agricultural laborers separately from landowning peasants. The All-India Agricultural Laborers Union it recently formed is not yet active in West Bengal.

Problems of Achieving Subnational Socialism

When the Left Front government was elected in 1977, it enjoyed close relations with the Janata government in New Delhi. Center-state relations quickly soured after Indira Gandhi's reelection in 1980. While Congress alleged that the communist government was unable to maintain political stability, the CPI(M) contended that Congress was disrupting law and order to create a pretext for dissolving the state assembly.[30] The Left Front government's relations with Congress after Rajiv Gandhi became prime minister were strained. The Janata Dal government, although more favorably predisposed toward West Bengal, was short-lived.

But regardless of which party is in power at the national level, the relation between central and state governments remains unequal. The constitution provides more extensive legislative powers to the center than to the states. Even those matters under state control are hedged with qualifications. Although agrarian reforms fall within the state government's jurisdiction, they can be overturned by the central government. Thus, in 1983 the West Bengal Legislative Assembly submitted an amended version of the Land Reforms Act of 1979 for presidential assent. After procrastinating for five years, the center finally approved a watered-down version of the act in 1987.

The governor of the state, whom the president appoints, has significant discretionary powers that indirectly give the center considerable influence. For example, he or she may reserve bills passed by the provincial Assembly for presidential consideration. The chief minister can also be confronted with serious resistance from central government bureaucrats posted to West Bengal. Asim Dasgupta pointed out to me that although the state government has some power to implement agrarian reform because of its control over land and labor, it is virtually powerless in the industrial sphere where capital is of greater importance.

Until the mid-1950s, West Bengal benefited from being situated near certain vital raw materials, notably coal. However, the union government deprived West Bengal of its comparative advantage by equalizing freight transportation costs for coal throughout India. The state government also alleges that Congress failed to increase West Bengal's capacity for thermal power generation in the 1960s and 1970s. Most important, the center has been reluctant to invest in industry and to grant West Bengal industrial licenses.

State governments are dependent on three sources of revenue: their own taxes, as denoted in the constitution; a share of centrally raised taxes, as specified by the Finance Commission; and Plan allocations. The Left Front government claims that the center has systematically deprived West Bengal of these resources. Between 1980–81 and 1984–85, per capita central Plan assistance was 132 rupees to West Bengal and an average of 214 rupees to other states. Moreover, 70 percent of its allotment was in loans with interest.[31] In 1984–85 a constitutionally mandated finance commission recommended that the center give West Bengal an additional $250 million, nearly 15 percent of the state's total budgeted expenditure. For what the Left Front government regards as contrived procedural reasons, the center rejected the commission's recommendations. As a result, according to Ashok Mitra, 40 percent of the state's total capital expenditure was channeled into debt repayment that year.[32]

The central government has also refused to share revenues from the corporate income tax, which is significantly more elastic than personal income tax. Moreover, rather than increase excise duty, which it shares with the states, the center has raised the administered prices of commodities like coal, iron, and steel, which central government monopolies produce. This rise in administered prices is partly responsible for inflation.

Given the enormous constraints imposed by the center, the Left

Front government has emphasized, in Biplab Dasgupta's words, that the government "is not in power but simply in office. Power rests with the Congress party in New Delhi." But this attempt to educate Bengalis about the impediments that Congress places before the Left Front government is likely to elicit the view that a peasant in Midnapur expressed: "The CPI(M) keeps telling us that it doesn't control power; Congress controls power. So we realized we should vote for the Congress party instead."

In continually highlighting central government constraints, the CPI(M) implicitly denies its own culpability. According to one senior government bureaucrat, the state government's inefficiency often prevents it from making full use of centrally allotted funds; by failing to submit "utilization certificates" for previously funded projects, it forgoes new allocations. In 1979–80, I heard government officials complain that the center was denying West Bengal food grains to which it was entitled under the Food for Work Program.[33] By 1985 the central government had replaced Food for Work with two similar but better funded schemes: the National Rural Employment Program and the Rural Landless Employment Generation Program. However, the center withheld the remaining entitlement because West Bengal had not used existing funds and lagged behind most states in implementing these programs.

Within the constraints that the center creates for state governments are opportunities the CPI(M) has only begun to exploit. As Kohli points out, the center possesses only a few formal mechanisms to influence state governments. It thus relies heavily on informal mechanisms of control through its party organization.[34] These have proved singularly ineffective in West Bengal because the state unit of the Congress party is rife with factional feuds.

Indeed, an important source of the CPI(M)'s repeated electoral success in West Bengal is Congress (I)'s growing weakness. The Congress party's dismal performance in the 1987 elections, when it captured forty seats, was particularly telling, for it had confronted more adverse conditions in previous elections. In 1969 it managed to win fifty-five seats although it faced the electorate's wrath at having connived with the governor to topple the first United Front government. Congress won twenty seats in 1977 when it encountered public outrage over the Emergency.[35] By contrast, although Congress went to the polls under comparatively favorable conditions in 1987, its disorganization, factionalism, and ideological incoherence all contributed to its overwhelming defeat.

The CPI(M)'s moderation exceeds the dictates of the external political environment. Compared to his mother, Rajiv Gandhi was more accommodating to opposition-controlled state governments. For example, he interpreted the governor's role as a nonpartisan figure, obligated to respect the wishes of state legislators rather than those of the central government. The short-lived Janata Dal government further eased whatever fears the CPI(M) may still have had about central government intervention.

Coalitions and Compromises

The dilemmas and constraints surrounding the CPI(M)'s approach to coalition building differ at the national and state levels. Given the weakness of the Opposition and the strength of Congress (I), the CPI(M)'s national leadership has endorsed electoral alliances with ideologically diverse political parties. The West Bengal unit has criticized the central leadership's alliance policy for compromising fundamental principles. In West Bengal, in contrast to other parts of India, the CPI(M) allies exclusively with other leftist parties. However, even in West Bengal, coalitions have entailed compromises and administrative inefficiencies.

For several years after the Left Front government's election in 1977, relations between its six constituents were relatively harmonious. (The three largest members were the CPI[M], the Forward Bloc, and the Revolutionary Socialist Party [RSP]; much less significant were the Marxist Forward Bloc, the Revolutionary Communist Party of India, and the Biplabi Bangla Congress.) Tensions have since mounted and become especially acute around elections. In preparation for the 1982 Legislative Assembly elections, the CPI(M) included the CPI, the West Bengal Socialist Party, and the Democratic Socialist Party within the Left Front. Echoing the West Bengal CPI(M)'s criticism of its central leadership, the older Left Front constituents criticized the CPI(M) for making the Front too broad based. Coalition partners also questioned the CPI(M)'s reallocation of ministerial portfolios.

Tensions further increased during the *panchayat* elections the following year over the extent to which the CPI(M) allowed coalition partners to nominate electoral candidates. With the 1984 parliamentary elections, divisions reemerged: its coalition partners joined oppositional forces in criticizing the CPI(M) for nonperformance in office and for poor interdepartmental coordination. The CPI(M) in turn blamed Front members for jealously safeguarding their ministerial prerogatives. "The basest instincts emerge in interparty feuds," commented former finance minister Ashok Mitra; "each minister says 'reform, streamlining, yes—but not in my ministry.' "

By the 1988 *panchayat* elections, disputes between coalition partners erupted in open, bitter rivalry. The CPI(M), RSP, and the Forward Bloc competed with one another for twenty-five thousand seats on which they could not reach agreement. Jyoti Basu described the demands of the Forward Bloc and the RSP for more seats as unjustified and urged voters to defeat those who were hurting left unity. Kamal Guha, agricultural minister in the third Left Front government ministry and member of the Forward Bloc, had slogans plastered around Coochbehar district that read: *Rajiv hatao, desh bachao, CPM hatao, gram bachao* ("Remove Rajiv to save the country, remove the CPI(M) to save the villages"). RSP leader Debabrata Bandhopadhyaya accused the CPI(M) of trying to annihilate its partners in a Stalinist manner. Ten days before the poll the CPI(M) claimed that the Forward Bloc and RSP had allied with Congress (I).

Even more significant disputes have emerged since 1987. One source is the policy question of whether Front partners have the right to launch agitations under their own party banners and in particular whether they have the right to launch agitations against the CPI(M). Another source of division has been allegations of CPI(M) corruption by coalition partners. Jatin Chakraborty, the RSP minister of public works, made the most damaging charge when he accused Jyoti Basu of privately instructing the government to promote the business interests of Bengal Lamps Works, in which Basu's son was active. The crisis threatened to destroy the government until the RSP instructed Chakraborty to resign. However, the Bengal Lamps scandal, along with another allegation of government kickbacks—to the Calcutta Teamways Company—have tarnished both the image of the chief minister and relations between Front partners.

Why should the CPI(M) continue to participate in a coalition government when it won an absolute majority of Legislative Assembly seats? Administrative inefficiency is a significant but still relatively minor inconvenience compared to the larger danger that coalition partners might undermine the Left Front from within. Old guard leaders fear that if leftist parties ceased to be allies, they could easily become enemies. Furthermore, the CPI(M) is eager to counter the image it gained under previous United Front governments by proving itself a trustworthy ally.

However, on balance, growing acrimony within the Front has not weakened the CPI(M). In fact, with the 1987 Legislative Assembly elections, in which the CPI(M) captured 187 of 294 Assembly seats, Front partners appeared to be virtually redundant. As a result the CPI(M) kept the major portfolios and took over housing, health, industry, and engineering from the RSP and the Forward Bloc. The Left Front government is much stronger and more durable than either previous United Front governments or coalitions in other parliamentary democracies.

The Hazards of Power

CPI(M) leaders frankly admit that they were not prepared to win the 1977 elections, let alone occupy office for three terms. One important hindrance to governing West Bengal was the party's relatively small size. Thus, at its Salkiya Plenum in 1978, the CPI(M) Central Committee decided to double the West Bengal unit's membership. Accordingly, it relaxed the strict criteria that had formerly governed admission to the party. Manoranjan Hazra, a high ranking CPI(M) leader in West Bengal, has sharply and eloquently criticized this policy. Hazra argues that although the CPI(M) had only 35,000 members in 1977, it won the Legislative Assembly elections and formed the Left Front government. However, despite having 118,000 members by 1984, Congress (I) emerged four times stronger in the parliamentary elections than it had been in 1980. In Hazra's words:

> Tragically, the Party has enrolled members without examining their past, aptitudes and motivations. All prospective members must be screened. But with the CPI(M) leaders at the branch and local committee levels eager to strengthen their own positions and push their personal interests, corrupt and anti-social elements have been enrolled as members. Such reckless enrollment has led to a phenomenal increase in numbers. Quality has suffered in the bargain.[36]

The CPI(M) has demonstrated greater laxity as its class coalition has broadened. For example, the Left Front government tacitly permits public employees to arrive at Writers' Building, the state government headquarters, toward 11 A.M. rather than 10 A.M. each day because of transportation difficulties. In fact, personal observations suggest that bureaucrats often arrive around noon and, after frequent tea breaks and a leisurely lunch, begin their exodus from the office by 3 P.M. A similar attempt to broaden its class coalition is evident in the rural areas, where the CPI(M) fears antagonizing the dominant classes. It makes electoral sense for the CPI(M) to direct its appeals to landowning peasants when agricultural laborers only constitute a fourth of the rural working population.

As long as the CPI(M) chooses to remain in office it will be forced to compromise certain ideals—although fewer perhaps than it believes: the Left Front government has scarcely tested the limits of tolerance in West Bengal. It is important to underline the element of choice in the CPI(M)'s strategy. Ashok Mitra, among the most radical party leaders, persuasively argued that the CPI(M) should risk electoral defeat in order to politicize the electorate. The longer the CPI(M) has remained in office, the more its exercise of power has become an end in itself.

The Inner Dynamics of Communist Parties

If as noted above the Left Front government has been weakened by its laxity, the CPI(M)'s overemphasis on discipline, to the detriment of creative grass-roots participation, has also been a critical source of its reformism.[37] The tendency is especially evident in communist parties that uphold democratic centralism. At its Vijaywada congress in 1982 and at a meeting of the West Bengal unit the following year, the CPI(M) reaffirmed its belief in democratic centralist principles. The Vijaywada report argues that a hierarchical chain of command is essential to combating central government repression and making the party an efficient instrument of change.

The CPI(M)'s commitment to democratic centralist principles seems to be born, above all, from its desire to maintain the party's cohesion. To some extent this strategy has borne fruit, for the CPI(M) is not plagued by the factionalism that characterizes other

Indian political parties. Democratic centralist principles have also enabled the CPI(M) to check opportunism, patronage, and corruption in the *panchayats*. A CPI(M) booklet published just before the 1983 *panchayat* elections justified the exclusive rights of top-ranking leaders to nominate candidates on grounds of democratic centralist principles.

However, democratic centralism justifies the unquestioned leadership of the party's old guard. Although theoretically the politburo's decisions are subject to ratification by the central committee, in fact it is commonly believed that several politburo veterans draft every major party decision. According to its own estimates, the CPI(M) dismissed 442 party members in West Bengal for corruption, lack of discipline, and antiparty activity after a "rectification campaign" in 1983.[38] Dissident party leaders refused, when questioned, to describe their activities.

As chapter 3 describes in greater detail, democratic centralist principles have enabled the CPI(M) to maintain strict control over its mass organizations. Manoranjan Rai justified such "top-down" control in the case of trade unions on the grounds that the party would ultimately be held responsible for the Centre of Industrial Trade Union's (CITU) actions. In any case, he asserted, it was unthinkable that there could be substantial differences between the party and union when a "people's government" occupied office. His comment betrays a widespread belief that such disparate groups as women, youth, workers, and peasants share identical interests, all of which the leftist government represents.

In short, democratic centralism is a critical source of the CPI(M)'s deradicalization. Deprived of significant influence or understanding of its inner workings, many of its lower-ranking cadres lack commitment. Isolated from the realities of peasants' lives, the party as a whole cannot champion their struggles. Its Vijaywada congress report acknowledges that the CPI(M) has failed to "give sufficient attention to the spontaneous struggles . . . by the common people against social oppression." Party activities have not facilitated "democratic participation of common peasants in decision making." The report notes that the party's sectarianism has impeded joint actions with other progressive forces.[39] Yet it does not recognize the link between the CPI(M)'s organizational weaknesses and democratic centralist principles.

Conclusion

If, in evaluating the Left Front government's record over the past thirteen years, the CPI(M) is judged by the standards specified by Panitch in the European context or by Rudra for India, it must be deemed a failure. Government reforms neither challenge the existing state and class structure nor create the groundwork for more radical alternatives. However, given the CPI(M)'s moderate intentions, coupled with the absence of revolutionary conditions in West Bengal today, these stringent criteria are irrelevant. It is more appropriate to analyze the extent to which the CPI(M) has fulfilled the reformist goals that Esping-Andersen and Stephens in the European context and Kohli in the Indian context consider as standards for social democracy.

The CPI(M)'s major achievement has been to enable the rural poor to obtain improved living conditions and a greater sense of dignity. A visit to arid, drought-stricken regions of western Midnapur in 1979–80 revealed that large numbers of villagers had left destitute family members to search for employment in the plains during the lean seasons. Five years later villagers in the same region spent these periods in their newly constructed homes, cultivating their own plots of land. Material betterment had increased their sense of efficacy. Despite the shortcomings in its conception and implementation, "Operation Barga" has unquestionably increased sharecroppers' incomes, provided them with greater security, and reduced their dependence on landlords.

The relative absence of violence against women, minorities, and the lowest castes and classes in West Bengal has not earned the CPI(M) the credit it deserves. "An absence" by definition constitutes an invisible achievement, especially because West Bengal has had a tradition of harmonious caste and "communal" relations since Partition in 1948, quite independently of the CPI(M)'s actions. However, there is little precedent or historical basis for some of the most virulent "communal" conflicts that have occurred elsewhere in India in the recent period. Given West Bengal's substantial Muslim population and the still bitter memories of the British partition of the province, Hindu-Muslim conflict could well have been severe under a less principled government.[40]

However, when one refers to the standards of successful social democracies, one finds that the Left Front government has scarcely implemented the most minimal reforms. As opposed to the dynamic that Esping-Andersen and Stephens suggest, the Left Front government sponsored its most ambitious reforms—concerning sharecroppers and the *panchayats*—in its first two years in office. These reforms gave the rural poor a sense of efficacy, strength, and optimism. Yet, as Ashok Mitra ruefully admitted to me several years later, "We failed to maintain our radical fervor. We failed to sustain the chemistry we created when we were elected."

One of the most frequent recent criticisms of the government concerns its lethargy, or, as it is often described, its "nonperformance." Although most evident in Calcutta, the problem is also apparent in the rural areas. For example, the central rather than the state government has introduced most programs designed to improve education, employment, and health facilities for scheduled castes and tribes, as they are officially designated.

It might be contended that West Bengal provides a poor test of Esping-Andersen's argument: the economy has not been expanding, the government does not control the business cycle, and the basis for the creation of a new class coalition does not fully exist; the peasantry has not shrunk nor the working class grown. Yet if the parallel is imperfect, the cases have enough in common for West Bengal's experience to illuminate Esping-Andersen's contention.

The Left Front government is among a small number of social democratic regimes that have occupied office for well over a decade. As Andrew Martin argues, a long, continuous tenure in office is critical to setting in motion the dynamic of spiraling reformism.[41] In contrast to most social democracies, which, as Przeworski notes, have never won sufficient votes to legislate without other parties' consent, the CPI(M) has secured an absolute majority of seats in West Bengal's Legislative Assembly for three consecutive terms. Moreover, in several respects that Esping-Andersen considers important, the Left Front government's experience resembles that of northern European social democracies: it came to power thanks to peasant support and has increasingly forged a coalition with the middling strata. Whatever the results of its efforts, it has seriously attempted economic expansion.

One can infer from Esping-Andersen that if social democracy is most likely to have radicalizing consequences during periods of growth, it must devise new reforms to maintain its momentum during periods of stagnation. To the extent that possibilities for economic growth are blocked, social democracies can provide their constituencies with nonquantifiable political benefits, such as workplace democracy. (The Meidner plan in Sweden provides a good example.) The CPI(M) has barely explored these options.

In keeping with Panitch's argument about the linkages between leftist parties' deradicalization and the diminution of working-class support, the CPI(M) suffered its worst defeats in Calcutta's urban-industrial belt both in the 1985 parliamentary elections and the 1987 Assembly elections. Many reports suggest that workers especially resented growing unemployment and the government's seeming favoritism toward middle-class public employees. However, given the relatively small size of the industrial working class, the CPI(M)'s growing reformism has not entailed electoral defeat. Indeed the CPI(M) has broadened its class coalition, as Esping-Andersen stipulates is necessary for social democracy to persist.

Both the structural constraints described by Przeworski and Offe and the strategic choices identified by Panitch are critical to explaining the Left Front government's growing moderation. However, for a variety of reasons it is difficult to evaluate the precise significance of each. Although many theorists consider "structural" synonymous with "economic," we have seen that radical reform is impeded as much by political as by economic factors, neither of which the CPI(M) fully controls. Take the example of the CPI(M)'s relationship to the central government. The Left Front government seems no less fearful of being overthrown than of being deprived of resources by the central government.

To make matters even more complicated, on the one hand the CPI(M) exercises greater control than may initially be apparent over "external" conditions, while on the other hand party leadership, organization, and ideology cannot simply be considered freely determined. For example, the CPI(M) exercises an unusual degree of control over coalition arrangements in West Bengal. Conversely, although democratic centralism represents a choice of strategy, it is in many respects predetermined by the trajectory of the international communist movement and the *bhadralok* base of the communist movement in West Bengal. Similarly, the extent to which the CPI(M) has chosen or has been forced by political circumstance to pursue a wholly electoral approach is debatable.

With these considerations in mind, it still appears that the major constraint upon the West Bengal CPI(M) emanates from the contradictory imperatives that are implicit in functioning at the subnational level. At the least this rules out the possibility of outright class struggle, large-scale political mobilization, and a direct challenge to the national state. But the example of Kerala indicates the possibility for a more radical strategy of land reform without necessitating the CPI(M)'s complete abdication of power.

The underdeveloped character of the West Bengal economy also ranks high among apparently intractable obstacles to a more effective reformist approach. However, large-scale capitalist agriculture of the Punjab-western U.P. variety is no more feasible than socialization of the economy. Although the CPI(M) has taken the initiative for political reforms to achieve further democratization, it has lagged much further behind with respect to democratization in the economic sphere.

If the small size of the industrial working class might be viewed as impeding the anticapitalist strategy that Panitch envisages, recall the contention of innumerable revolutionary theorists within the Third World context: the rural proletariat can play a parallel role to industrial workers when the transition to capitalism is incomplete. Indeed, landless agricultural laborers have been a prime source of rural militance in India. Like industrial workers in the Marxist formulation, agricultural laborers have nothing to lose from their radicalism, for they do not own or control the means of production. Laborers' militance is often heightened by their experience of subjugation along both caste and class lines. But the CPI(M) has sacrificed the interests of agricultural laborers in much the same way that Panitch argues social democratic parties have sacrificed workers' interests in Western Europe.

Even if the three constraints described earlier—emanating from the unitary features of the federal system, the challenge posed by West Bengal's impoverishment, and the imperatives of coalition building—effectively precluded significant reform, they would still not explain the CPI(M)'s failures with respect to women, the landless, and *adivasis*. To better understand these failures we must consider the consequences of the CPI(M)'s electoral bent and its adherence to democratic centralist principles set against the backdrop of its *bhadralok* leadership and middle-class base.

If, as Panitch notes in a different context, the CPI(M)'s actions have not been wholly dictated by the logic of liberal democracy, it is easier to suggest the need for an uncompromising yet feasible strategy than to provide specific guidelines. How might the CPI(M) have avoided succumbing to conservatizing constraints in order to creatively exploit the potential for radical change?

Not only, as noted above, are constraints more malleable than they appear, but a progressive strategy would involve transforming constraints into opportunities. In reviewing the situation of West Bengal, two quite different spheres—agrarian production and cultural relations—provide important illustrations. Although certain aspects of both spheres stifle progressive change today, they contain emancipatory possibilities that the CPI(M) could realize only if it possessed greater political will and vision.

Consider agricultural production. In a densely populated, overwhelmingly agrarian state, land reform must be among a leftist government's highest priorities. As described above, however, the Left Front government has pursued land reform in a manner barely distinguishable from that of Congress governments at the national and state levels. Such an approach is not wholy dictated by legal, constitutional, or economic realities. By rejecting producer cooperatives, for example, the Left Front government denies itself a potentially valuable opportunity to make optimal use of key economic resources, disseminate socialist ideology, and forge solidaristic relations among the rural poor.

If the Left Front government frequently cites the conservatizing weight of the central government and overarching capitalist context, it seems oblivious of the extent to which Bengali *bhadralok* culture shapes its actions. Important instances include the government's failure to organize agricultural laborers on a separate basis, frontally attack the dowry system, and support *adivasi* identity movements. The government thereby renounces an opportunity to mobilize the most oppressed groups.

In an age of skepticism regarding socialist possibilities, it is noteworthy that the Left Front government has survived for so long. Yet the manner in which it has done so is strikingly reminiscent of northern European social democratic governments. In both cases, success in the current period has been achieved through increasing moderation and the depletion of hard-earned cultural and political capital.

Chapter Three

Democratic Centralism in the Home and the World: Bengali Women and the CPI(M)

"We see the CPI(M) as our family. Like our family it protects us."
Purna Das, executive member of the West Bengal Democratic Women's Association

"The essence of Stalinist communism," argues Ronald Tiersky, "is its monolithic internal politics, and Stalinism is the attempt to make *all* politics into internal politics."[1] Imagine then the possibilities of extending the realm of internal Communist party politics when democratic centralist principles are already prefigured in the private sphere. Like the CPI(M), the Bengali Hindu family is organized along strictly hierarchical lines: the men who occupy its highest rungs exercise the most power. Yet the family, like the party, mystifies such inequality and projects itself as a solidaristic unit whose members share identical interests. Democratic centralist principles in the home fortify the CPI(M) in the world, at the cost of perpetuating sexual inequality.

If the CPI(M) in West Bengal now accepts women's subordination within the family, the communist movement has not always done so. As sectarian as it might have been in its early stages, the CPI was far more willing than the CPI(M) is today to challenge "bourgeois practices" that sometimes included traditional gender relations. Although communist leadership has always been drawn from the *bha-*

dralok, its identification with middle-class interests and commitment to electoral success have grown simultaneously. Ironically, the party and its affiliated women's organization have become instruments of Sanskritization.[2]

The political sources of Bengali women's quiescence are rooted in the CPI(M)'s democratic centralist principles of organization, electoral preoccupations, and class reductionist ideology. Clearly, certain facets of West Bengal's economic and social structure strengthen the CPI(M)'s approach. For example, women's primary and often exclusive identities as wives and mothers—the product in turn of both economic and social influences—cannot be disassociated from the CPI(M)'s tendency to neglect women's political interests, underrepresent them in the party and the government, and project their maternal roles onto the public arena. The more difficult question is whether the CPI(M) can escape these socioeconomic influences.

Rather than challenging women's subordination, the CPI(M) has expediently built upon it. Tacit acceptance of female seclusion, which as noted earlier has its roots in upper-caste traditions, benefits the CPI(M) in several ways: it accords with the CPI(M)'s attempt to create a cross-class coalition in which middle-class interests will predominate. The stability of women's roles as wives and mothers reassures those who fear radical change and demonstrates the CPI(M)'s sympathy for traditional practices. Most important, by accepting the roles that Bengali Hindu society prescribes for women, the CPI(M) can demonstrate its allegiance to Bengali cultural identity in the face of a pervasive fear of domination by the Hindi-speaking heartland.

The Romance of Bengali Communism

Given the formidable barriers they had to overcome, communist women were more audacious in the 1940s than they are today. Moreover, they clearly struggled harder to resolve contradictions between their public and private roles. However, the bleaker reality is that the CPI never seriously challenged sexual inequality, cultivated female leadership, or addressed the problems of poor rural women.

The account that follows is based on reminiscences of the first generation of Bengali communist women.[3] Virtually all of those who were interviewed spoke of the risk and romance entailed in becoming a CPI member between 1939 and 1942. Most of the young women who joined the CPI during this period were from wealthy, conservative families. Many had been active in the so-called terrorist movement, a violent, anti-imperialist struggle in the first two decades of the twentieth century. Consider the account of Bani Dasgupta, who joined the CPI Student Federation in 1939.

> It is difficult to describe my sense of excitement when some students told me about the Communist party. You see my father was from a big *zamindar* [landlord] family. I used to hear laborers screaming with pain when they were beaten for being lazy and dishonest. . . . Here was a party which would put an end to such injustice. I began to attend the student meetings. When my relatives found out they locked me in my room at night. When they realized that they could not stop me, they drove me out of the house—beat me with shoes—because they said I was an insult to the family.

Dasgupta arrived in Calcutta in 1941 with a letter of introduction to party leaders and the two rupees (approximately a nickel) she had left after paying her train fare. Like many other young, middle-class women who had left their homes to work for the party in Calcutta, she moved into a communally organized home that was headed by Manikuntala Sen, the senior-most woman in the CPI at the time. The fifteen men and women who shared the house lived in an extremely egalitarian fashion, sharing meager incomes and ample household responsibilities. Dasgupta recalled that often they could not afford to eat for several days at a time. At the suggestion of CPI comrades she gave up graduate studies to work as a full-time party member for a monthly salary of twenty rupees (about seventy-five cents).

The first generation of Bengali communist women did not question the party's neglect of gender issues. Having taken the radical step of severing ties with their parents, they sought camaraderie and protection from male comrades. Many were financially dependent on the party. But the more important explanation for their silence was that they considered the CPI the major font of opposition to women's oppression.[4]

Communist men and women attempted to organize their personal lives in an emancipated fashion. Breaking with traditional practice, they rejected arranged marriages, lavish weddings, and the dowry and often married across religious and caste lines. In some areas where the communist movement was strong, party members consecrated marriages with an exchange of garlands rather than through religious ceremonies. In striking contrast with their present stance, communist men tended to marry women who were full-time political activists. Although these women were primarily responsible for housework and child care, their husbands encouraged their political activism.

One can only speculate about why the chasm grew between party members' private and public lives. The CPI seems to have increasingly absorbed dominant cultural values once it became incorporated into the formal political arena. In Gita Mukherjee's view, from the 1950s the CPI undermined the autonomy of mass organizations among women and other groups by relying upon them for electoral mobilization. More broadly, in West Bengal as in numerous other contexts, women's activism tended to be confined to periods of political crisis. In the absence of revolutionary upheaval, women were not compelled to perform men's jobs in fields, factories, or battlegrounds. But even in its heyday, the CPI was ill-equipped to challenge gender inequality, particularly among poor rural women. There was a deep cultural abyss between urban, educated, upper-class communist leaders and the rural poor. The rift was compounded by the CPI's alienation from indigenous cultural traditions, in part because of its close links with the Soviet Union.

The Formation of the Mahila Atma Raksha Samiti

The period 1944–48 represents the high watermark of CPI mobilization in West Bengal. During this period, the communist movement was closely identified with a renaissance in Bengali theater, film, and literature. After the government legalized the CPI in 1942, it created a number of mass organizations, including the Mahila Atma Raksha Samiti (MARS, or Women's Self-Defense League). Although only 112 women attended its first meeting in 1942, its membership had risen to 43,500 by its second annual meeting two years later.

MARS's first major contribution was to rehabilitate poor rural and urban women during the tragic Bengal famine in 1943. It created orphanages, formed soup kitchens, opened first-aid centers, and organized demonstrations against hoarders and black marketeers. Manikuntalla Sen described MARS as having been especially active in relief work because women were the worst victims of the famine.

Needless to add, women's organizations were the first to engage in charitable social work.[5]

MARS's other major commitment was to antifascist organizing in response to the threat of a Japanese invasion of India and Germany's attack on the Soviet Union. At this time the CPI's declaration that the "imperialist war" had become a "people's war" was doubly ironic: the CPI's refusal to challenge British imperialism alienated it from the Congress-led nationalist movement, which was mobilizing peasant men and women on an unprecedented scale. Moreover, opposition to Nazi Germany had little meaning to poor rural women. Because of its reluctance to criticize the Allies, the CPI did not even expose British complicity in creating the famine.

In contrast to the Union of Italian Women (UDI) and other European women's organizations that grew out of the Resistance, MARS derived much less political capital from its antifascist work. In part this was because Indian women were less affected than Italian women by fascism. In Italy, not only were the communist and socialist parties outlawed, but fascist legislation forced women out of schools, the work place, and political life. Thus, as Judith Hellman argues for Italy, the antifascist struggle became synonymous with a struggle for the restoration and expansion of women's roles.[6] The challenge that MARS did not meet in India was to oppose the deterioration in rural women's economic conditions as a result of colonial domination.

Today some CPI members like Bani Dasgupta criticize the CPI's war-time stance. But Kanak Mukherjee, an old-time communist who subsequently became a member of the CPI(M) Central Committee, adamantly defends the CPI's position: "You cannot judge the correctness of a party line by whether the people are behind you. Otherwise we would always be running after the people."

Under the aegis of the communists' peasant organization, the Bengal Provincial Kisan Sabha, in 1946 sharecroppers put forward the demand *"Adhi nai, tebhaga chai"* ("We want two-thirds, not one half" [of the harvest]). In fact, under the *adhi*, or *barga*, system of produce rent, tenants gave landlords most of the crop as rent and bore the entire costs of cultivation. Sharecroppers traditionally had no rights to the land.

Most accounts of the Tebhaga movement (1946–48) indicate that peasant women demonstrated extraordinary militance, particularly in later phases of the movement, as government repression increased.

Women formed *nari bahinis*, fighting troops, which confronted landlords, encircled the police, and forcibly harvested the paddy. They played an especially important role in organizing communication by transmitting messages between activists, hiding cadre who had gone underground, and sounding alarms when police were approaching.

Women's activism in the Tebhaga movement provides an excellent illustration of the dual significance of socioeconomic and political influences. On the one hand, local women leaders mainly comprised those who had escaped the strictures of seclusion: *adivasis*, Rajbansis (low castes), and widows.[7] An excellent example is Bimala Maji, who overcame the restrictions her in-laws imposed on her after her husband's death and became the leading female activist in Midnapur district. Maji reported that many women became conscious of their own interests through attempts to protect their families. Thus they demanded income from the labor they had performed; some of them also spontaneously protested sexual harassment by landlords and even by their own husbands.

On the other hand, emphasis must also be accorded to the political forces that permitted women's fleeting but significant activism. MARS played a relatively minor role in the Tebhaga movement, largely because of its urban, middle-class composition and its distance from poor rural women. However, in the early stages of Tebhaga the CPI was in its radical phase and did not discourage women's spontaneous protest. After the fall of 1947, when the CPI appealed to peasants to reject direct action and rely upon legal channels, women's militancy subsided.

By the early 1950s, MARS's dependence on the CPI inhibited recognition of the transcendent nature of women's oppression across class, caste, and party lines. During periods of sectarianism, the male party leadership would rein in its mass organizations and thereby undermine the gains they had achieved. Moreover, government repression was not confined to the CPI but also directed at its mass organizations. Thus, although MARS was often led by noncommunist women and included members with diverse political affiliations, it was forced to go underground when the government declared the CPI illegal as a result of its decision to pursue an insurrectionary path; MARS subsequently became small and isolated.

Similarly, for years communist women participated in the Congress Party–affiliated All-India Women's Conference (AIWC), which comprised a broad cross-section of women. Vidhya Munshi described it as an important national forum in which communists could disseminate their ideas, make contacts with otherwise inaccessible women, and influence relevant legislation. Thus they could fight in parliament for the passage of the Hindu Code Bill, which gave women legal rights to divorce, remarry, and inherit property. In *Communists in Indian Women's Movement*, Renu Chakravarty suggests that communist women transformed the AIWC from an urban, elite organization into a mass organization.[8] Communist women relinquished an important resource by leaving the AIWC in 1949.

In accordance with CPI policy, which called for revolutionary opposition to the Nehru government, MARS worked underground between 1947 and 1951. During this period it encountered a great deal of opposition. Police shot and killed four communist women at a demonstration in Calcutta in April 1949; numerous women were killed in the districts throughout this period.

A Split within the Split: The Formation of the PBGMS

After the CPI emerged from its sectarian phase, women formed the National Federation of Indian Women (NFIW) in 1954. Vidhya Munshi reported that communist men initially opposed the creation of the NFIW for they feared that it would divide and weaken the party. Women overcame their resistance: the NFIW became affiliated to the Soviet-based Women's International Democratic Federation, which by no means espoused independent feminist goals. MARS, which was reconstituted as the Paschim Bangla Mahila Samiti (PBMS) in 1953, became the most important constituent of the NFIW in West Bengal. The NFIW poured its energies into constructive activities and establishing contacts with communist-bloc women's organizations. It explicitly refrained from organizing agitational movements among the rural poor.

More damaging yet to communist women's organizing efforts were rifts within the communist movement. Although dissident Communist party members formed the CPI(M) in April 1964, women members of the two parties worked jointly in the PBMS until 1971. Relations between them became estranged as a result of the downfall of the CPI(M)-led United Front government in 1971 and attendant strains between its constituents. The PBMS remained affiliated with the CPI, whereas the Paschim Bangla Ganatantrik Mahila Samiti (PBGMS) was established as a separate organization, linked to the CPI(M).

The PBGMS, born of the split, was more sectarian than its predecessor. The contrasts between the two communist women's organizations became particularly marked after the Left Front government was elected in 1977. The CPI was not a constituent of the Left Front coalition at this time; it had been severely discredited because it had supported the Congress party's declared national Emergency. Its marginalization from the formal political arena freed the CPI-affiliated PBMS, unlike the official PBGMS, to join feminist groups in struggles against women's oppression.

PBGMS influence on the CPI(M) further declined during the Left Front government's tenure in office. The CPI(M) increasingly used the PBGMS as a vehicle for securing electoral support and discouraged the PBGMS from organizing agitational movements. Furthermore, the CPI(M) became less responsive to women, who now constituted only one part of a large and heterogeneous constituency. In short, added to the CPI(M)'s earlier economic reductionism was its growing political reductionism: its tendency to narrow the scope of confrontational activities because of electoral imperatives.

Women under the Left Front Government

If the undivided Communist party created a counter-community for a small group of urban, middle-class women in the 1940s, the CPI(M) has replicated its efforts, this time for rural women in the 1980s. Indeed, one of its major achievements is to have imparted feelings of dignity to poor rural women. This intangible gain is apparent at government rallies in Calcutta. The women who arrive in party-sponsored buses from the surrounding villages clearly attend these demonstrations for their entertainment value. But equally unmistakable is their sense of solidarity, efficacy, and pride that "their" government is in office. Their sentiments grow out of a political context that is relatively free from police repression, caste and "communal" conflict, and violence against women. For example, in contrast to north Indian states in which the incidence of dowry deaths is high and rising, in West Bengal the Left Front government has helped contain their escalation by appointing dowry prohibition officers in all the districts. It is also committed to hiring women police officers to investigate cases of dowry-related harassment and murder.

The Left Front government has achieved several small but significant improvements in the conditions of rural women. It has expanded the scope of the West Bengal Social Welfare Advisory Board (SWAB), which is financed and staffed jointly by state and central governments. SWAB activities include social work, rehabilitation programs, and vocational training. The board also sponsors thirty-four women and child welfare programs that organize nonformal education, nutrition classes, nursery schools, and craft centers in the villages. SWAB has formed village committees, each of which includes a female *panchayat* member and a director of programs for rural women.[9]

With central government assistance, the West Bengal government has recently provided poor rural women loans to promote income-generating projects.[10] It has provided women with opportunities for employment in small-scale and cottage industries, particularly in handloom cloth production. It has increased pensions for widows from thirty to sixty rupees a month. The Legal Aid Department provides free legal services to widows, prostitutes, and destitute women.

In the sphere of education, the Left Front government provides free tuition to the twelfth grade, textbooks to the fifth grade, and, on an experimental basis, midday meals. According to Kanti Biswas, minister of education, since 1977 the government has opened twelve thousand schools and appointed forty-six thousand teachers; it has increased the proportion of school-age children attending school from 69 percent to 96 percent. As a result, literacy rates increased from 34 percent to 40 percent between 1971 and 1981.

Resolutions from recent party congresses reveal an increased commitment to women's political participation. At its eleventh congress in 1982, for example, the CPI(M) identified women's struggles as "not just a struggle for social reform but an integral part of the Indian people's struggle for democracy and socialism."[11] The same congress passed a resolution that stated that membership in the All-India Democratic Women's Association, the national women's organization that is affiliated with the CPI(M), would be open to nonparty members.[12] Within West Bengal, the Left Front government nominated sixteen women to contest the Legislative Assembly elections in 1987; fourteen were elected, twelve on the CPI(M) ticket and two from other leftist parties.

Overall, however, when compared with the efforts of autonomous women's organizations and socialist governments elsewhere, the CPI(M) has scarcely attempted to restructure women's economic, political, and social roles.

The Sphere of Production

Ironically, the CPI(M) has been insufficiently Marxist in ignoring the links between women's propertylessness and sexual inequality. Thus it has not questioned women's limited inheritance rights under Hindu law and in Bengali social custom. Moreover, it has redistributed land only to household heads, who are generally male. Thus, its most striking failure with respect to women is its major achievement with respect to men: tenancy reforms.

Shortly after the government had initiated "Operation Barga," an independent women's organization, the Center for Women's Development Studies (CWDS), organized a workshop for rural women in Bankura district. At this meeting, a landless *adivasi* woman said, "Babu, it is all well and good to give *puttas* [land titles] to our husbands. But if they leave us, we become landless again." A participant in the workshop, D. Bandhopadhyaya, land reforms secretary to the West Bengal government at the time, persuaded the central government to include the principle of joint *puttas* in the seventh five-year plan. New Delhi left the initiative for implementing this proposal to state governments. Yet by early 1988, the West Bengal government was registering only the names of households heads on land records.

Resistance to joint *puttas* clearly reflects men's fear of women's economic independence. But given the fact that *adivasis* and *dalits*, who are less prejudiced, are the major recipients of land titles, the more significant obstacles must be sought elsewhere. Despite Bandhopadhyaya's encouragement, the PBGMS did not mobilize peasant women around this critical issue. Ironically, even top-ranking PBGMS members often opposed joint land titles. Kanak Mukherjee commented, "If we give *puttas* in women's names, next children will be demanding land in their names. And what will happen if the couple separates? The land will become even more fragmented."

By bestowing land titles on household heads, the CPI(M) exacerbates economic disparities between men and women and buttresses male domination. Since Hindu women can neither remarry nor easily return to their natal families, women whose husbands abandon them are rendered impoverished. The problem is compounded by the government's failure to significantly increase credit facilities and employment opportunities for women. Nor has the PBGMS demanded that women should be recognized as sharecroppers in their own right, although such a designation is legally permissible. Although women toil alongside their husbands on leased land at a range of cultivation tasks, Shyamali Gupta, the PBGMS secretary, argued that people would reject the notion that women work as hard as men.

One frightening manifestation and consequence of the Left Front government's tendency to ignore women in pursuing land reform is female malnutrition. A survey of two West Bengal villages by Amartya Sen and Sunil Sengupta reveals that, ironically, girls suffered more severe malnutrition in Kuchli village, which had experienced land reform, than in Sahajapur village, which hadn't.[13] Yet boys' nutritional level was much better in Kuchli than Sahajapur village. Severe female malnutrition could have been curtailed by direct nutritional intervention in the form of supplemental feedings to boys and girls alike. Such a program among *adivasis* in Sahajapur not only improved children's nutritional level but also significantly reduced the sex bias.

Bengali women's dependence is compounded by their inability to secure loans for cultivation and self-employment. The Left Front government has neither provided women with credit facilities nor helped them secure central government loans. In 1984 and 1985 only 5 percent of the beneficiaries of Indian Rural Development Program (IRDP) loans (the major central government assistance to the families below the poverty line) were women. Although the proportion of female beneficiaries increased to 10.4 percent in 1985–86 and 14.4 percent in 1986–87, it still fell far short of the stipulation of the central government that 30 percent of the beneficiaries should be women. Far from setting a precedent among India's twenty-two states, West Bengal was one of the ten states whose performance was poorest in providing IRDP loans for women. (See tables 3 and 4.) The dearth of female beneficiaries must be attributed in part to the *panchayats'* failure to execute central government directives. According to Prasad Rai, director of *panchayats*, banks have also resisted provid-

TABLE 3 *Women Beneficiaries of IRDP Loans in India*

State	*1985–86 (%)*
Lakshwadeep	47.29
Meghalaya	34.46
Tamil Nadu	30.39
Manipur	22.87
Gujarat	16.87
Maharashtra	16.55
Assam	14.78
Orissa	14.58
Karnataka	12.86
Andhra Pradesh	12.50
Haryana	12.02
Himachal Pradesh	10.92
Punjab	10.69
Uttar Pradesh	10.47
West Bengal	10.40
Kerala	9.03
Tripura	3.63
Sikkim	3.25
Bihar	2.89
Rajasthan	2.82
Jammu and Kashmir	2.75
Madhya Pradesh	0.93
India (as a whole)	9.07

Source: Interview with Land Reforms Officer.

ing women loans for self-employment, a core component of the IRDP package, for fear that women are apt to default. Yet Asim Dasgupta informed me that repayment rates for women were much better than for men.

Despite its rhetorical claim that the key to women's emancipation lies in their incorporation into social production, the PBGMS has not seriously attempted to increase employment opportunities for women or to improve their working conditions. It has not challenged

TABLE 4 *Women Beneficiaries of IRDP Loans in West Bengal*

District	*1985–86 (%)*	*1986–87 (%)*
Bankura	12.78	24.93
Birbhum	6.98	7.70
Burdwan	9.72	9.21
Cooch Behar	17.74	1.21
Darjeeling	19.76	17.04
Hooghly	16.65	20.42
Howrah	14.20	22.93
Jalpaiguri	11.39	37.90
Malda	5.60	11.61
Midnapur	7.17	9.95
Murshidabad	8.56	6.45
New Dinajpur	26.85	9.41
Purulia	16.28	23.71
Twenty-four Parganas	4.98	18.63 N 8.05 S

Source: Interview with Land Reforms Officer.

the displacement of women in industry as a result of plant closings, nor in agriculture as a result of mechanization. It has not brought female agricultural laborers under the purview of labor legislation. Nor has it experimented with intermediary technology that could increase women's productivity and alleviate their work load. The government's only significant achievement in this domain is the attainment of equal wages for male and female agricultural laborers in a few scattered regions within West Bengal.

The Left Front government's attitude toward women's work reflects its conservative conception of female roles. The major employment opportunities it has sought to create for women are in such home-based forms of production as knitting, sewing, and weaving. This poorly paid activity contributes to the notion that women work for "pocket money" rather than stable wages, that women's work is an extension of their housework, and that paid manual labor is degrading to women. The CPI(M) imposes on peasants implicitly middle-class conceptions of what constitutes women's work.

That women can greatly profit from employment in nontraditional jobs is evident from the experience of *adivasi* women in eastern Bankura district. Few employment opportunities were available to men or women in this arid, drought-prone region during most of the year. In 1980 the CWDS organized a number of income-generating activities that used local materials, such as manufacturing disposable plates from pressed leaves. Women's cooperatives were responsible for all stages of the production and marketing process: manufacturing the items, managing the accounts, and corresponding with distributors in Calcutta. Women's roles as the principal income earners also increased their stature within the family.

The Political World

Women have similarly been invisible and confined to narrow, sex-linked roles in the political realm. There were only two women in the previous Left Front government (1982–87), both low-ranking ministers responsible for "soft" portfolios: a minister of Relief and Social Welfare and a minister of state for Education. In the present government, only one of thirty-two cabinet ministers is a woman: Chaya Bera, who heads Relief, one of the weakest ministries in the government. Given the unprecedented number of women who were elected to the Legislative Assembly in 1987, women's underrepresentation in the cabinet is especially striking.

Unlike many socialist and communist governments, the Left Front government has not created a women's ministry. Manjari Gupta, the president of the All-India Democratic Women's Association, the national women's organization affiliated with the CPI(M), opposed "artificially separating the problems of women and of men." Other PBGMS members believed that the Social Welfare Ministry could adequately address issues concerning women. Yet a quick review of Social Welfare programs reveals that few address the fundamental socioeconomic needs of the vast majority of women; most attend to women under extreme duress, such as vagrants, widows, and prostitutes. Moreover, programs are generally devised and funded by the center and poorly implemented by the state government.

An official in the Social Welfare ministry, who preferred to remain anonymous, noted that lack of coordination among departments made it difficult to address women's interests. He felt that a women's ministry could centralize, coordinate, and process information pertaining to women. Yet, far from creating a women's ministry, the government has placed "Jails" within the jurisdiction of the Social Welfare ministry and thereby diluted its responsibility to women.

Nor has women's political representation been much greater at the local level.[14] As with Operation Barga, this failure is especially glaring because the government's major political reform has been to overhaul the *panchayats*. The Left Front government decreed in 1978 that at least two women must serve on each village *panchayat*. The government was authorized to nominate them if they were not elected in the general balloting. As a result of charges of partisanship in the selection of candidates, the government later decided that the dominant political party in each *panchayat* should designate women to fill the reserved seats if they were not elected.

However, according to Prasad Rai, women remain greatly underrepresented, particularly at the village level. Given a total of 3,305 *gram panchayats*, at least 6,610 women should have become members after the 1983 *panchayat* elections; instead, the total female membership was 4,300. In West Bengal's 339 block-level *panchayat samitis*, the female membership was 600 rather than 678 and women occupied only 10 seats in the district level *zilla parishads*. Women's representation improved only slightly in the third *panchayat* ellections in 1988, to 5,707 out of 52,529 members of the 3,227 *gram panchayats*, 470 out of 9,127 members of the *panchayat samitis*, and 24 out of 658 members of the 15 *zilla parishads*.[15]

Antipathy to women's political representation is further evident from the fact that a large proportion of women who serve on the *panchayats* are nominated rather than elected. In the 1978 elections, for example, 47,527 members were elected to West Bengal's 3,242 *gram panchayats;* a total of 97 women were elected and 5,803 women were nominated. Shyamali Gupta admitted that local party cadre often openly opposed women's candidacy.

Two consequences of the CPI(M)'s failure to sponsor female candidates are especially noteworthy. It perpetuates the electorate's prejudice against women's participation in public life. It also contributes to women's timidity: the women who are appointed to the *panchayats* have not gained the sense of efficacy that is associated with political contestation. Personal observation suggests that women *panchayat* members tend to be much more reticent than male members to express their views during *panchayat* deliberations.

As the previous chapter describes, the government's State Planning Board has recently introduced further decentralization reforms. Although including women in the newly formed committees at the district, subdivisional, and block levels would seem an important aspect of ensuring wider representation, A. K. Ghosh, the chairman of the board, admitted that no mechanism had been created to include women. He concluded pessimistically that the underrepresentation of women was inevitable in a patriarchal society.

Not surprisingly, few women are included among the upper echelons of CPI(M) leadership. At the national level, there are no women in the politburo and only four women on the Central Committee: Sarala Maheshwari, Kanak Mukherjee, Godavari Parulekar, and Ahilya Rangnekar. Five of the ninety-seven members of West Bengal's State Committee are women: Nirupuma Chatterjee, Aarti Dasgupta, Shyamali Gupta, Rekha Goswami, and Kanak Mukherjee. A few of the district committees include women but they generally constitute only two or three of up to forty members.

When asked about women's invisibility in the political sphere, the CPI(M)'s female leadership often dismissed the problem. "Women's political participation should not be measured by counting heads," Kanak Mukherjee quipped. "The more important question is: How active are women in political struggle?" Sarala Maheshwari commented, "We had a woman prime minister for fourteen years and it did nothing for the majority of women. More women in our ministry would not automatically improve the status of Bengali women." Nor has the male leadership been attentive to women's interests. Most of those who were interviewed treated the question with levity and scorn; several asserted that the issue was irrelevant because the family constituted an indivisible unit.

Although the women who occupy political office need not *automatically* represent women's interests, female representatives visibly manifest women's identities as social actors. Moreover, if CPI(M) male and female leaders hold similar views, peasant men and women do not. Thus, even the most subjugated women, Mahishyas in Tamluk, expressed grievances at women's limited life chances. Nor should culturally relativist perspectives be employed to deny inequality. That Bengali women eat less nutritious and smaller quantities of food than their husbands may be customary but is also unjust.

The Social Domain

In both private and public spheres, the CPI(M) has accepted as natural the prevailing sexual division of labor and thus perpetuated women's sex-linked roles. For example, the government has sacrificed both the quality and the scope of girls' education. Kanti Biswas reported that the government had introduced mandatory vocational training programs in schools for boys in carpentry, woodwork, and agriculture, and for girls in needlework and handicrafts. In his view, girls were more dexterous than boys. Although he recognized that textbooks might contain slurs on religious minorities (indeed he had appointed a commission to remove incriminating material from textbooks), he did not conceive that they might contain sexist material. Nor did he see any value to including women's history in textbooks. Biswas reported that the government had created eight thousand new schools for boys and only half that number for girls. He proudly added that West Bengal has a ratio of 34:66 female to male teachers, which was higher than the ratio of 30:70 for India as a whole!

The CPI(M) has failed to question women's subordination in the family, as manifested through the taboos surrounding divorce, widow remarriage, and women's infertility. It has not attempted to educate rural women about the everyday forms of sexual inequality they experience and perpetuate: restrictions on their physical mobility, feeding their families before they eat, and their exclusion from major religious rites. Nor has the PBGMS devoted much attention to violence against women. It has ignored newspaper reports of families who have performed sex-selection tests in order to abort the female fetus. It has only recently begun to protest the growing incidence of dowry deaths in Calcutta. (The CPI-affiliated PBMS has been much more active around the latter issue.)

The fact that women are primarily responsible for housework and child care has seriously constrained their political activism. Shyamali Gupta noted that women displayed low levels of political consciousness because they had little time to devote to reading, study groups, and party activity. As a result, very few PBGMS activists felt that they were in a position to criticize party policy.

The Sources of the CPI(M)'s Sexism

Which facets of the CPI(M)'s ideology, organization, and strategy have fostered its tendency to ignore, underrepresent, and even disparage women's interests? At the simplest level of analysis, male and female leaders are often oblivious to the varied manifestations of sexual inequality. When the issue was raised with CPI(M) men, it often allayed their fears about being interviewed by either a CIA agent or a Congress stooge. They simply did not consider women's issues serious political questions.

The CPI(M) leadership's theoretical justification for the party's passivity is the familiar reference to Engels: women cannot be emancipated until socialism is achieved, at which point their liberation is assured.[16] It also justifies inaction by appealing to another Marxist tenet: the notion of class conflict as the motor force of history. Aarti Dasgupta, the most prominent female leader in the CPI(M)-affiliated CITU argued: "As trade unionists we work for the laboring class as a whole and do not make invidious distinctions between men and women; to do so would be wrong and anti-Marxist." The CPI(M) opposes reserved seats and special quotas for women, *dalits*, and *adivasis*. Shambunath Mandi, the minister for scheduled castes and tribes and an *adivasi* himself, argued that it would be preferable to reorganize the quota system on a class basis. "As long as there is no legal bar on women's participation, there is no question that they will come up in political life and there is no need for reservation," Kanak Mukherjee argued. Yet, as the Congress government at one stage recognized in instituting the system of reserved seats, meritocratic principles do not govern competition for positions in education and employment. Nor, as we have seen earlier, is the Left Front government's own composition free of gender bias. Not surprisingly, the Left Front government has failed to fill its reservation quotas.

More significant than the CPI(M)'s economic reductionism is its political reductionism. As the CPI(M) has become increasingly committed to the exercise of power, its relationship to women has become highly instrumental: women should be seen, particularly on election day, but not heard! Electoral considerations also contribute to women's invisibility in the formal political arena. When asked why the CPI(M) did not nominate more female candidates, several party members responded that women were less likely than men to be elected. Those women who are appointed to political office often project women's nurturing roles to avoid alienating the electorate.

Contrary to the common assumption that Marxists oppose the family, in West Bengal as in the Soviet Union, China, and Italy, communist parties have strengthened familial loyalties to their own advantage. Judith Stacey argues that the Chinese Communist Party made concessions to patriarchal morality in order to facilitate acceptance of its mass-politics line.[17] By recognizing the class status of families rather than individuals, it prevented women from realizing the direct benefits of land redistribution. Judith Hellman argues that the Italian Communist Party presented the family as a key element in the reconstruction of postwar Italian society and was loath to intervene in its members' "private lives."[18] Similarly, the CPI(M) fears male opposition if women were to acquire independent land holdings. Given an environment charged with religious conflict, it fears being voted out of office if it were to propose far-reaching reforms of the religious laws that govern the family.

At the level of organization, democratic centralism is the major source of the CPI(M)'s sexism. Democratic centralist principles explain: (a) the subordination of the PBGMS to the CPI(M), (b) inequalities between urban, middle-class PBGMS leaders and poor rural women, and (c) female CPI(M) members' subordinate position within the party hierarchy.

If growth is indicative of strength, the PBGMS has flourished since the Left Front government attained office. According to Shyamali Gupta, PBGMS membership grew from 250,000 in 1979 to over 1,250,000 in 1987. But the more it has grown, the more closely it has become linked to the CPI(M). Whereas in the past, the women's organization included noncommunists, today the PBGMS consists entirely of CPI(M) members and supporters. The close relationship between the CPI(M) and its mass organizations is best exemplified by the fact that the CITU, the PBGMS, and the All-India Kisan Sabha (AIKS), the CPI(M)-affiliated peasant organization, occupy the same building complex in Calcutta.

Karen Beckwith argues that by forging a close relationship with the communist and socialist parties, the UDI gained access to the formal political arena in Italy.[19] This proved especially important to passing legislation favorable to women in parliament. However, in India, as we have seen, communist women were most effective in the formal political arena during a period in which mass organizations were relatively autonomous from the CPI. Today the CPI(M) and the Left Front government deprive the PBGMS of the political space from which to put forward feminist demands.[20]

The PBGMS's dependence on the CPI(M) greatly magnifies inequalities between the two organizations. A very large proportion of PBGMS activists are married to men who are active in the CPI(M) and generally outrank their wives. Once again we observe the interplay of democratic centralism in the home and the world: PBGMS members are unlikely to challenge the CPI(M), since doing so would require them to question the superiority of both male party members and their own husbands. Furthermore, interviews revealed that the most talented women could devote the least time to women's issues because they were preoccupied with party and government responsibilities. Chaya Bera, minister of Relief, described herself as responsible for her department as a whole, not for women's particular concerns. Kanak Mukherjee's presidency of the PBGMS has become virtually an honorific position since she became a member of parliament.

The PBGMS in turn reproduces democratic centralist principles when organizing poor rural women. Through close consultation with party officials, PBGMS leaders in Calcutta generally decide which issues to raise throughout the state. They then convey directives to the district level women's organizations, which in turn convene meetings at the block and village levels. Nando Rani Daal, president of the PBGMS for Midnapur district, reported that the major demands of demonstrations between 1980 and 1985 included greater state autonomy vis-à-vis the center, higher prices for agricultural produce, equal wages, reduced inflation, and global peace. With few exceptions, rural women thus have little opportunity to organize around the problems they confront in their daily lives.

Democratic centralist principles further buttress female seclusion. For example, women can generally become politically active in the CPI(M) only with their husbands' consent. Thus, virtually all the husbands of the married women who were CPI(M) members or supporters were involved in party activity themselves. But even then, politically active women are suspect in the public eye. Chaya Bera noted, "A serious disadvantage for women is that they can be maligned and gossiped about more easily than men. When I was contesting the election this time [1987], Congress (I) made up a lot of unspeakable, slanderous stories about me. People like to believe such stories about women."

The CPI(M) is hardly in a position to create greater public acceptance for women when it upholds their traditional roles in both the party and the family. CPI(M) members often tolerate glaring contradictions between their public and private lives. For example, while publicly denouncing the dowry system, many party members participate in it. The PBGMS has not challenged the dowry system through political education and mobilization.

One explanation for the CPI(M)'s sexism may be its adaptation to Bengali social values. Because Hindus consider women the repositories of tradition, the CPI(M) can demonstrate its indigenous character by upholding female seclusion and subordination. Numerous CPI(M) leaders took great pains to dissociate themselves from feminism, which they believed was a Western import. The CPI(M)'s domestication of Marxism has protected it from a widespread criticism of the pro-Soviet CPI: that it is alien. The cost entailed in this approach is the CPI(M)'s acceptance of "indigenous inequality."

The Consequences of Democratic Centralism in the Home

The CPI(M) apparently assumes that issues concerning women are "social" while issues that concern men are economic. Such a distinction underlies the division of labor between the PBGMS and CITU. The PBGMS attends to "social" issues that are of little relevance to women from working-class and agricultural laborer families. Conversely, CITU attends to "economic" matters, primarily among male workers, thereby neglecting female workers and men's "social" concerns.

Such distinctions mystify the intimate relations between the social and economic spheres. They also falsely imply that the CPI(M) could radically challenge class inequality but adopt a conservative approach to gender. In fact, the CPI(M)'s acceptance of sexual inequality provides a key to explaining its conservatism in other spheres. Two examples are illustrative. The PBGMS distances itself from the rural poor by upholding middle-class conceptions of women's roles. Conversely, CITU's neglect of gender is linked to its narrow conception of class.

The PBGMS projects an image of womanhood that is based on upper-caste, upper-class norms. Its assumption that women are economically dependent, socially secluded, and politically inactive is reflected in its emphasis on home-based income generation projects and sex-linked constructive activities. This urban elite ideal ignores the greater independence of women from lower castes and classes in the rural areas. Given their need to engage in wage labor, many female agricultural laborers who were interviewed had little time for what they considered recreational activities. Thus, the communists' conservative views of gender roles are closely linked to their conservatism with respect to class.

Conversely, CITU is weakened by its underrepresentation of women. CITU restricts itself to the organized sector of the economy in which male workers predominate. But workers in the informal sector, in which women are concentrated, especially need trade union support, for wages are abysmally low, working conditions are wretched, and they are excluded from the purview of labor legislation. Moreover, in neglecting to organize in the informal sector, CITU weakens its own potential for expansion and fails to tap incipient militance among exploited workers.

In a twist on Lenin, economistic tendencies do not arise spontaneously among workers and peasants but are imparted from without by CITU. Underrepresenting women and their specific concerns reinforces CITU's tendency to focus on short-term material gains for economically defined classes, rather than noneconomic quality of life issues such as child care, maternity leave, and sexual harassment at the workplace. Thus, CITU neglects some of the most vital and complex matters regarding the reorganization of relations of production and of the larger society. Similarly, the AIKS's lack of female membership and inattentiveness to women's problems narrow its focus to wages, land, and tenancy, to the neglect of issues concerning relations between production and social life.

The CPI(M)'s response to *adivasi* struggles is reminiscent of its approach to autonomous women's movements. It has opposed the Jharkhand movement's demand for a separate state for the *adivasis* who inhabit Midnapur, Bankura, and Purulia districts. It has similarly opposed the Gurkha National Liberation Front (GNLF) demand for regional autonomy for Darjeeling's Nepalese inhabitants (termed "Gorkhas" by the GNLF). It has ignored these ethnic movements, termed them divisive, and failed to recognize their legitimate demands. Ironically, given its commitments to Marxist ideology, it has overlooked the material bases of ethnic conflict. The CPI(M) has also failed to appreciate and achieve proportional political representation of *adivasis* (as of women) in state and local office.

The communists' concern for the problems of ethnic minorities, like those of women, has diminished over time. In 1946, when West Bengal was ruled by the Congress party, the CPI(M) initiated a demand for greater regional autonomy for the Gorkhas within the state of West Bengal. Even its 1982 Vijaywada party congress supported regional autonomy for "compact tribal areas." Since then the CPI(M)'s stand has changed dramatically.

The CPI(M)'s adherence to Marxist principles has been most doctrinaire and least adaptive to Indian realities where women and minorities are concerned. Pragmatic considerations reinforce theoretical deficiencies. Minorities, like women, lack political clout and—unlike women—numerical significance. By terming GNLF demands for greater regional autonomy secessionist and arousing fears of a second partition of Bengal, the CPI(M) plays upon and enhances Bengali regional identifications. Although it accurately blames the Congress party for fomenting separatist goals in northern Bengal, by terming legitimate minority demands separatist to gain electoral support of the majority community, it has itself exacerbated ethnic conflict and separatist tendencies.

Conclusion

In considering the balance sheet of progress for women under the CPI(M)'s leadership in West Bengal, due significance must be accorded to women's increased sense of dignity, efficacy, and material security. Moreover, only a narrow reading of "women's interests" could ignore the fact that "communal" conflict, political corruption, and criminal violence are much less extensive than in northern India.

However, the CPI(M)'s achievements with respect to the rural poor as a whole mask growing inequalities within the family as male household heads alone have gained landownership, credit facilities, and agricultural technology. The PBGMS perpetuates the sexual division of labor within the home and the world by confining its demands to incremental, sex-typed reforms and accepting its subordinate role within the communist movement. The CPI(M)'s preoccupation with electoral success and its democratic centralist principles have been especially damaging for women. But the influence between party strategy and female subordination is not unidirectional. The CPI(M)'s obliviousness to gender inequality and sex-typing of women's roles narrows its approach to class inequality and contributes to its overall conservatism.

It would be misleading to attribute women's quiescence exclusively to the CPI(M)'s approach. In countries like Italy, where the Communist party has become increasingly responsive to women's issues in recent years, a vibrant women's movement has forced the Left to confront sexual inequality. As chapter 4 shows, *adivasi* women forced the Shramik Sangathana to address their concerns in Dhulia district. Not only are autonomous women's organizations relatively weak in West Bengal, but economic and political conditions are not propitious for rural women's spontaneous militance. Consider by contrast the crisis that engulfed Bengal in the 1940s and underlay the emergence of the Tebhaga movement.

In its defense, the Left Front government is constitutionally prohibited from legislating certain reforms that could improve women's conditions. Most notably it has no control over the entire gamut of laws governing the family. Moreover, the fact that the disjunction between the home and the world is so great in Bengali Hindu society might suggest that the CPI(M) simply caters to public opinion, when for example it projects women's maternal roles onto the public arena. Evidence for the culturally bound character of the CPI(M) women's organization in West Bengal is the greater militance of its sister organization, the Janvadi Mahila Samiti, in New Delhi. Similarly, the PBGMS can scarcely be held responsible for its *bhadramahila* composition when the entire Bengali communist movement owes its existence to the *bhadralok*.

However, there is not simply one monolithic, internally consistent cultural paradigm in West Bengal. Women's freedom increases as one moves down the caste and class hierarchies. Thus, instead of imbibing *bhadralok* values, which are heavily laden with upper-caste snobbery, disdain for manual labor, and male chauvinism, the CPI(M) and PBGMS could appropriate the sexually egalitarian traditions of *dalits* and *adivasis*.

As a result of its economic reductionism and cultural conservatism, the Left Front government has failed to create a popular radical culture. Instead, the government's cultural style reinforces social hierarchies. This is particularly ironic in light of the fact that West Bengal has long been India's progressive cultural capital, in the vanguard of theater, music, literature, and film. Indeed, one of the greatest achievements of the early communist movement in West Bengal was to draw upon and enrich this vitality in order to challenge conservative Indian traditions. Bereft of an alternative vision in a nation rich with diverse popular cultures, the communist movement is immeasurably weakened.

Perhaps the CPI(M) has discouraged autonomous women's mobilization for fear of a spiraling cycle of feminist activity. Women's attainment of joint *puttas* could lead them to demand equal rights to inheritance and other forms of property ownership. This in turn could free women from their dependence on the family. To understand why the CPI(M) is reluctant to undertake such reform, we must shift our attention from structural to political constraints. The prospect of women's economic independence could prove costly to the CPI(M) in electoral terms. Even more disturbing to some, might "decentering" the family eventually threaten the edifice of democratic centralism in the world?

Chapter Four

Decentering Democracy: *Adivasi* Women and the Shramik Sangathana

Unite all you workers and brothers,
Get rid of your liquor,
Oh workers and brothers,
Get rid of your gambling . . .

Shramik Sangathana song

The river cannot change the taste of the ocean; rather, it loses its sweetness when it merges with the sea.

Marathi song

Introduction

To those who criticized the CPI(M) for having become reformist, centralized, and patriarchal, the Shramik Sangathana appeared an ideal alternative. Through the early 1980s, the Shramik Sangathana seemed to constitute a model of radical democracy: whereas the CPI(M) was culturally conservative, the Shramik Sangathana was culturally radical; whereas the CPI(M) organized landowning peasants, the Shramik Sangathana organized landless laborers; whereas the CPI(M) was preoccupied with electoral success, the Shramik Sangathana was committed to grass-roots mobilization. Yet by 1987, when the CPI(M) triumphantly returned to office for a third term in West Bengal, the Shramik Sangathana and its affiliated women's organization were in shambles. What explains the Shramik Sangathana's early success and subsequent inability to sustain its momentum?

This chapter opens with a discussion of the Bhil tradition of social reform, which shows that *adivasi* militance long predated the Shramik Sangathana's formation. Indeed, in many respects its attention to social reform, democratic methods, and women's emancipation was patterned after Bhils' earlier struggles. Women's protest, which is analyzed next, illustrates the extent to which the Shramik Sangathana built upon these earlier traditions. In keeping with the movement's goal of creating political spaces outside the domain of state power, women politicized vast arenas of private life. Faithful to the movement's rejection of economic reductionism, women emphasized nonmaterial demands and cultural forms of resistance.

The Shramik Sangathana's organizational weakness, incoherent leadership, and excessive localism might lead one to question the viability of a decentralized, democratic, nonelectoral approach. However, in some respects the Shramik Sangathana's downfall resulted from its inability to forge a fully democratic approach. If in the early 1980s most observers could scarcely distinguish between the beliefs and practices of *adivasi* and middle-class activists, a decade later it became clear that middle-class activists had always monopolized power within the organization.

It may be useful to analyze the Shramik Sangathana in a broader theoretical and comparative context to highlight the dilemmas that it shares with other grass-roots political movements. Activists in the Shramik Sangathana, as in other grass-roots movements in India, acknowledge the influence of new social movements in the West upon their own struggles.[1] Comparisons are facilitated by a substantial body of scholarship on the new social movements in the United States and Western Europe, which, unlike literature on European social democracy, largely concurs on their genesis, significance, and outcomes.[2]

Many scholars associate the new social movements in the West with the failures of Marxism because of its acceptance of a vanguard political party, insistence upon a single historical agent, and neglect of social divisions based on race and gender.[3] In contrast the new social movements have addressed a broader range of issues: peace, ecological preservation, women's liberation, and human rights. Activists largely operate outside the party, trade union, and sometimes even the parliamentary arena through decentralized democratic methods, direct action tactics, and diffuse cultural revolt. Yet these very strengths have resulted in fragmentation, utopianism, and marginality. Thus, many of the organizations that were founded in the mid-1970s have suffered defeat and decline.

However, although the above description aptly characterizes the experiences of the Shramik Sangathana and SSMS, most scholarship considers the new social movements products of "post-industrial" societies. The Shramik Sangathana's trajectory illustrates the complex manner in which the combined features of capitalism and liberal democracy provide fertile soil for the emergence of grass-roots movements transnationally.

The Genesis of the Shramik Sangathana

The Shramik Sangathana must be viewed against the backdrop of the Maharashtrian Bhils' indigenous tradition of protest against abuse by Hindu cultivators (described in chapter 5); sexual exploitation of *adivasi* women was an especially important catalyst. The early social reform movements often assumed religious forms and sought millenarian outcomes. Despite its secular ideology and more radical stance, the Shramik Sangathana was deeply influenced by this tradition.

The most eminent Bhil social reformer was Ambersingh Suratvanti (1940–74), more commonly known by the term of respect Ambersingh Mahraj. In 1962 Ambersingh joined the Sarvodaya Sangh, a Gandhian organization that had been established in Dhulia district six years earlier. In some respects, Gandhian traditions complemented *adivasi* attempts to combine social reform and political struggle. However, according to Shramik Sangathana activists, Ambersingh felt that the Sarvodaya Sangh's constructive activities were ineffective in curtailing exploitation. He left the Sarvodaya in 1968 and began organizing independently among *adivasis*. Ambersingh's rejection of formal organization was to influence the Shramik Sangathana.

Ambersingh was apparently radicalized when some rich Hindu peasants in his native village raped a group of women and they criticized him, as the most educated villager, for his silence. Ashamed of his inaction, Ambersingh contacted the superintendent of police, who found eight Gujars guilty of committing atrocities against *adivasi* women.[4] The verdict was subsequently overturned in court. Although it is noteworthy that Ambersingh was politicized by the exploitation of *adivasi* women, he characteristically sought to preserve women's honor rather than encouraging women's own activism.

Ambersingh subsequently dedicated himself to eradicating *adivasi* oppression. In 1970 he formed the Bhil Adivasi Seva Mandal (Society for the Service of Bhil Adivasis). But his efforts at improving conditions for *adivasis* through peaceful, legal means were fruitless. A brutal assault on *adivasis* by Hindu cultivators persuaded him to intensify the struggle. On 2 May 1971 several hundred starving *adivasis* visited Vishram Hari Patil, the largest landlord in Patilwadi village, Shahada *taluka,* to request a loan of twelve kilos of grain each, for this was a severe drought year. Patil pretended to comply but in fact called the police, who arrested the *adivasis*.

Following the "Patilwadi incident," Ambersingh asked the Sarvodaya Sangh to recruit volunteers to work with him. The men who arrived in Dhulia district in November 1971 founded the Shramik Sangathana the following January: Vijay Kanhare, who had recently received his bachelor's degree; Kumar Shiralkar, an engineer; and Dinanath Manohar, a writer. All three had been working with the social reformer Baba Amte in Chandrapur district. The volunteers' arrival marked a turning point in the movement. Until then, *adivasis* had largely organized independently in a dispersed and isolated fashion. The enthusiasm the movement generated among middle-class supporters in Bombay, some of whom had excellent contacts with the press, provided the movement visibility, material support, and protection from repression.

Ideology and Approach

Before creating the Shramik Sangathana in 1972, the volunteers who settled in Shahada worked with a Sarvodaya-sponsored village improvement association, the Gram Swarajya Samiti (GSS). Whereas the GSS was influenced by Gandhian precepts and committed to nonviolent, accommodative politics, Shramik Sangathana activists were Marxists. Although Ambersingh mediated relations between them, tensions increased after his death in 1974 and the two organizations severed ties in 1977.[5]

Deeply critical of their most likely allies, the communist parties, Shramik Sangathana activists decided to forge an independent path.

Although they criticized the parliamentary communist parties for their reformism, they believed that even the Naxalites, despite their more radical stance, differed little from the CPI and CPI(M) with respect to their centralized organization, preoccupation with the state, and neglect to engage in sustained grass-roots mobilization. Dinanath commented to me: "I felt that the Marxist parties were too concerned with the question of who should struggle and not interested enough in how they should struggle. I did not believe that ends justified means or strategy justified tactics."

One of Ambersingh's first objectives was to bridge the gap between urban middle-class activists (they rejected the term leaders) and the *adivasi* community as a whole, particularly by recruiting *adivasis* as full-time organizers. After Ambersingh's death, the urban activists remained committed to this ideal. By 1980, nine of the fourteen activists were from rural areas; six of the nine were *adivasi* agricultural laborers and poor peasants. At times the Shramik Sangathana's objective of forging solidarity between *adivasi* and middle-class activists conflicted with its other major objective: creating an open, democratic decision-making structure. For example, the full-time activists held closed weekly or biweekly meetings in order to reduce inequalities among themselves and strengthen collective decision-making procedures.

In 1976 the Shramik Sangathana further decentralized the movement by creating *tarun mandals*, or youth committees, at the village level. The *tarun mandals*, which were modeled after the traditional Bhil *panch* (council of elders), initially sought constant advice from full-time activists but became increasingly autonomous. Two years later the Shramik Sangathana created regular channels of communication between *tarun mandal* members and full-time activists by organizing monthly meetings, which up to a hundred representatives from youth committees in a given *taluka* would attend. These meetings provided a forum in which *tarun mandal* members could air their concerns.

The Shramik Sangathana also sought to democratize the movement by eliminating disparities in living standards both among the activists and between activists and villagers. Initially the full-time activists all lived in the main headquarters of the Shramik Sangathana, a spacious mud hut with a thatched roof in the town of Shahada. The meals, which they cooked together and shared with anyone who was passing through, consisted of the customary Bhil fare of *jowar roti* (a coarse bread), *chatni bhakri* (a very hot chili pickle), and a watery *dal* (lentils); they could not afford fresh vegetables or meat. As the movement expanded, most of the activists came to Shahada only for meetings and otherwise lived with villagers, rotating frequently among villages and *talukas* to dissuade villagers from identifying the movement with particular individuals. The activists' meager subsistence allowances, like funding for the organization as a whole, came from villagers' membership fees (of one rupee annually) and from sympathizers' contributions.

Objectives: Wages, Employment, and Land

The period 1972–75 represented the high watermark of the early Shramik Sangathana movement. During these years it challenged Hindu cultivators' appropriation of *adivasi* land, laborers' receipt of subminimum wages, and state restrictions on *adivasis'* cultivation of forest land. The activists believe that in the early years their objectives were dictated by the extreme oppression of *adivasis*.

The twin issues that the movement first addressed were *adivasis'* landlessness and abysmally low wages. With the Sarvodaya Sangh's support, Ambersingh sponsored a Bhu Mukti Andolan (Land Liberation Rally) on 30 January 1972, which over five hundred *adivasis* attended. The purpose was to organize *adivasis* to regain land they legally owned that landlords had taken over. Within six months, *adivasis* recovered nearly two thousand acres from Hindu cultivators.[6] Partially in response to the Shramik Sangathana's demands, the Maharashtrian government passed two pieces of legislation in 1974–75 that returned land to *adivasis* and helped them retain the land that was in their possession.[7]

To pressure the government to legislate the restoration of *adivasis'* land and minimum wages, the Shramik Sangathana organized a campaign to cast invalid ballots in the 1972 Legislative Assembly elections. Vijay explained that in contrast to an electoral boycott, this campaign required active citizen participation and thus politicized the electorate.[8]

On the question of agricultural wages, the Shramik Sangathana organized an Ekta Parishad (Unity Conference), which ten thousand people attended. The rally demanded higher wages for agricultural laborers and *saldars* (annual contract laborers).[9] Landlords granted these demands in about thirty villages; *saldars*, agricultural laborers, and poor peasants went on strike in seventy villages where landlords did not comply. The following year, before employers contracted *saldars'* services, laborers' committees successfully negotiated with employers for higher wages and other benefits. Landlords agreed to formal contracts for the first time.

However, as the Shramik Sangathana's demands escalated, landlords responded with repression. The most dramatic confrontation occurred in April 1974 in Prakashe village, where the Shramik Sangathana had organized fifteen thousand peasants to demand higher wages, the cancellation of *saldars'* debts, and the inclusion of *saldars* under the Minimum Wage Act. During the conference and a subsequent ten-day strike, landlords organized a counterdemonstration, which culminated in an attack on Kumar. They also sent a delegation to the chief minister, demanding that he ban the Shramik Sangathana, and registered a police complaint that resulted in the arrest of 138 *adivasis*. Although the Home Minister promised to oversee the implementation of the Minimum Wage Act, he also doubled the police force in Dhulia district to maintain law and order.[10]

Struggles for drought relief. In 1972 and 1973, Dhulia district was struck by a severe drought and famine. According to a survey of one *taluka*, 94 percent of the population was earning less than the subsistence wage of thirty-three rupees a month.[11] The drought revealed the government's biased approach to rural development. Most of the state's irrigation facilities were designed to benefit large landowners who grew cash crops for export. Food grain supplies were soon depleted in the subsidized shops and the government did not procure grains from districts that were unaffected by the drought. Employment in government scarcity relief projects was inadequate, hazardous, and distant from workers' homes. Laborers claimed that their supervisors rarely paid them on time and siphoned off funds intended for relief support. Even if both husband and wife obtained relief employment, their joint wages did not cover the family's subsistence.

The Shramik Sangathana organized numerous demonstrations demanding increased public employment and improved working conditions. Largely through its efforts, the government allotted more relief employment to Dhulia than to any other district in Maharashtra.[12] After the government had introduced the Employment Guarantee Scheme (EGS) granting lean season work to the unemployed in 1972, the Shramik Sangathana kept up pressure for the implementation of EGS and liberalization of its provisions.[13]

Struggles for fallow forest land. Thirty-three percent of the land in Dhulia district, compared with 18 percent in Maharashtra as a whole, is covered by forests. Approximately four thousand *adivasis* earned their livelihood principally from cultivating forest wasteland and thousands more relied on the forests for food, firewood, and fodder.[14] *Adivasis* also have deep emotional ties to the forests, which provided them refuge during periods of political repression.

In the early 1970s, the Shramik Sangathana most directly confronted the state in demanding *adivasis'* rights to cultivate government-controlled forest land. Although the government periodically regularized a few *adivasi* "encroachments," it excluded commercially valuable land that was under the forest department's control. On other occasions the government stationed Special Reserve Police in Dhulia district to forcibly evict *adivasis*. In organizing struggles around *adivasis'* rights to cultivate forest land, the Shramik Sangathana collaborated with several other leftist leaders. Most important among these was Sharad Patil, who headed the CPI(M) until 1977, when he broke away to form the Satya Shodhak Communist party in the heavily forested Sakri, Nawapur, and Akkalkuwa *talukas*.

The Emergence of Women's Resistance

Several women participated in the early struggles of the Shramik Sangathana for land, wages, and employment, but most were politically inactive. To permit women to explore their grievances and demands independently, the activists convened a three-day women's meeting in April 1973. One hundred and fifty women from thirty-one villages attended the camp. They described the difficulties that they faced in their villages: sexual harassment by landlords, watchmen, and the police; long hours of work within and outside their homes; and their husbands' alcoholism and abusive behavior.

One speaker galvanized the meeting when she appealed for help in stopping liquor production in her village. Despite the activists' opposition, the women immediately marched to the village en masse and proceeded to smash the liquor vessels. They then surrounded the home of the *panchayat* chairman, who had encouraged drinking, and cordoned off the village to prevent bootleggers from escaping. This dramatic incident provided a precedent for women's repeated struggles against alcoholism.

Adivasi men had always been heavy drinkers, particularly during periods of mourning and festivity. However, alcoholism increased as the commercialization of agriculture disrupted traditional social relations. Numerous *adivasi* women felt that alcoholism was encouraged by traders for commercial reasons and by rich peasants because it blunted *adivasi* militance.

Women's opposition to men's excessive drinking foreshadowed their subsequent forms of protest. Women did not create a structured organization, hold regular meetings, or appoint leaders. But through their informal network, they could quickly assemble large groups. Women's militance assumed distinctive forms: rather than using force, they would humiliate their opponents, thereby reflecting their own experience of degradation. It often found expression through cultural media, above all through their composing and singing of songs that described their experiences of oppression.

> We used to be afraid of the rich
> Now we are no longer afraid
> Oh, Ambersingh, the times have changed.[15]

For *adivasi* women, singing was a powerful vehicle for expressing hope, resistance, and collective spirit. The Shramik Sangathana validated this tradition by opening and closing its meetings with songs.

The Shramik Sangathana's emphasis on change at the level of cultural relations had important implications for women. For example, the activists decided to celebrate May Day in 1979 by organizing a group wedding ceremony, for *adivasi* weddings were generally expensive and its rituals were sexist. The Shramik Sangathana issued a bulletin that read:

> Laboring Brothers and Sisters,
>
> From start to finish, *adivasis'* marriages involve great expenditure and a lot of trouble . . . men say, "we have bought this girl," so she is not considered a human being. . . . According to the old customs, the girl is not asked whether or not she likes the boy. If the girl doesn't like her husband she must run away to her parent's home or find another husband of her liking.

Adivasis have come to realize that this form of marriage is unnecessary. They lose their land to moneylenders and rich farmers and their poverty increases. Marriage expenses are beyond our means.

The Shramik Sangathana has taken the initiative to end these traditional customs which oppress *adivasis*. Girls and boys who belong to this organization will freely choose their marriage partners. There will be no bride price, no presents, . . . no liquor, no ceremonial lunches. The marriage will take place within one day. The principle should be to keep expenses to a minimum. If some cannot afford even these, all the laborers should help them meet the expenses.

Down with long marriage ceremonies!
Down with the bride price and liquor!
Change the old customs!
Long live the unity of the laborers!

In important ways, the Shramik Sangathana's approach was ideally suited to organizing *adivasi* women: its democratic character legitimated women's expression of their grievances without stifling their spontaneity. However, its very respect for *adivasi* traditions prevented it from challenging many forms of male domination.

The Shramik Stri Mukti Sangathana

The catalyst for the creation of the SSMS was the brutalization of a Muslim woman by her employer in Shahada town in 1979: seven hundred women organized a protest rally. As the incident that led to its creation signified, the SSMS was committed to organizing women across caste and class lines to challenge the varied manifestations of sexual inequality.

The SSMS was in many respects a more decentralized, democratic version of the Shramik Sangathana. It encouraged all the women who attended meetings to participate in its deliberations. The *adivasi* women—Hirkana, Tagibai, Saraswati, Bhuribai, Surtanbai, Sukmabai, Vimlabai, and Pitabai—who played leading roles wielded no formal authority. It rejected fixed membership, office holders, and subcommittees.

In 1982 the SSMS invited Nirmala Sathe, a feminist from Bombay, to help broaden its focus. Nirmala initially organized a seven-week workshop for the SSMS and subsequently spent about ten days each month in Dhulia organizing meetings that would address various facets of the situation of *adivasi* women. The issues ranged from rape and sexual harassment to the patriarchal character of Bhil ritual and superstition, women's lack of control over their own bodies, and the unequal division of labor within the home. These meetings provided opportunities for regular contact between *adivasi* women and urban feminists.

One of the major questions that the SSMS addressed, over two long study camps in March 1983, concerned the benefits and disadvantages of *adivasi* customary law when compared with Hindu law and of the judicial system compared with the *adivasi panchs*. They agreed that *adivasi* law was in most respects superior to Hindu law but that it needed to be revised to prohibit polygamy, give mothers custody of children upon divorce, eliminate the bride price, and provide for women's representation in the *panchs*. They also favored marriage at an older age to partners of the couple's choosing. *Adivasi* women preferred not to go to court for they felt it was expensive and time-consuming; instead they demanded inclusion on the *panchs* on an equal basis unless the *panch* addressed issues concerning women, in which case they demanded greater representation. Most important, they felt that *adivasi* law should encompass *adivasi* women's inheritance rights.

The SSMS worked closely with the women's wing of the Satya Shodhak Communist party, which advocated bringing *adivasi* women under the purview of the Hindu Code Bill on the grounds that Hindu law was preferable for women to *adivasi* customary law. But the SSMS feared that their inclusion would result in the further assimilation of Bhils into caste Hindu society. As a result of SSMS pressure, the writ petition, which the Satya Shodhak Communist party filed in the Supreme Court, demanded the immediate formulation of a new *adivasi* personal law and the ultimate formulation of a uniform civil code that would apply to all women.

As the SSMS grew stronger, it felt increasingly constrained by its relationship to the Shramik Sangathana. An incident in April 1982 heightened its concern for safeguarding its autonomy: some *tarun mandal* members tried to stop the SSMS from confronting a landlord who had raped an *adivasi* woman. After a heated discussion, the SSMS persuaded the Shramik Sangathana to accept its authority on all matters relating to women. However, according to Nirmala, the principle of organizational autonomy was never fully realized. The male activists continued to expect the SSMS to consult the Shramik Sangathana before planning their activities. Furthermore, since the Shramik Sangathana was the "parent" organization, most *adivasi* women were reluctant to oppose its decisions.

As Nirmala pointed out, ironically the principle of SSMS autonomy in some respects further marginalized women's concerns from the movement as a whole for it enabled the Shramik Sangathana to simply relegate all women's issues to the SSMS and to define class issues ever more narrowly. For example, the Shramik Sangathana could more easily exclude gender when addressing the concerns of agricultural laborers once the SSMS had come into existence. Conversely, the principle of autonomy prevented the SSMS from working with male activists.

The Electoral Challenge

The government's declaration of a state of national emergency in 1975 marked a turning point for the Shramik Sangathana movement. The Emergency brought into sharp relief the movement's small size, isolation, and lack of control over the larger political environment. Although the events that preceded and followed the Emergency persuaded the Shramik Sangathana to participate in the electoral process, doing so further accentuated its weaknesses.

The national Emergency enabled the dominant classes to reverse *adivasis'* recent gains. Earlier attempts at repression by Dhulia's most powerful landlord, P. K. Patil, had failed. In September 1973, Patil had proposed to other landlords the creation of the "Purshottam Sena," a paramilitary force.[16] However, when the scheme became public, widespread opposition led the government to block the plan. The restrictions that the Emergency placed on activists, along with the repressive climate that it created, enabled Hindu cultivators to take more punitive measures. Never having gained Congress support, Gujar landlords joined the Janata party after its electoral victory at the center in 1977 and thus forged links with party and government officials at state and national levels.

Adivasi support for Congress increased partly in reaction to Gujar support for the Janata party. Furthermore the Congress party's "Twenty-Point Program" included such measures designed to benefit *adivasis* as the elimination of bondage and the liquidation of their debts to unlicensed moneylenders. Although the government did not implement these proposals, the activists wrote moneylenders countless letters threatening to have them arrested under the Maintenance of Internal Security Act if they did not return *adivasis'* mortgaged goods. Ironically, these measures further increased *adivasi* support for Congress.

The experience of the Emergency made the activists rethink their relationship to the electoral process. Vijay explained to me:

> Our boycott of the 1972 Legislative Assembly elections implied we thought that parliamentary democracy was meaningless. We began to realize that this angry response did not recognize the influence of parliamentary politics on the class struggle. There were major differences between the Congress and Janata parties and which of them was elected would affect our actions. We also felt that leftist parties had failed to educate people about the differences between political parties, about the meaning of parliamentary democracy. To simply consider them all "bourgeois parties" was naive.

The Shramik Sangathana sponsored two candidates for the 1977 Legislative Assembly elections. Both were *adivasis*—Vaharu Sonalkar, an activist who had been with the Shramik Sangathana since its formation and had worked closely with Ambersingh, and Bhuribai, among the most militant *adivasi* women. The Shramik Sangathana election manifesto stated simply:

> Until now we have not used our democratic rights to participate in elections. We now feel that we should take advantage of these rights without compromising with landlords or political parties. We are not going to promise you employment or loans. Our work will remain the same whether or not we are elected. We think that to become MLAs [Members of the Legislative Assembly] is the right of the people and we are committed to the people.

Accordingly, the Shramik Sangathana spent only three thousand rupees over a period of a month campaigning for its candidates. The election results were predictably a disaster for the Shramik Sangathana. Its candidates lost by a wide margin and, by splitting the Congress vote, inadvertently helped elect the Janata candidate.[17]

The Shramik Sangathana again nominated Bhuribai to contest the 1980 parliamentary elections. Although it recognized that she would doubtless lose, its electoral strategy remained uncompromising. It did not appeal to a multiclass constituency but only to landless laborers and poor peasants. Its electoral slogans insisted that it was not interested in winning at any cost: "Elections are only a tool—the united movement of the laborers is our goal." "We will not bargain with you—to develop the area in exchange for your votes."

Not only was Bhuribai defeated by a large margin by a Congress party candidate in the parliamentary elections, but Congress swept the polls once again in the Legislative Assembly elections that followed in May 1980.[18] Congress (I) won eight of nine assembly seats in Dhulia district; to add to the injury the Shramik Sangathana thereby suffered, the one seat Congress lost was to the Shramik Sangathana's worst adversary, the Janata party's P. K. Patil. The elections revealed not only the Shramik Sangathana's lack of support in the urban areas and among non-*adivasi* peasants; even many *adivasis* who supported the Shramik Sangathana had obviously voted for Congress candidates.

Adivasis voted for Congress because of their great reverence for Indira Gandhi, who had campaigned in Dhulia district several times, and quite simply, because the Congress party bought votes with meat, liquor, and cash. But many *adivasis* also felt that Congress had more to offer them than the Shramik Sangathana. Ironically, one of the activists noted, *adivasis* who had been militant participants in political struggles tended to credit the government for what they had achieved. However much the Shramik Sangathana dismissed the electoral results as inconsequential, its poor performance inevitably demoralized the activists. Moreover, with the CPI(M)'s growth in the aftermath of the Emergency, the Shramik Sangathana's anti-electoral stance became harder to maintain.

From Grass-Roots Democracy to Democratic Centralism

By 1980 the activists had become deeply divided over their relationship to the party system and the parliamentary arena. Although four activists remained committed to an independent path, the remaining five believed that the Shramik Sangathana would collapse if it did not ally with a political party. They pointed out that whereas the CPI(M) occupied office in two Indian states and was active in many more, the Shramik Sangathana was only active in about fifty-nine villages (eight in Nandurbar, twenty-five in Shahada, eighteen in Taloda, and eight in Akkalkuwa); its membership was fifteen thousand. They proposed an eventual alliance with the CPI(M) and an interim alliance with its trade union, CITU.

The activists agreed upon a referendum of *tarun mandal* members to decide on the Shramik Sangathana's possible affiliation with CITU. In November 1982, following a month in which each faction campaigned for its respective position, the majority voted to support a CITU–Shramik Sangathana alliance. Shortly thereafter, five of the nine activists who had been secretly meeting with party officials joined the CPI(M) on the grounds that an affiliation with the CPI(M) would link the Shramik Sangathana to the national political arena. Although they believed that the Shramik Sangathana had functioned successfully as a "mass organization," they did not think it could function independently as a "political" organization. Conversely, they believed that the Shramik Sangathana could act as a leftist pressure group within the CPI(M).

Following the split, the activists who had refused to join the CPI(M) became members of the Shramik Mukti Daal, an independent Marxist organization based in Sangli district. This affiliation was designed to lessen the isolation of Shramik Sangathana activists who had remained independent by providing them with linkages to nonparty organizations elsewhere in Maharashtra. But apart from its symbolic value, this affiliation could scarcely reduce the Shramik Sangathana's marginality, for the Shramik Mukti Daal did not have roots in Dhulia district.

The decision by several activists to join the CPI(M) further aggravated the crisis that it was designed to resolve. It was in the nature of party activity that CPI(M) members would devote more time to participating in conferences and meetings throughout the state than to grass-roots organizing in Dhulia district. Kumar Shiralkar visited Dhulia frequently but spent most of his time traveling in other parts of the state as did other Shramik Sangathana members who had joined the CPI(M). Symptomatic of the CPI(M)'s insensitivity to local conditions, the largest demonstration that it organized in Dhulia district in 1986 was to oppose the proliferation of nuclear arms! Rai Singh, a *tarun mandal* member from Fatehpur village commented, "In trying to get at the national level, the CPI(M) has abandoned the local level, not realizing that without the local there can be no national." Even many *adivasis* who had supported the Shramik Sangathana's affiliation with the CPI(M) became disillusioned by its inactivity in Dhulia district.

Factional disputes within the Shramik Sangathana became associated with distrust and suspicion, further eroding its democratic character. Although in theory the two factions agreed that they would recruit new activists jointly, when the Shramik Mukti Daal activists proposed that the Shramik Sangathana hire a man by the name of Dhanaji as a full-time activist, the CPI(M) rejected his candidacy on the grounds that it would strengthen the Shramik Mukti Daal faction.

The split inevitably divided *adivasis*. Many resented the CPI(M) because the Janata party, with which it was allied, had spearheaded repression in Dhulia district. Ironically, the Legislative Assembly candidates whom the CPI(M) and Shramik Sangathana jointly sponsored in 1985 obtained fewer votes than Shramik Sangathana candidates had received eight years earlier. By 1987, activists estimated that the Shramik Sangathana's membership had fallen to between three thousand and five thousand, and even this figure had lost its earlier significance, for the CPI(M) tended to recruit new members into the Shramik Sangathana rather than into CITU because subscription costs were lower and the criteria for membership were less stringent.

It is difficult to assess the extent to which the Shramik Sangathana radicalized the CPI(M) because those who joined the party generally refused interviews with external observers. There is no question that the CPI(M)'s desire to affiliate with the Shramik Sangathana reflected its growing concern for organizing among *adivasis*, women, and the landless, in part because of the cumulative pressures exerted by grassroots organizations. However, activists in Dhulia district expressed great skepticism as to the likely consequences. One of them summarized his views by paraphrasing an old Marathi song: "The river cannot change the taste of the ocean; rather, it loses its own sweetness when it merges with the sea."

Shortly after the split, the Shramik Sangathana was engulfed by a crisis of a different kind. The activists accused Dinanath, among the Shramik Sangathana's most prominent members, of sexual harassment of Bhuribai. The details of the incident were never made public, but the activists expelled Dinanath and made him leave Shahada immediately. Shortly thereafter a similar incident occurred: the activists discovered that two of the *adivasi* activists, Tagibai and Chander Singh, were living together. Since Chander was already married and had children, the activists expelled them both.

The Shramik Sangathana was greatly weakened by the expulsion of three activists and the loss of Bhuribai, who joined the Satya Shodhak Communist party shortly thereafter. But more important, the two incidents challenged assumptions about the Shramik Sangathana's democratic character. The full-time activists did not even consult either the *tarun mandals* or the SSMS in making these vital decisions. Deeply demoralized, the SSMS demanded, to no avail, that those male activists who had made the unilateral decision concerning Dinanath should be suspended. As details surrounding the incident unfolded it became evident that the activists had been swayed by Kumar's desire to oust Dinanath because of his fierce opposition to affiliating with the CPI(M).

Both incidents also revealed the costs of assuming that activists could completely sacrifice their personal lives for political causes. Indeed, by questioning the notion that their political commitments represented sacrifices at all, the Shramik Sangathana denied the activists any personal freedom. For example, one of the reasons that the turnover among middle-class activists had traditionally been so high was undoubtedly that the activists found it difficult to sustain long periods of separation from their families and friends. By and large, however, the activists were more capable of making great personal sacrifices when the movement was strong; as the movement waned, these costs became less tolerable.

The erosion of the Shramik Sangathana's democratic character was further manifested by the attempts of middle-class activists to impose sexually puritanical attitudes upon *adivasis*. To some extent this was a result of the tension between achieving a democratic structure on the one hand and a relatively egalitarian, nonexploitative relationship between *adivasis* and urban, middle-class activists on the other. The Shramik Sangathana generally frowned upon sexual relations between middle-class male activists and *adivasi* women for fear of further magnifying inequalities between them; indeed, before the creation of the SSMS, the activists even refrained from discussing contraception with *adivasis* lest they be misconstrued. The very fact that neither *adivasi* men nor urban women activists figured in their discussions is indicative of the male activists' sexual double standard. Ironically, the activists' puritanism also represented a form of cultural domination in which restrictive attitudes toward sexuality were imposed upon more emancipated *adivasis*. In the incidents involving Dinanath as well as Tagibai and Chander, the Shramik Sangathana revealed the extent to which it had imbibed and was now transmitting upper-caste Hindu values.

The Recurrence of Repression

Previously constrained by the movement's widespread popularity, the dominant classes greatly increased their repression against the Shramik Sangathana in the aftermath of the split. Three major riots occurred in December 1983 alone. In each case, hordes of armed young men ransacked *adivasi* homes, ravaged *adivasi* shops, and attacked *adivasi* men and women. In the third riot they also attacked Muslims who had previously sheltered *adivasis*. Three months later the most serious massacre of *adivasis* that Dhulia had ever experienced took place in Shahada *taluka*. Armed landlords descended on Shelti village one night and killed five *adivasis*, some of whom, they claimed, had stolen a bundle of dried cotton sticks with which to light a fire for a Holi festival.

The character of repression in Dhulia district, as in other parts of the country, was markedly different in the 1980s than it had previously been. The dominant classes broke out of their isolation and formed linkages with statewide political organizations; for example, P. K. Patil, who had masterminded the "Purshottam Sena," became president of the Maharashtrian Janata party. Dhulia's dominant classes also forged linkages with the Patit Pawan Sangathana, a Hindu revivalist organization that had linkages with the Shiv Sena and the Bharatiya Janata Party at the state level. The PPS attracted support across caste and party lines among such diverse groups as wealthy landowners, *panchayat* members, shopkeepers, small merchants, and unemployed youth in the towns.

The failure of the police to make any arrests after the December 1983 riots paved the way for the Shelti massacre. Despite significant evidence to the contrary, the superintendent and deputy superintendent of police strenuously denied in interviews the involvement of the Janata party and the PPS in the violence, expressed disdain for *adivasis*, and demonstrated solidarity with wealthy cultivators. Although the chief minister ordered a judicial enquiry into the Shelti massacre and dissolved the local unit of the PPS, he contributed to its rise by ignoring its earlier activities.

Electoralism and the Displacement of Women

Given women's commitment to decentralized, democratic methods, it is not surprising that they displayed greater opposition than *adivasi* men to the proposed affiliation of the Shramik Sangathana with CITU. The significance of women's stance is ambiguous and two-sided: women may have in part opposed the affiliation out of a conservative desire to cling to the past but also out of their recognition of the dangers of co-optation. Furthermore, given the CPI(M)'s inattention to women, the dearth of female electoral candidates, and the absence of state-sponsored reforms concerning women, they had little incentive to become active within the formal political arena.

A few women attempted to revive the SSMS by organizing a demonstration, which about a hundred women attended on 8 March 1987. Among them were Chaya Suratvanti, Ambersingh's widow who had remained with the Gram Swarajya Samiti; Bhuribai, who had joined the Satya Shodhak Communist Party; and Tagibai, who the Shramik Sangathana had expelled. However, the CPI(M) obstructed the demonstration because of not having been consulted in planning it. Conflict with the CPI(M) activists also caused Nirmala to stop working with the SSMS in 1984. Although some of its veteran activists revived the SSMS in 1988, it never regained its former vitality.

As a result of the dependence of the SSMS on the Shramik Sangathana, women's political concerns became increasingly marginalized. As men's attention shifted away from the arena of community to the formal political sphere, women's illiteracy, lack of exposure, and immersion in the politics of daily life placed them at an increasing disadvantage. In all these respects, women epitomized the precarious situation of *adivasis* as a whole.

The Demise of the Shramik Sangathana and the SSMS

Why did a political movement that appeared to provide an ideal leftist alternative to the CPI(M) flounder and ultimately fail? To what extent were the demise of the Shramik Sangathana and the SSMS inevitable?

The crisis that engulfed the Shramik Sangathana appears in many respects to have been preordained, because its very success in eradicating exploitation was also the source of its demise. For example, the Shramik Sangathana's ascendance coincided with the unfolding of acute contradictions between capitalist Hindu landlords and *adivasi* wage laborers in Dhulia district. The older activists agreed that by the mid-1980s, *adivasi* youth lacked political commitment in part because they had not experienced the extreme forms of exploitation of the earlier period. Whereas middle-class activists may have upheld an ideal of continuous struggle that they themselves could not withstand, *adivasis* were more explicitly committed to concrete demands and immediate gains.

In other respects as well, the Shramik Sangathana's very strengths were the source of its demise. For example, closely identifying itself with *adivasis* radicalized the Shramik Sangathana but also restricted its influence. To a large extent the problem appears to have been insurmountable, for the greater radicalism of *adivasis* than caste Hindus was not simply a product of Shramik Sangathana strategy but of the nexus of social, economic, and cultural influences that have been discussed in earlier chapters.

Similarly, the isolation conferred upon the Shramik Sangathana as a result of its decision to operate largely outside the parliamentary arena, which appeared initially to be one of its major strengths, later proved to be a major weakness. Leslie Calman argues that the Shramik Sangathana's nonconfrontational approach enabled it to extract significant concessions from the state without incurring repression.[19] Although this argument may be true for the early phases of the movement, the Shramik Sangathana's failure to create a consistently oppositional stance toward the state was ultimately a major reason for its demise.

The Shramik Sangathana's attitude toward the state oscillated between two poles. On the one hand, it refused to accord centrality to the state in order to politicize arenas of social life outside the purview of state power. It also hoped that rejecting parliamentary participation would provide some protection against co-optation and reformism. On the other hand, recognizing the dangers of marginalizing itself completely from the formal political arena, it attempted to delegitimate the state. The Shramik Sangathana found itself at a continual disadvantage, for it could not afford to be as audacious as Congress. For example, the government could violate the constitutional protection of private property by appropriating land from private landowners and returning it to *adivasis*. But for Shramik Sangathana activists to initiate such an action would result in their imprisonment.

Furthermore, Congress provided *adivasis* invaluable protection against repression by the dominant classes. Over the years the government had made a number of concessions to *adivasi* demands for drought relief, restoration of agricultural land, increasing agricultural wages, and regularizing "encroachment" on forest land.[20] Like other grass-roots organizations, the Shramik Sangathana dismissed these on the grounds that they were reformist measures, without recognizing their importance for impoverished groups.

Nor, as Calman asserts, did the Shramik Sangathana's approach protect it in the long run from political repression. Although in the early years, the exclusion of Dhulia's dominant classes from state power ensured *adivasis* a modicum of government protection, over time the dominant classes gained greater influence over the state. As the Shramik Sangathana's commitment to an independent stance waned, it lost the support it had formerly enjoyed among the urban middle classes. For example, although repression was more severe in the 1980s than it had been a decade earlier, it received far less media attention than it had in the past.

However, if from one perspective the Shramik Sangathana's demise seemed to result from being excessively democratic, from another perspective the Shramik Sangathana was not democratic enough. The Shramik Sangathana's decision to ally with CITU suggests that personalities played a more critical role than ideas in determining organizational strategy. Despite stated commitments to egalitarianism, Kumar, who proposed the merger, had always been the most influential activist in the organization. The secretive manner in which he and other activists decided to join the CPI(M) contradicted their professed commitment to openness.

The events surrounding the split also made manifest deep-rooted inequalities between the activists and followers and among the activists themselves. The Shramik Sangathana had so fully presented itself as an organization of the people, that those who were active in the movement were wholly unprepared to address the organizational crises it experienced. Having had little contact with the CPI(M), *adivasi* activists lacked the information with which to make an informed decision. In hindsight, Dinanath reflected that middle-class activists had often been more vocal, aggressive, and influential than the *adivasi* activists: "We found we were walking a tight rope. We wanted tribals to play a leading role but we did not want the movement to slacken because tribals were less pushy than middle class activists. This became our justification for being more aggressive."

Vijay similarly questioned how democratic the Shramik Sangahana had in fact been. Earlier he had thought that institutional mechanisms to ensure democratic representation were unnecessary, for when the movement was powerful, its supporters had kept a close check on the activists. But as the movement languished he was more aware of the dangers that were implicit in a self-selected leadership. In retrospect he was also more aware of inequalities between urban and rural activists. Although the urban activists could fall back on resources that enabled them to leave, *adivasi* activists were more confined by material circumstances to existing surroundings.

The Shramik Sangathana's demise appears also to have been accelerated by its far from inevitable theoretical impoverishment. Its disdain for theorizing resulted from a suspicion of orthodox Marxist abstraction as well as its inclination toward learning from the people. Dinanath commented in an interview:

> We felt that left intellectuals were more engrossed by what was said and meant by European thinkers decades ago than by what is happening in India today. . . . And we were so engrossed in the movement that we couldn't theorize our experience in any real sense. Now I think that we activists who were close to rural reality and who were able to think in relation to actual practice should have been more concerned with the theoretical implications of our practice. If we had made more strenuous efforts to understand our practice theoretically instead of only being active at the level of movement

and totally dependent on our urban colleagues for that task, we might have avoided the present impasse.

Once the Shramik Sangathana had reached a juncture where the vibrancy of the early phase had waned, the costs of its lack of theoretical reflection became fully evident.

Vijay later commented, "We were operating in a time lag. We did not anticipate the changes which were occurring and respond to them quickly enough." For example, although initially the Shramik Sangathana had achieved great success in reviving *adivasi* cultural identity, it did not sufficiently challenge the growing assimilation of *adivasis* into dominant cultural values as manifest by the growing popularity of Hindi films in Dhulia district. Another example, further illuminated in chapter 8, was the movement's failure to challenge the new forms of exploitation that were generated by changing employment patterns. "The problem was not that the movement had run out of issues," Dinanath reflected; "in a capitalist society there are always inequalities and the potential for struggle." Rather, he blamed the Shramik Sangathana's failure of imagination.

To an even greater extent than the Shramik Sangathana, the SSMS had yet to confront a vast array of issues. Nor could the SSMS's demise be explained by the personality conflicts or the sense of enervation that crippled the Shramik Sangathana. Whereas the Shramik Sangathana suffered from an excess of middle-class leadership, the SSMS suffered from a dearth of middle-class activists. Consider by way of contrast the success of grass-roots organizations in which women were substantially represented in addressing gender inequality.

The Chhatra Yuva Sangarsh Vahini, a Gandhian Socialist Youth organization that became active in Bodh Gaya district, Bihar, in 1977, is often cited as a success story in this regard. Because four of its ten urban activists were women, the Vahini addressed a range of women's issues from the start. Women activists subjected the Vahini's internal workings to close scrutiny, drawing attention to interpersonal dynamics, meeting times, and domestic responsibilities among the activists. The most path-breaking move, probably attempted for the first time in India, was women's demand that the land the Vahini had appropriated from a vast Hindu *math* ("temple, monastery complex") should be distributed to female laborers rather than to their husbands. Although Chetna, one of the women activists, conceded that in fact the Vahini had distributed land to women in only a few villages and elsewhere jointly to men and women, she believed that the presence of women activists provided the crucial impetus for addressing the issue.[21]

The question of whether peasant movements can sustain themselves in the absence of outside support has been hotly debated.[22] On the one hand, *adivasis* seem to have been much more active than the peasantry as a whole in autonomous political organizations; the tradition of *adivasi* protest in Dhulia district in the nineteenth and early twentieth centuries provides eloquent testimony.[23] On the other hand, only with the formation of the Shramik Sangathana did *adivasis* gain a sufficient sense of efficacy to shift their attention from social reform to opposition directed at the state and the dominant classes. Furthermore, the Shramik Sangathana created a framework for sustained political mobilization in place of the sporadic, issue-oriented struggles that had preceded it.

In the case of women's struggles among *adivasis*, urban feminist support seemed initially unnecessary because *adivasi* women in Dhulia district had such a good understanding of their own oppression. However, its importance increased as *adivasi* women sought to broaden their own agenda from questions of violence against women to the more subtle sources and manifestations of sexual inequality. Urban feminist support was also critical to reducing SSMS dependence on the Shramik Sangathana and providing it with the kind of resources that the Shramik Sangathana acquired through its linkages with the Shramik Mukti Daal and the CPI(M).

The Shramik Sangathana and the New Social Movements

To return to the questions posed at the beginning of this chapter, to what extent does the Shramik Sangathana resemble the new social movements in the United States and Western Europe? What light does the social movement literature shed on the sources of the Shramik Sangathana's emergence and demise? Does this literature illuminate the particular dilemmas of women's organizations?

One might argue that these questions are irrelevant: it is much more fruitful to explore the Shramik Sangathana's genesis by analyzing conditions in Dhulia district than to apply theoretical approaches that emerge from entirely dissimilar contexts. Without attempting an exhaustive explanation here, the analysis must include a discussion of the long tradition of *adivasi* resistance and, particularly in this context, its cultural forms of expression. With respect to ideological influences upon the movement, although the Shramik Sangathana sharply differentiates its approach from that of the reformist Sarvodaya, it has been strongly influenced by the Gandhian attempt to infuse politics with morality, reconcile means and ends, combine social reform with direct action, and incorporate marginal groups into political activity.

However, situating the Shramik Sangathana exclusively within its immediate environment neglects the cross-fertilization of ideas among political activists transnationally since the late 1960s as well as the shared dilemmas and constraints of all decentralized democratic movements. To appreciate the similarities among social movements, consider, to begin with, their social composition. As Claus Offe argues, at their core are well-educated, middle-class activists who enjoy relative economic security. The durability of the alliances that they form with other social strata significantly shapes their future prospects.[24] As noted earlier, the inability of both the Shramik Sangathana and particularly the SSMS to form durable cross-class alliances represented a critical weakness.

The resemblances also pertain to the issues that social movements have addressed and the values that they uphold transnationally. Not only have questions of women's liberation, ecological preservation, and social justice been of paramount importance in both sets of movements; the Shramik Sangathana, like its Western counterparts, has also sought to reaffirm traditional identity while forging new cultural patterns, to affirm pluralism while democratizing socialist goals, and, particularly in the case of women, to forge solidarity while enhancing autonomy.

Perhaps the most significant parallels concern the forms that these movements have adopted. Like the Shramik Sangathana, Western social movements have created small, decentralized local organizations that rely heavily on direct action tactics and large-scale mobilization. By largely bypassing the formal corridors of power, social movements attempt to break with the bureaucratic state in favor of a more informal, open, participatory style. Indeed, Offe argues that these movements are located in an intermediary space between the public and private spheres—the realm of noninstitutional politics—which is absent in the doctrines and practices of liberal democracy.

Given similarities in their methods and goals, grass-roots movements, in both the East and West, have experienced similar problems and dilemmas.[25] Many scholars link the decentralized character of social movements to factionalism and fragmentation.[26] Portraying a path of development that is strikingly reminiscent of the Shramik Sangathana's experience, Jo Freeman describes the tendency for larger, more centralized organizations to dominate small, decentralized women's groups in the United States during the mid-1970s.[27] Moreover, given the intensity of interpersonal relationships, these women's organizations tended to become mired in personal conflicts that sapped the activists' energies and limited their effectiveness in the outside world.

The "tyranny of structurelessness" was especially damaging to the SSMS because it rejected all forms of organization in favor of a highly ad hoc decision-making process.[28] However, by virtue of women's experience of patriarchal domination, the SSMS avoided romanticizing *adivasis'* indigenous culture and checked the Shramik Sangathana when it did so. More generally, the SSMS continually exposed the unequal nature of its relationship with the Shramik Sangathana.

The very striking resemblances between the Shramik Sangathana and its Western counterparts challenge the assertion by most theorists that the new social movements are postindustrial and post-Marxist.[29] Their basic argument is that production in postindustrial societies is no longer organized along purely economic lines but through increasing integration of economic, political, and cultural structures. This generates new social cleavages along nonmaterial lines and, correspondingly, new forms of mobilization. "Issues of economic redistribution," Herbert Kitschelt argues, "are likely to be supplemented or even displaced by conflicts over the relative autonomy of social relations from central control by the economic and political core of modern societies."[30]

It is curious, on the one hand, that "post-Marxist" scholars should implicitly concede to the economically reductionist notion that production in modern, industrial societies was organized along purely economic lines and that class inequality formed the locus of political conflict. On the other hand, in its reflexive anti-Marxism, the new social movements literature underemphasizes the structural bases of grass-roots political movements. Although Touraine and Laclau and Mouffe concede that the new social movements are associated with capitalist expansion, they exaggerate the postmodern character of the new social movements.[31]

The notion that the new social movements result from cleavages and address issues that are devoid of material-class conflict is equally misleading. In the postindustrial context, the most significant social movements have attempted to demonstrate the linkages between racial and class inequality, ecological destruction and capitalist development, and militarization and imperialism. Conversely, theorists' contention that cultural forms of struggle are particularly well articulated in the postindustrial context is ironic when one considers the rich cultural symbolism of protest in modern India.

Post-Marxist scholarship also paradoxically makes concessions to modernization theory by accepting the "modernity-tradition" divide. Alain Touraine argues, "In the past actual social claims and protest were disjointed because they always fought an actual social opponent but appealed at the same time to a representative of a metasocial order. Dependent laborers fought against their masters, their landlords, or the merchants but called upon the justice of the priest or that of the king."[32] In his view postindustrial society is characterized by a disappearance of the sacred and traditional and the generalization of social conflicts.

As Offe comments about the Western context, in the Third World as well, the values of the new social movements are neither postmodern, in the sense that they are not yet shared by the whole society, nor premodern, in the sense that they adhere to remnants of a romanticized, prerational past.[33] Rather, these movements provide a modern critique of modernization that is rooted in traditions of humanism, historical materialism, and the emancipatory ideas of the Enlightenment.

A new subfield of anthropology, which points to the obsolescence of conventional distinctions between the traditional and the modern, is extremely germane in the context of Dhulia district.[34] Bhil protest dating back to the early nineteenth century offers an excellent example of indigenous resistance. But Bhil social reform movements demonstrated *adivasis'* acculturation into caste Hindu society even while they were struggling to preserve their autonomous identity. In the contemporary period, the confluence of two distinct traditions of radicalism—that of *adivasis* and that of urban middle-class youth—cannot be understood in terms of traditional versus modern, new versus old, indigenous versus alien.

The challenge for theorists of social movements is to look beyond the now familiar experiences of Western industrial societies and identify relations between structural conditions and political choices that nurture grass-roots struggles transnationally. One way to begin is by learning from the achievements and defeats of actual social movements like the Shramik Sangathana.

Chapter Five

Societal Dimensions of Seclusion and Solidarity

Caste relations have profoundly influenced patterns of political mobilization in both West Bengal and Maharashtra. In West Bengal the weakness of Brahminic orthodoxy and the faint public expression of caste identifications have weakened Congress and strengthened the communist movement but perhaps also contributed to its reformism. Given the absence of caste polarization, the communists have not been forced to mobilize *dalits* and *adivasis*, the most subordinate and potentially radical groups.

In Maharashtra, in sharp contrast to West Bengal, caste boundaries are rigid, Brahminic traditions are powerful, and a single caste, the Marathas, exerts economic and political control. The Maratha-led Congress party plays a hegemonic role whereas the Brahmin-dominated communist parties are relatively weak. Within this context, Dhulia district represents an anomaly: its dominant caste is not Maratha but Gujar, a caste from a neighboring state that is politically insignificant in Maharashtra; roughly a third of its population is *adivasi*, much larger than in other districts within the state. These twin facets of Dhulia's caste composition—its substantial *adivasi* population, coupled with dominant castes that possess economic resources but lack state power—help explain the Shramik Sangathana's strength and radicalism.

However, caste ideologies have differing implications for women and men. If, on the one hand, the weak public expression of caste has strengthened the Bengali Communists, the strength of caste ideology in the private domain underlies female seclusion. A firm delineation between public and private spheres and women's primary identities as wives and mothers are critical sources of Bengali women's political quiescence. Conversely, if the very strength of the Maharashtrian caste system has lessened communists' political influence, it has opened up spaces for grass-roots political activity among *adivasis*, particularly among *adivasi* women.

The contrasts between Bengali Hindu and Maharashtrian *adivasi* women are striking: the price paid for Bengali Hindu women's "protection" from the dangerous world outside is their subjection to oppressive family norms.[1] Devoid of such protection, *adivasi* women have experienced greater exploitation but also greater sexual freedom. Bhil women have been more apt to challenge sexual and class exploitation whose source lies outside their community than to challenge oppression by Bhil men.

As the preceding chapters suggest, the CPI(M) and the Shramik Sangathana absorb, reflect, and reinforce these societal influences. While the CPI(M) largely accepts the material and ideological underpinnings of women's seclusion and subordination, the Shramik Sangathana encourages women's solidarity and activism without challenging certain Bhil practices that perpetuate women's subjugation.

Caste Structure and Communist Mobilization in West Bengal

Various aspects of Bengali ecology, geography, history, and social structure have contributed to the fluidity of caste boundaries, the weakness of orthodox Hinduism, and the acceptance of heterodox beliefs. Population pressure, a monsoon climate, and adverse technological conditions have inhibited elaborate social stratification.[2] Its location on the fringe of the upper Gangetic plain placed Bengal beyond the reach of the Vedic Aryans,[3] although Bengal later experienced diverse social influences as a result of migration by the Kols, Dravidians, Mongolians, and Aryans, as well as through a series of invasions: the Pathans (twelfth century), Mughals (seventeenth century), and the British (eighteenth century).

Bengali history has been characterized by cyclical challenges to Brahminical domination, followed by Hindu revivalism. The cumulative effect of this pattern, however, has been to empower the lower castes while weakening the Brahminical elite. During the middle ages, the lower castes revolted against the caste system by converting en masse to Islam. Muslim domination in turn gave rise to numerous religious reform movements, largely because the Brahmin cleric was too weak to prevent egalitarian cults from permeating the Great Tradition. A resurgence of Hindu orthodoxy, first in the late sixteenth century and again in the seventeenth and eighteenth centuries, was followed by the Brahmo Samaj social reform movement's attempt to synthesize medieval devotionalism with Western rationalism. In reaction, orthodox Hindus revived Puranic traditions of the middle ages.

By the early nineteenth century, British colonialism further eroded rigid caste boundaries. Opportunities for capital accumulation through collaboration with foreign rulers promoted some indigenous entrepreneurship. Colonialism further weakened the caste system by disempowering traditionally dominant castes.[4] This period was marked by the emergence of the *bhadralok*, an educated urban elite drawn from the intermediary and upper castes, who subsequently became Bengal's intelligentsia and political leaders.[5]

Today, caste remains a weak basis for political organizing, in part because Brahmins—who in any event constitute but a small minority of the Bengali population—control neither property nor political power.[6] Moreover, none of the intermediary castes is as powerful as the Marathas in Maharashtra. In Midnapur district, for example, the economically dominant castes range from the Mahishyas in Tamluk to the Sadgopes in Debra to the Mahatos in Jhargram. Thus, the upper castes have not been sufficiently cohesive to create a party that could represent their political interests. The only attempt of this kind was the ill-fated Bangla Congress, born of a split in the ranks of Congress in 1965. Similarly, at the lower end of the caste hierarchy, *dalits* have not organized movements against caste domination.

Since the late nineteenth century Sanskritization may have institutionalized incremental reform of the caste system. For example, between 1921 and 1931 the Mahishya population grew by 770,000 because Chasi Kaibartas described themselves as Mahishyas in the 1931 census.[7] This example of upward caste mobility was not unique: thirty-one castes upgraded their status that year. They also formed the Jat Pat Torah Mandal, which persuaded its followers to change their caste status in the 1931 census.

In the villages of Midnapur district that were studied, several castes had upgraded their position. The Mahatos had attained Kshatriya status by identifying themselves with the Kurmis.[8] The Sadgopes had abandoned pastoral pursuits for agriculture and simultaneously placed themselves among pure Sudras. The Goalas, traditionally a caste of cattle rearers and milkmen, had elevated themselves above the Sadgopes.

As caste mobility movements have improved men's conditions, they have further confined women. In emulation of Brahminic customs, upwardly mobile castes have prescribed female seclusion, which entails restricting women's manual labor, prohibiting divorce and widow remarriage, and replacing the bride price with the dowry. Perhaps within alternating currents of social reform and religious revival, women's roles within the family provided a semblance of stability. One might further speculate that their very inability to control political institutions led the upper castes to exercise even greater control over the family.[9]

The nineteenth-century social reform movements improved women's position without fundamentally challenging the sexual division of labor. Thus, for example, while social reformers advocated greater women's education so that women could become the "helpmates" of their husbands, they did not expand women's employment opportunities. The tenacity of traditional social norms, the influence of Victorian ideology, the paternalism of social reformers, the movement's elite social base, and the requisites of male-female solidarity in the early stages of the nationalist movement, all restricted women's emancipation in nineteenth- and twentieth-century Bengal.[10]

Social Mobility and Female Seclusion

A central foundation of sexual inequality among Bengali Hindus is the system of *purdah* (literally "curtain"), which implies the strict and unequal division between male and female spheres. Women's seclusion had roots in Islam but became widespread during the late eighteenth and early nineteenth centuries when upper castes migrated from rural areas to Calcutta and feared for women's safety. British Victorian ideology later reinforced Bengali Hindu puritanism.[11]

Among affluent families, *purdah* traditionally entailed women's confinement to the *antahpur*, the inner sanctum of the home. The nineteenth-century social reform movements abolished the formal institutions of *purdah* without eradicating its ideological and material underpinnings. The abolition of *purdah* seemed undesirable because women's sexuality was thought to make them both vulnerable and potentially dangerous; seclusion protected their modesty, guarded them against shame, and minimized the risks of "wanton" behavior. Interestingly, even most upper-class women seemed unaware of their newly won rights. The principles underlying seclusion still powerfully influence gender relations.

Within Midnapur district, the strength of Brahminic Hindu norms appeared to increase with the proximity of villages to Calcutta. Moreover, the greater upward mobility castes had achieved, the greater was women's seclusion. Thus, the most secluded women interviewed were Mahishyas, the dominant caste in Tamluk subdivision, eastern Midnapur, which borders Calcutta; *adivasi* women in Jhargram subdivision, western Midnapur, were the least secluded.

In regions which contain substantial *adivasi* populations, such as western Midnapur, bordering the *adivasi* belt in Bankura and Purulia districts, women enjoy much greater independence than among caste Hindus. However, *bhadralok* values have so deeply permeated the rural areas that to varying degrees all of the *adivasi* groups that were interviewed—Santals, Lodhas, Sabhurs, and Kharias—had adopted Sanskritic practices; some had rejected widow remarriage, others had given up the bride price in favor of the dowry. The more Sanskritized the group, the greater deference women displayed. Many *adivasi* groups that have experienced upward caste mobility have acquired *dalit* status. Thus, from being external to the caste system, they have joined its lowest rungs, where they are more likely to internalize inferiority.

The Meaning of Marriage and Motherhood

Marriage. If marriage is designed to fulfill a religious obligation and solidify alliances between kin groups for all Hindus, its significance for women and men differs greatly. As Lina Fruzetti notes, the male place in the line is fixed whereas women come and go in and out of lines.[12] Although men form alliances and create families, women represent objects to be exchanged and receptacles for the continuation of the male line. Among Bengali Hindus, marriage is designed to sustain the male *bangsa*, or "line" in the most literal sense, for Bengalis consider physical nature and behavioral codes inseparable. Thus, they believe that blood (*rakta*) is the physiological source of life.[13] Women are considered guardians of purity, for they transmit blood to the offspring, who continue the birth group. The metaphor that Bengalis use to depict women's relationship to the male lineage is as follows: women are the field that men own and cultivate; women receive men's seeds and bear their fruit (children).[14]

Along with the "gift of the virgin," the central ritual of the Bengali Hindu marriage act, the bride's family offers the groom's family other unreciprocated gifts, the most important of which is the dowry. In theory, the higher the dowry, the greater the worthiness of the groom's family and thus the greater the prestige of the bride's family. In fact, however, the dowry has come to signify the degradation of the bride, the price her parents must pay to rid themselves of an economic liability. Because she is considered a burden, the bride's in-laws expect gifts from her natal family after marriage, and from her brothers after her father's death.

Bengali Hindus believe that if a husband's principal commitment is to his wife, he will neglect his brothers and parents. Thus, while he must feel *sneha* (protective, parental love) for his wife, she should feel *bhakti* (supreme love or devotion) for him.[15] Upon awakening in the morning, wives must do *pranam*—a religious ritual that entails touching the deity's feet—to their husbands. They should not refer to their husbands by name but rather use the honorific pronoun *unni* as a sign of deference. The major life-cycle rituals associated with birth, marriage, and death, as well as the daily *bratas* (resolutions or vows), all assign structural superiority to men. Unmarried girls perform the Saivratir *brata* in the hopes of having a husband like the lord Siva; married women worship Sasthi, the deity of fertility, in the hope of being blessed with many children.

Motherhood. The major festivals in Bengal, including Durga, Laxmi, Kali, and Saraswati puja, all center around the mother goddess. In the Great Tradition, images of women as deity and as mortal conflict strikingly. Consider, for example, how the goddess Durga violates the model of Hindu womanhood: Durga saps the potency of male gods in her heroic exploits on the battlefield, where she is depicted as a woman astride a lion slaying the buffalo demon. Or recall the terrifying image of Kali in the cremation ground, where she insatiably consumes life. How can these images of women's power and danger be reconciled with social norms of female subservience?

Susan Wadley cogently argues that the energy of female goddesses is a source of danger unless it can be harnessed and controlled by male consorts.[16] Once it is channeled into motherhood, women's power becomes a benevolent, procreative, nurturing force. The corollary of the deified mother are unwed, barren, and widowed women, who are despised and feared. Indeed, the mother's venerated position in Bengali Hindu society may be a source and manifestation of Bengali women's powerlessness. Several scholars have remarked on mothers' dependence on their sons in situations in which they are powerless in the public arena. Similarly, some scholars have argued that the commitment of an older generation of Chinese women to traditional family structures, which in their view centered around their relationships with their sons, may explain their opposition to communist family reforms.[17]

If all Bengali Hindus worship the mother goddess, folk traditions, especially among *dalits*, who have been more militant than the higher castes, do not consider the unrestrained female deity a source of danger. Rather, she is seen as a stabilizing force, whereas male deities play disruptive roles. Moreover, community rituals among the *dalits* are more sexually egalitarian than among upper castes; some *dalit* festivals, like Bhajo, explicitly provide women sanction to vent their grievances against male domination.[18]

However, even among the Bengali upper castes, as among groups in other regions where public and private spheres are sharply delineated and women's mothering roles are valorized, women's domestic roles have inspired political activism that preserves the distinctions between male and female, madonna and whore, and public and private.[19] An important example is women's participation in so-called terrorist activities in early twentieth-century Bengal.[20]

One might speculate that the veneration for women as mothers protects them from the violence, sexual objectification, and debasement they have experienced in northern India, at the same time denying them political agency. Much more widespread than women's actual political involvement is the association between the image of mother and the Bengali homeland. The works of the most esteemed Bengali writers, such as Bankim Chandra Chatterjee and Rabindra-nath Tagore, developed this theme during the *swadeshi* movement against the partition of Bengal and during the nationalist movement. In "Amar Sonar Bengal," which has become the national anthem of Bangladesh, Tagore equates the mother with the beautiful, fertile Bengali homeland. In his film *The Home and the World,* an adaptation of Tagore's "Ghare-Baire," Satyajit Ray analyzes the close association between impassioned, ultimately destructive nationalism and the female principle. Today, the association of motherhood and Bengali nationalism remains a powerful theme, as the CPI(M) has closely identified with Bengali cultural identity.

Caste Structure and Congress Dominance in Maharashtra

In contrast to West Bengal, where communist parties are strong, Congress is weak, and political conflicts are highly ideological, Maharashtra is characterized by communist party weakness, Congress party dominance, and personalized political rivalries. There have been more conflicts between Congress party factions than between parties of divergent ideological persuasions in Maharashtra. Although the communist party successfully extended its influence from the cities to the countryside and from trade unions to the parliamentary arena in West Bengal, it failed to do so in Maharashtra. What explains the reversed roles of Congress and the communist parties in West Bengal and Maharashtra? Yet why, in a state in which Left parties are weak, has Dhulia district experienced radical protest?

Because caste barriers are much stronger in Maharashtra than in West Bengal, the Maharashtrian communist parties have been unable to mobilize extensively along class lines. Furthermore, in contrast to West Bengal, where none of the intermediary castes is politically dominant, the Marathas, who form over 40 percent of Maharashtra's population, are the dominant caste and the backbone of the Congress party. Caste exclusivism has also handicapped communist leadership to a much greater extent in Maharashtra than in West Bengal. Whereas the *bhadralok,* comprising various intermediary castes, constituted the undivided Bengali Communist party's leadership, Brahmins dominated the Maharashtrian communist movement.

By contrast, the Marathas forged close ties with the lower castes in their long and bitter struggle against Brahminical dominance initially by supporting the Satyashodhak Samaj, which Jyotiba Phule founded in 1873. The Non-Brahmin party emerged from the Satyashodhak Samaj in the 1920s; it disintegrated around 1930, when Congress absorbed its constituency and demands.

Once the Marathas had gained control over the Congress party, they organized the Samyukta Maharashtra movement, demanding that the national government create a state in which they would predominate. By the 1960s, with the bifurcation of the Bombay presidency into Maharashtra and Gujarat, Marathas' dominance in Maharashtrian state politics was unrivaled. Alongside their control over a network of political institutions at the village level, the Maratha *kunbis* also became prosperous peasant proprietors.[21] Although the CPI benefited in the short run from participating in the Samyukta Maharashtra movement, it was ultimately undermined by the creation of the Maratha-dominated state.

Caste dynamics also help explain why grass-roots political movements have emerged in Maharashtra. As in West Bengal, the most significant traditions of political radicalism have emerged among groups that have escaped the strictures of caste Hinduism: *dalits*, particularly the Mahars, and above all *adivasis*.[22] Political uprisings among the Warli *adivasis* in Thana and the Bhils in Dhulia district date back to the late nineteenth century.

Adivasi Radicalism in Dhulia District

The relative weakness of caste domination is a critical ingredient of political radicalism in Dhulia district. As in West Bengal but unlike in most districts of Maharashtra, Dhulia's dominant caste varies from one village to the next. Although Dhulia's largest landowners are Gujars, they are followed closely by Marathas and Rajputs. Caste conflicts among dominant groups, particularly between the Gujars and Marathas, have prevented them from unifying to defend their shared class interests; traditionally Marathas supported Congress whereas Gujars supported the Janata party.

The local Gujar-dominated Janata party, led by Dhulia's single largest landowner, has spearheaded repression of the Shramik Sangathana. The movement has survived these assaults because the local Janata party has failed to enlist the state government's support. In fact, following a brutal massacre of *adivasis* in 1984, the state government established a committee to investigate Janata-party complicity in the violence. The Maratha-dominated Congress government may be particularly unsympathetic to Gujars, who as migrants from Gujarat are outsiders to the state.

However, weak domination at the top of the caste hierarchy simply eliminates a deterrent to protest. The most important positive impetus to political radicalism derives from Dhulia's large *adivasi* population. As subaltern historiography has shown, *adivasi* radicalism often originated and persisted independently, although it may have intersected Congress activity. The very autonomy of *adivasi* protest, alongside its religious-spiritual character, may explain the insignificance it has been accorded by conventional accounts.[23]

Various aspects of the Bhils' social structure and history have nourished their opposition to class and gender inequality. The Bhils proudly describe themselves as India's oldest inhabitants. Once rulers, with kingdoms in Gujarat and Rajasthan that are thought to date back fifteen hundred years, they fiercely believe in their right to self-determination.[24] Although the Bhils were governed by chieftainships that are by definition relatively centralized, their village councils, presided over by headmen, functioned autonomously from central authority in day-to-day village affairs. *Adivasi* villages were relatively unstratified, for land was plentiful and collectively farmed by methods of shifting cultivation.

A further source of their radicalization was the Bhils' experience of continuous encroachment by outside forces—the Mughals (sixteenth and seventeenth centuries), Marathas (eighteen and early nineteenth centuries), British (nineteenth and mid-twentieth centuries), and Gujars (late nineteenth century on). These invasions, prompted by Dhulia's location on major trade routes and unusually fertile agricultural land, subjected the Bhils to great cruelty. Maratha invasion destroyed the local administration, destabilized the economy, and heavily taxed the peasantry. With British colonization, Khandesh was penetrated by market forces; from the 1850s on it became linked to the chain of commercial capital emanating from Britain. Henceforth, the state played a critical role in facilitating exploitation of *adivasis*.[25]

Commercialization of the region dispossessed *adivasis* from the forests to facilitate timber export and from agricultural land to encourage commercial cultivation. As P. V. Paranjape notes, although *adivasis* regarded land as a source of livelihood, Gujars, who had a developed sense of property, saw land as a source of gain and thus appropriated *adivasis'* most fertile land holdings.[26] Sexual and class exploitation of the Bhils were often closely linked. British officials admitted to kidnapping Bhil women in order to gain their husbands' acquiescence. Hindu cultivators who wanted a permanent work force would include women's names on labor contracts so that male laborers would not flee.

The forms of Bhil resistance varied with the forms of domination they experienced during successive conquests. In response to the Marathas' cruel methods of subjugation, the Bhils organized themselves into armed bands that struck and plundered the invaders. Once the Bhils ceased to fear physical extermination by Marathas, they confronted more subtle forms of domination through assimilation by the British colonizers. The Bhil response, which was expressed from the early twentieth century on through movements of social reform, was also more complicated than it had previously been. Inspired by Hindu belief and practice, the Bhils repudiated liquor, meat, gambling, and theft. Even if social reform movements entailed a measure of Sanskritization, the *bhakti* tradition, with which the Bhils identified, represented the most egalitarian face of popular Hinduism. Social reform movements may have also been the most feasible means for Bhils to claim equality with caste Hindus.[27]

Ramdas Mahraj radicalized the religious festivals that his brother Gulya Mahraj had initiated in the 1930s by making them into political forums. The gatherings urged *adivasi* men and women to challenge exploitation—particularly sexual exploitation—by caste Hindus. As a result the movement encountered fierce opposition; the dominant castes shaved the heads of *adivasis* who attended the *arati* festivals and fined them fifty rupees.

A cruel incident in 1938 aptly illustrates the extent to which Hindu exploitation of *adivasi* women was a recurrent source of *adivasi* protest. A forest guard, while riding his horse through the woods, carelessly injured a woman who was going to visit Ramdas Mahraj and left her unconscious. Ramdas filed a complaint with the police, who did nothing. When the injured woman died, enraged *adivasis* assaulted the forest guard. The collector of Dhulia persuaded Ramdas to withdraw his charges but considered charges against *adivasis* for attacking the forest guard. The police arrested eighteen women and six men from Ramdas's Samaj a few days later; several thousand *adivasis* protested outside the court. The police and feudal chieftain persuaded the government to ban the *arati* festivals in 1941 and the government exiled Ramdas the following year to the neighboring Holkar state. Although the *arati* festivals were legalized by the following year, they never regained their former vitality.

The Bhil legacy of spiritualism and social reform is crucial to explaining the Shramik Sangathana's concern for organizing women and challenging gender inequality. It provided the foundations for women's direct participation in religious worship and simultaneously made religious festivals into political affairs. Furthermore, in keeping with the early social reform tradition, the Shramik Sangathana coupled its emphasis on class struggle with social reform within the *adivasi* community.

The Sources of Adivasi Women's Militancy

In exploring the sources of Bhil women's political radicalism, the conditions discussed earlier in the context of Bengali women will be considered: the place of marriage and motherhood in women's lives, and their implications for women's relationship to the public arena. Although Bhils' relative sexual egalitarianism is the major source of *adivasi* women's militance, a danger in Hindu-*adivasi* comparisons is the tendency to understate sexual inequality among the Bhils. The discussion that follows will indicate both the extent and limitations of *adivasis'* sexually emancipatory attitudes.

Marriage and motherhood. Compared with caste Hindus, Bhil women have a greater choice of marriage arrangements. Elopement, which often occurs at the woman's initiative since it is the most favorable arrangement from her perspective, is approved by the village when the couple returns a month or so later. The most unfavorable is the practice of the groom abducting the bride during certain festivities when such activity is sanctioned. Most commonly, the families of the bride and groom arrange the match.

One reason why Bhil women, unlike most Hindu women, are not considered economic liabilities, is that Bhil men pay a bride price to the bride's family at the time of marriage; the average bride price in Dhulia district in 1980 was about six hundred rupees for an agricultural laborer family; marriage expenses, mainly incurred to entertain the entire village, averaged about nine hundred rupees. If the groom cannot afford the bride price he may live and work in his in-laws' home until he has repaid his debt.

The bride price has mixed significance for Bhil women.[28] On the positive side, as Y. V. S. Nath suggests, the Bhils consider the bride price an indemnity paid to the bride's kin for the loss of their daughter. Among the Ratanmal Bhils the bride price was distributed among the bride's relatives and the local community. The bride's mother, unlike male recipients, was supposed to either keep this amount or, underlining the woman's respected position, distribute it to her daughters. Nath emphasizes the reciprocal nature of the bride-price system, which requires recipients to make gifts to the bride even after her marriage.

On the negative side, however, the bride price is given to relatives and community members rather than to the bride. Moreover, interviews revealed husbands' expectations of services from the wives whom they had "bought" and resentment at money wasted on wives who did not perform their duties. With the infiltration of Hindu influences, the bride price has acquired certain features of the dowry. It has increased from a small symbolic sum to a burdensome amount. Whereas in the past a bride's physical appearance was irrelevant, today the more beautiful the bride, the higher the bride price.

After marriage most Bhil couples settle in the husband's village. Although the bride retains relatively close ties with her natal family, her day-to-day relations tend to be confined to her husband's relatives. However, the groom may live with his wife's relatives when the bride's parents do not have sons or have an infirm daughter whom they would like to support. Because such an arrangement makes the bride heir to a portion of her father's property and thus represents a clear infraction of patrilineal descent rules, it requires the explicit consent of the two lineage groups as well as the bride's village community. The groom may also move into the bride's natal home when he is unable to afford the bride price. Once he has worked several years for his in-laws and repaid his debt, the groom generally returns with his bride to his kin group's village. In such cases the couple forms an economically independent nuclear family.

The notion that the marital contract is dissoluble provides *adivasi* women considerable freedom before, during, and after marriage.

Divorce, which the wife may initiate, simply requires returning the bride price to her husband. If a woman remarries, her new husband gives her ex-husband the bride price. Because *adivasi* women are not considered the "guardians of purity," they may have premarital and extramarital sexual relationships; younger widows may remarry a year after their husbands' death. Polygamy is acceptable but uncommon among the Bhils, for most men do not have the means to provide each wife with a bride price and separate residential arrangements. Moreover, although sons are desirable because they will continue the family descent line, daughters will become economic assets once they marry and fetch a bride price.

The home and the world. The Bhils have not escaped the equation of women with private and men with public; Bhil women are primarily responsible for housework and child care and men for managing public affairs. Although women may attend meetings of the *adivasi panch*, which adjudicates disputes within the community, they are excluded from decision making. Women are also unable to preside over religious activities.

However, despite women's lack of formal authority in the public domain, they exercise considerable informal influence. Women control and manage the family income and perform most of the same economic activities as their husbands. Although the most important Bhil deities are male, a few like Kalika, the mother of the universe, are female; women's influence is much greater with respect to nature worship and witchcraft.[29]

Women's presumed skill derives, in the Bhils' view, from their susceptibility to evil influences because they lack moral integrity and spiritual strength. Once a woman has been diagnosed as a witch she must either leave the community or undergo a painful purification process. Nath suggests that the association of women with witchcraft results from patrilocal living arrangements. The fact that only women who marry into agnatic families are accused of witchcraft reflects the assumption that they remain strangers to the family. Personal observation also suggests that widows tend most often to be accused of practicing witchcraft, particularly when they have demanded their share of inheritance.

The status of Bhil women is thus complex and multifaceted. Granted, they have escaped the restrictions that Bengali Hindu women face on their sexuality, physical mobility, and economic independence. Yet the influence of patrilineal descent and patrilocal residential arrangements within an overarching patriarchal context should not be underestimated.

Conclusion

Comparing the political implications of the Bengali and Maharashtrian caste structures reveals several paradoxes. The first concerns the dichotomous structuring of gender roles in West Bengal. On the one hand, fluid caste boundaries, weak Brahminical domination, and a history of anti-orthodox movements have enabled the communist movement to flourish. On the other hand, the constitution of women's roles according to Brahminic Hindu norms is linked to Hindu women's seclusion from the political arena. A related paradox concerns the fact that in Maharashtra, where caste boundaries are rigid, Brahminic traditions are powerful and a single caste is politically dominant, grass-roots movements have flourished. The relative freedom that women enjoy in *adivasi* communities has contributed to their consciousness and activism.

Differing caste structures are a key to explaining communist strength in West Bengal in contrast with Congress electoral dominance coupled with extraparliamentary grass-roots movements in Maharashtra. Caste barriers are sufficiently weak in West Bengal to permit communists to organize along class lines. In Maharashtra, by contrast, communist parties have been less able to mobilize the lower classes because caste solidarities are much greater. As a result of Maratha support, Congress has enjoyed a hegemonic position in Maharashtrian politics since Independence; caste elitism has prevented the communists from organizing extensively among the lowest castes in the rural areas.

Grass-roots movements have emerged in the regions that contain few Marathas at the upper end of the caste hierarchy and numerous *dalits* and *adivasis* at the lower end. Dhulia district represents such an anomaly. Its dominant caste is Gujar, a caste from a neighboring state that is politically insignificant in Maharashtrian politics; *adivasis* constitute over a third of its population. The Shramik Sangathana has been energized by an indigenous tradition of *adivasi* militancy.

The most significant contrast that this chapter describes is between the quiescence of Bengali Hindu women and the political activism of Maharashtrian *adivasi* women. The first source of this contrast is in the relationship between private and public spheres. Among Bengali Hindus the two domains are sharply differentiated: women are relegated to the private sphere, while men monopolize the public sphere. By contrast, among Maharashtrian *adivasis*, these arenas interpenetrate to a much greater extent; although women play the primary role within the domestic sphere, this does not preclude their participation in the public domain.

The Hindu emphasis on female seclusion derives from the conception of a world fraught with dangers: women are in need of protection from the hostile outside world to preserve men's honor. The price paid for Bengali Hindu women's "protection" is oppression by their own community. Although *adivasi* women are severely exploited by the outside world, the Bhils cannot afford the costs of female seclusion and have little investment in women's modesty. Bhil women have been radicalized both by the fluidity of public-private boundaries as well as by sexual and class exploitation.

In both West Bengal and Maharashtra, the twin institutions of marriage and motherhood place far greater constraints on the freedom of women than of men. Patrilocal marriage arrangements make women outsiders to their natal families and place them in a position of vulnerability after they are married. Moreover, women seldom exercise choice over marriage partners and the normative ideal is marriage and motherhood, regardless of women's other roles.

However, the extent to which married women retain control over their own lives differs significantly among Bengali Hindus and Maharashtrian *adivasis*. The notion that women are simply powerless objects to be exchanged is crystallized within the Sanskritic practice of the gift of a virgin with no thought of reciprocal gifts. By contrast, the bride price among *adivasis* implies that the loss of a daughter must be compensated. Although patrilocality is the rule, *adivasi* women can remain within their natal homes.

Compared to Bengali Hindu women, Bhil *adivasi* women have a stronger sense of both their individual and collective interests. In part this is the result of the predominance of the nuclear family among Bhil *adivasis* as opposed to the joint family among caste Hindus. It also has to do with the stronger sense of social hierarchy among Bengali Hindus than among Bhil *adivasis*.[30] Married women, who do not compare their husbands to deities, are much freer than Hindu women to defend themselves against abusive treatment. Because the marriage contract is easily dissolved, Bhil *adivasi* women enjoy much greater freedom than Bengali Hindu women before, during, and after marriage.

Social structures provide crucibles in which collective identities are forged and interests developed. However, social patterns are not monolithic or static: by selectively highlighting certain elements within given cultures, political organizations may reinforce or reshape dominant patterns. A key instance is provided by the way that political organizations interpret the place of women: upholding women's traditional roles often places inherent limits on the potential for radical change. Conversely, an organization that appropriates emancipatory themes from subaltern traditions stretches the limits of the possible in ways that go beyond conventional leftist agendas.

Chapter Six

The Political Economy of Protest

It is tempting to explain the greater militance of the Shramik Sangathana than of the CPI(M) by higher levels of capitalist development in Maharashtra than in West Bengal. However, this explanation leaves too many questions unresolved: Why have more developed capitalist regions like the Punjab, Haryana, and western Uttar Pradesh not experienced greater political protest? Conversely, what explains the durability of communism, albeit of a reformist variety, in West Bengal? Moreover, why within West Bengal, as chapter 7 analyzes, have more developed capitalist regions not experienced greater political protest?

The experiences of Maharashtra and West Bengal suggest the possibilities of agrarian mobilization in divergent social formations; they also suggest the importance of devoting more attention to its *form*. Although agrarian stagnation has not hindered communist activity in West Bengal—indeed, I will argue the contrary—it has seemingly contributed to the CPI(M)'s reformism. Conversely, class polarization as a result of capitalist development in Dhulia district seems to have radicalized the Shramik Sangathana. The picture is further complicated by social and political influences. The relationship of caste to class cleavages has heightened polarization in Dhulia district and lessened it in West Bengal.

With respect to the class composition of political movements, in both cases the rural poor form the backbone of movements for wages and land, although agricultural laborers can be more clearly differentiated along economic and political lines in Maharashtra than in West Bengal. However, matters are more complex for women, whose rights to inheritance and control over family income are not determined by their labor-force participation but rather by rules of caste and kinship. Although inheritance laws foster dependence among most women, Maharashtrian Bhil women possess greater control over their earned income than Bengali Hindu women.

The questions that have received the most attention in the study of agrarian social movements concern its material basis: what are the consequences of capitalist development for class stratification and agrarian radicalism?[1] What have been the respective roles of middle peasants compared to agricultural laborers in agrarian struggles?[2] Important as these questions are, they share a tendency to construct both the economic and the political too narrowly.

As the focus on gender suggests, material conditions can only be properly understood in light of mediating social, cultural, and political influences. For example, the greater spread of capitalism in Dhulia district, Maharashtra, than in Midnapur district, West Bengal, is partly a function of differing caste relations in the two regions. Similarly, relationships between class identities and political consciousness are mediated by gender. A broadened understanding of economic relationships lends itself to a richer conceptualization of political resistance.

This chapter comprises two sections: the first contrasts the extent and political consequences of capitalist development in Maharashtra and West Bengal, devoting particular attention to differences in class relations in the two regions. The second section focuses on the relationship between gender and class: What are the determinants and political correlates of women's labor-force participation? To what extent are women's labor-force participation and political activism a function of their class as opposed to caste identities? How do differences in the sources and forms of propertylessness among men and women necessitate a reconceptualization of class?

Capitalist Development and Agrarian Protest

One of the most influential explanations for regional differences in economic development points to the critical influence of ecological conditions in shaping population densities and social structures.[3] Regions of wet cultivation like West Bengal, the argument runs, historically supported dense populations, complex social structures, and large proportions of agricultural laborers. Such elaborate hierarchies may have impeded agricultural innovations because local landowners preferred to leave cultivation to *adivasi* and low-caste agricultural laborers.[4] By contrast, in sparsely settled dry regions where irrigation was restricted, including much of Maharashtra, peasants generally worked their own land and the proportion of agricultural laborers was small.

The prospects for agrarian commercialization under the colonial impact differed in the two regions. Once-prosperous wet localities often became arenas of slow agricultural growth as a result of population pressure, diminishing space for expanding cultivation. By contrast, after powerful warriors were eliminated, the dry regions prospered through cash-crop cultivation and export. Newly emergent capitalist farmers turned agrarian wealth into political power.

This astute contrast between wet and dry regions is wanting in two respects: first, it underestimates political influences, particularly of the colonial state, in fostering capitalist development in some regions while stifling it in others.[5] During the colonial period, differences between the land-tenure systems that the British created, the *ryotwari* system in Maharashtra and the *zamindari* system in Bengal, had enduring economic, social, and political consequences. Second, even if, as David Ludden suggests, certain contrasts between *ryotwari* and *zamindari* systems are overdrawn, the two systems differed greatly with respect to what Ludden notes is fundamental to economic development, namely the creation of irrigation systems, which were much more developed in *ryotwari* than *zamindari* regions. The two land-tenure systems also established the bases for very different forms of state intervention in the postcolonial period.

Maharashtra

Khandesh, as Dhulia district was formerly known, is the northernmost of the Bombay Deccan districts. Although it was a frontier region, located between Maharashtra proper and Gujarati and Rajasthani regional cultures, Khandesh became a separate kingdom ruled by the Faruki dynasty during the early Muslim period. In the sixteenth century, the region was incorporated into the Mughal empire; in the eighteenth century it came under Maratha control.

If ecological conditions—particularly Dhulia's abundant, fertile agricultural land—favored capitalist development, British colonialism played the decisive role. Ravinder Kumar shows that the British deliberately created a rich peasant class through the *ryotwari* system in the first decades of the nineteenth century.[6] Whereas the Marathas had made the payment of land revenue a collective responsibility, the British freed *ryots* from obligation to the village community and enabled them to amass vast profits. With the growing demand for cotton after the mid-nineteenth century, the British attracted Hindu cultivators to the area by lowering revenue assessments, building new railways, and overhauling the administrative apparatus.[7] After 1853 the administration constructed 227 kilometers of railway line and 160 kilometers of paved roads.[8] By the 1870s the district had acquired regular postal service from Bombay and a network of fifty-three post offices.

As peasants migrated to the area, population increased, from just over a million in 1872 to 1,237,308 in 1881 to 1,427,832 in 1901. Tillage correspondingly shot up, from a bare 7 to 9 percent in 1852 to 72 percent in Nandurbar, 60 percent for Shahada, and 78 percent for Taloda *taluka* in 1878.[9] However, this intensification of cropping patterns was highly class differentiated; although food production stagnated, the principal cash crops, namely wheat, cotton, and gram, accounted for 35 percent, 33 percent, and 46 percent of the total cropped area in Nandurbar, Shahada, and Taloda respectively.[10] By the First World War, cotton acreage occupied a third of the land farmed in Khandesh.

The growth of cultivation created a labor shortage. Through *jalap*, in which laborers would pledge crops six months in advance, traders secured cotton for export to Lancashire. Similarly there developed the *saldari* system, whereby laborers would mortgage their services to wealthy landlords, often for several years at a time, to repay old debts. The British assisted cultivators by creating judicial civil courts to transfer *adivasi* land and passed legislation that made breach of an employment contract a criminal offense. Government forest enclosures forced thousands of *adivasis* to migrate to the plains; between 1873 and 1878 timber imports to Khandesh fell from 536 tons to 240 tons, while timber exports rose from 10 to 112 tons.[11] Forest enclosures and clearing reduced *adivasis'* access to grass for cattle and wood for fuel, building materials, and implements. More significant for household budgets was the loss of *adivasis'* income from forest products, including liquor, medicines, fibers, dyes, and tannin.

After Independence, the Indian government enacted legislation that further empowered rich peasants and impoverished the poor. The Bombay Prevention of Fragmentation and Consolidation of Holdings Act (1947, amended in 1956), allowed wealthy cultivators to acquire *adivasis'* land, compensating them with arid plots in the hills. The Bombay Tenancy and Agricultural Lands Act of 1948 encouraged landlords to evict their tenants on a massive scale to prove that they were owner-cultivators. Former tenants either lost their land and became wage laborers or, in a reversal of previous tenancy arrangements, leased it out to wealthier landowners because they were unable to afford cultivation costs. The 1948 act originally included a "Tribal Land Protection Clause," but in face of landlord opposition, the government conceded to *adivasi* land sales under specified conditions. With the 1956 amendment, tenants became owners of only 24 percent while landlords regained nearly 56 percent of the leased land in noncoastal areas. The government acquired very little land for redistribution.

Changes in the class structure, particularly the growth of the agricultural labor force, transformed the *saldari* system along capitalist lines. As the labor shortage ceased, *saldars* were freer to choose their employers.[12] A study of twenty-one villages in Shahada *taluka* in 1976 found that of 596 *saldars*, 462 had worked less than five years with one employer and only 38 *saldars* had worked for the same employer for over fifteen years.[13] Moreover, in contrast to past arrangements, more of *saldars'* wages were paid in cash than in kind. One further evidence of the compatibility of the *saldari* system with capitalist relations was that *saldars* constituted up to 25 percent of the work force in agriculturally prosperous villages but no more than 15 percent of the work force in less economically developed villages.[14]

Simultaneously, the government transformed various institutions in order to strengthen rich peasants. (See tables 5, 6, and 7.) In 1960 it created *zilla parishads*, local administrative entities that functioned independently of the centralized bureaucracy in Bombay. The *zilla parishads* became responsible for allotting mechanization, fertilizer, fuel resources, and other agricultural inputs necessary for commer-

TABLE 5 *Distribution of Outstanding Debt according to Size of Landholding and Credit Agency in Dhulia District*

Class	*I (%)*	*II (%)*	*III (%)*	*IV (%)*	*Total (%)*
Government	8.8	13.3	18.4	13.2	14.8
Cooperative and commercial banks	41.2	32.8	14.0	16.0	26.3
Relatives	19.9	21.1	18.4	18.9	20.2
Landlords	4.3	5.0	4.8	0.9	4.6
Agricultural moneylenders	4.1	4.7	8.5	13.2	6.2
Professional moneylenders	17.9	18.6	32.5	34.0	23.6
Lenders and commission agents, etc.	3.8	4.5	3.4	3.8	4.1
Total	100%	100%	100%	100%	100%

The total cultivators covered in the survey were classified into decile groups according to the size of landholding. Class I refers to the top 10 percent (decile) cultivators; class II includes the next two deciles; class III the middle four deciles; and class IV the bottom three deciles.

Source: Adapted from table 1 in P. V. Paranjape, "Kulaks and Adivasis: The Formation of Classes in Maharashtra," *Bulletin of Concerned Asian Scholars* 13, no. 1 (Jan.–March 1981), p. 17.

TABLE 6 *Agricultural Credit Societies in Dhulia District*

	1957–58	*1971–72*	
Agricultural credit societies (no.)	672	765	
Membership (thousands)	48.60	110.75	
Share capital (lakhs)	39.36	209.07	[97.70]
Reserves (lakhs)	27.79	70.84	[33.10]
Working capital (lakhs)	129.9	664.93	[310.70]

The figures in brackets give the amounts in 1971–72 corrected for inflation between 1957–58 and 1971–72, during which time the consumer price index rose by 214 percent.

Source: Adapted from table 3 in P. V. Paranjape, "Kulaks and Adivasis: The Formation of Classes in Maharashtra," *Bulletin of Concerned Asian Scholars* 13, no. 1 (Jan.–March 1981), p. 17.

TABLE 7 *District Central Cooperative Bank in Dhulia District*

	1957–58	*1971–72*	
Member societies (no.)	777	1,598	
Share capital (Rs. lakhs)	10.64	98.02	[45.80]
Reserves (Rs. lakhs)	—	33.68	[15.74]
Working capital (Rs. lakhs)	118.78	884.67	[413.40]

The figures in brackets give the amounts in 1971–72 corrected for inflation between 1957–58 and 1971–72, during which time the consumer price index rose by 214 percent.

Source: Adapted from table 4 in P. V. Paranjape, "Kulaks and Adivasis: The Formation of Classes in Maharashtra," *Bulletin of Concerned Asian Scholars* 13, no. 1 (Jan.–March 1981), p. 17.

cial agriculture. Cooperative societies became responsible for fertilizer distribution, dairy production, animal husbandry, agricultural operations, and, above all, sugar production. By 1983 there were four cooperative sugar factories and two factories under construction in Dhulia district.[15] In compliance with regulations, cooperatives would advance loans to poor peasants; they would then finance the earlier loans but require poor peasants to pay interest in perpetuity on their outstanding debts, thereby generating a ready source of capital for rich peasants.

With this background in mind, it is possible to speculate about the political repercussions of changes in the agrarian political economy. The Shramik Sangathana's creation followed the significant growth of mechanization, irrigation, and cash-cropping. Moreover, this growth was especially marked in Shahada, the *taluka* in Dhulia district in which the Shramik Sangathana was founded and has been most active. (See table 8.) Capitalist development was also significant in Taloda and Nandurbar, the two other *talukas* in which the Shramik Sangathana was active, but was negligible in Akkalkuwa, where the movement found no support.

With the Shramik Sangathana's formation, both the demands and the locus of *adivasi* struggles significantly changed. *Adivasis'* demands broadened from their earlier focus on questions of identity and dignity to include class issues concerning land and wages. This shift accompanied a significant growth of the agricultural labor force. Whereas social reform movements among the *adivasis* had primarily occurred in the underdeveloped hill regions, the focus of the Shramik

TABLE 8 *Agricultural Modernization in Shahada Taluka*

	1951	*1961*	*1971*
Population (thousands)	134.5	155.5	183.7
Gross cropped area[a] (thousand hectares)	85.2	93.4	84.3
Percentage of gross irrigated area to gross cropped area[a]	6.8%	8.1%	20.6%
Intensity of cropping[a]	110	115	113
Engines with pumps (no.)	283	1,008	2,228
Electric pumps (no.)	1	50	801
Tractors (no.)	8	13	109[b]

[a]Averaged over 1952/53–1953/54, 1960/61–1961/62, and 1970/71–1971/72.
[b]According to the Livestock Census, 1966, the number of tractors in Shahada *taluka* was 136.
Source: Adapted from table 6 in P. V. Paranjape, "Kulaks and Adivasis: The Formation of Classes in Maharashtra," *Bulletin of Concerned Asian Scholars* 13, no. 1 (Jan.–March 1981), p. 18.

Sangathana's efforts was the capitalist plains. Both personal observation and activists' reports suggest that within the plains' villages, wage laborers were the most militant participants in Shramik Sangathana struggles.

However, far from supplanting caste inequality, capitalist development exacerbated caste domination by encouraging Hindu cultivators to migrate to Dhulia district.[16] Caste and class inequality have subsequently become so intimately linked that they can scarcely be disentangled. For example, tensions between rich peasants and agricultural laborers might with equal justification be ascribed to either class or cultural differences; unlike *adivasis*, Gujars, as a cultivating caste, have a strong sense of property ownership.[17] Similarly, the fact that greater mobilization has occurred in the plains than in the hills might be attributed either to capitalist development or to extensive caste inequality in the plains' region.

West Bengal

In the search for historical origins, students of modern Bengal concur that the roots of agrarian stagnation can best be identified during the era of British colonialism. Rajat Ray shows that from 1870 to 1914, while a modern industrial complex emerged around Calcutta, agricultural growth rates declined in the Bengali countryside.[18] Although Bengal's population grew by 11 percent, its gross acreage under cultivation contracted by 4 percent and agricultural productivity, particularly in rice production, declined between 1901 and 1921.[19] In Midnapur district, for which the most reliable statistics are available, not only was there a decrease in cultivated area from 2,587 to 2,443 square miles between 1870–75 and 1910–18, but colonial rule transformed an agriculturally diversified region into a monocrop paddy economy.[20]

The greatest impediment to agrarian capitalist development, and ironically an important subsequent influence on the Bengali communist movement, was the land revenue system, which the British introduced.[21] Framers of the Permanent Settlement erroneously assumed that like English landlords, *zamindars* were landowners who, if given the right incentives, would intensify agricultural production. In fact, the *zamindars* had traditionally served as revenue collectors who paid a tribute to nawabs: *jotedars* effectively controlled the land. The British replaced the nawabs, weakened the *jotedars*, and conferred proprietary rights on *zamindars* in 1793.

However, rather than giving *zamindars* full property rights in land, the British simply gave them the right to land revenue. Ray argues that the divergence between the structures of revenue-collecting rights and effective control of land and labor obstructed capitalist transformation of the agrarian order. Their lack of ownership rights discouraged *zamindars* from investing in the land and encouraged them to migrate to the urban areas; layers of intermediaries then extorted the peasantry. Socially, Permanent Settlement destroyed the possibility of an organic relationship between *zamindars* and agrarian producers. Instead it gave rise to the *bhadralok*, the Bengali leisured and cultured urban classes who derived an income from land revenue but derided manual labor and the entrepreneurial ethic and devoted themselves instead to the arts, philosophy, and even radical politics.[22]

Politically, Permanent Settlement contributed to Congress party weakness and communist strength. At the upper end of the class hierarchy, it fostered deep resentment of *zamindars* among the *jotedars*. Traditional caste differences, along with new sources of economic competition, further divided *jotedars* and *zamindars* and prevented the emergence of a unified dominant class.[23] Although by abolishing the *zamindari* system after Independence the Congress party gained *jotedar* support, it remained weak because the *jotedars* were internally divided and unwilling to forge alliances with either the *bhadralok* or with industrialists.[24] Meanwhile, the *bhadralok*, who were drawn into the communist movement, isolated the *jotedars* and mobilized support among the rural poor.

Within the urban context, commerce and industry came to be dominated by non-Bengalis: first the British and then Marwaris and Parsis. Non-Bengali entrepreneurship limited the spread of capitalism and strengthened the communists because industrialists were politically inactive. Yet, the tacit alliance between industrialists and the communists probably contributed to the communists' reformism.[25]

If thus far the focus has been on the dominant classes, the discussion of agrarian poverty and communist mobilization rests equally upon an analysis of subordinate groups. Biplab Dasgupta estimates that the laboring population in the precolonial period constituted less than 1 percent of the village population.[26] According to the Dufferin report, by the last quarter of the nineteenth century, wage labor provided a primary source of income for 25 percent and a secondary source of income for another 13 percent of all rural households.[27]

However, the growth of the agricultural labor force was not synonymous with its proletarianization. Van Schendel points out that because of their weakness vis-à-vis small holders and the colonial state, *jotedars* were unable to dispossess peasants from the land, the classic pattern associated with rural proletarianization. Instead they allowed peasant production to persist while intensifying exploitation through both wage labor and sharecroppers. As further analyzed below, the incomplete nature of rural proletarianization and the absence of class conflict are closely related.

Many of the trends that emerged during the colonial period are still evident in its aftermath. The sheer magnitude and character of poverty in West Bengal help explain the seeming paradox of communist strength in the absence of class conflict. To convey, by way of background, the dimensions of rural poverty in West Bengal, the exponential growth rate for agricultural output fell from 4.35 percent in 1957–64 to 1.36 percent in 1965–72 and then rose slightly to 2.57 percent in 1973–80.[28] In the contemporary period, West Bengal is one of two major states in which rural poverty has significantly increased. By 1973–74, 66 percent of West Bengal's rural population was living below the official poverty line, the highest percentage of any Indian state.[29]

Poverty is closely linked to wage labor and landlessness. Wage labor constituted the principal source of income for 30 percent and a secondary source of income for another 25 percent of rural households.[30] (See table 9.) Each agricultural holding is subdivided into numerous smaller holdings, and a single holding of about two acres consists of five or more noncontiguous plots. Seventy-eight percent of West Bengal's households own 27 percent of the land, with average plots of less than 2.5 acres per family.

Poverty and class inequality have not fostered militant class conflict for a variety of reasons. First, West Bengal's disarticulated economy not only entails economic inefficiencies but may also hinder large-scale collective organizing by dispersing agricultural laborers.[31] Second, the rural poor are divided between sharecroppers and agricultural laborers, who may be casual or attached and with or without land. Their partially opposing interests may generate divergent political positions. Although sharecroppers and rural laborers may share antagonisms toward credit-giving *jotedars*, sharecroppers also employ wage labor.[32] In a study of 110 villages in West Bengal, Bardhan and Rudra find that in villages in which labor agitation had occurred, about three-fourths of the attached laborers (who comprise approximately 16 percent of the agricultural laborers they interviewed) had not participated because, they reported, of ties to landlords. As we will see below, similar forms of dependence constrain Bengali women's political activism.

Third, under conditions of pauperization, employers are increasingly apt to intensify exploitation of wage laborers and reject their demands. Agrarian stagnation coupled with population growth has significantly impoverished the largest group of rural employers, namely middle peasants, without reducing their reliance on wage laborers.[33] The working conditions of agricultural laborers have correspondingly deteriorated—as signified by the shorter duration of their contracts and higher turnover rates—and their bargaining power has declined.[34]

To conclude this section, is the argument linking agrarian capitalist development and agrarian mobilization substantiated in the case of West Bengal? Prima facie evidence suggests the contrary: that the very absence of agrarian capitalism helps explain the strength of the communist movement. However, the lack of class polarization and

TABLE 9 *Percentage Distribution of Households and Area of Operated Land in West Bengal, 1971/72*

Farm size (acres)	*% Households*	*% Area*
Landless	30.94	0
0.01–2.5	42.22	24.79
2.51–5.0	15.77	28.94
5.01–10.0	8.95	31.05
above 10.0	2.12	15.22

Source: Adapted from a table in Kirsten Westergaard, "People's Participation, Local Government, and Rural Development: The Case of West Bengal, India" (Research Report no. 8, Center for Development Research, Copenhagen, March 1986), p. 11.

the communists' reformism may in fact be linked. The absence of class polarization, divisions among the rural poor, immisiration of agrarian employers, leftist inclinations of the Bengali *bhadralok*, and dependence of the rural poor on dominant groups are among the explanations elaborated above.

Given the extent of uneven regional development within West Bengal, it is worth exploring the possible linkages between agrarian capitalism and political protest at the district level. There is indeed some correlation between party strength and capitalist development in that Burdwan, a bastion of CPI(M) support, has experienced the most extensive capitalist development within West Bengal; at the other end of the spectrum, the CPI(M) is relatively weak in Bankura and Purulia, which are among the most impoverished districts; Midnapur falls between these two poles, judged both by its level of economic development and CPI(M) strength.

However, the problem with a purely economic explanation is that it equates CPI(M) strength and political radicalism. It is thus unable to explain why the Jharkhand movement (a militant *adivasi* movement) finds support in Bankura and Purulia districts or why the CPI and CPI(M-L) have been so active in regions of Midnapur where the CPI(M) has traditionally been weak. These puzzles can only be resolved by shifting attention from the narrowly economic to the social and political. The caste composition of the districts and the roles played by various political parties strongly influence the extent and character of political conflict.

Thus, if one objective of this chapter is to suggest the influence of structural arrangements upon prospects for agrarian radicalism, another is to question economically reductionist explanations. To the extent that economic arrangements are shaped by social and political conditions, the latitude for political intervention increases. If, for example, Bengal's impoverished agrarian economy limits the likelihood of overt class conflict, it invites the yet unexplored possibility of creating rural cooperatives. Both the inefficiencies that result from fragmented landholding patterns and the limited benefits of irrigation facilities would be alleviated through collective control over water and land.

Women and Production

Most scholarship on agrarian social structure and movements ignores the influence of gender on peasant-class formation and resistance. Scholarship on Indian women has scarcely filled the lacunae in this field. To what extent has capitalist development proletarianized rural women? What if any are the linkages between women's wage labor and their political activism? How are women's economic roles shaped by social relations based on family, caste, and kinship?

Published in 1978, Gail Omvedt's "Women and Rural Revolt" remains the strongest argument we have linking capitalist development with women's proletarianization and protest.[35] Omvedt argues that between 1961 and 1971 there was an accentuation of a trend toward women's proletarianization, which she defines as their relegation to the class of wage laborers rather than self-employed cultivators. With the exception of West Bengal, Omvedt argues, the states in which there has been the most labor militancy in recent years are the states that have experienced the greatest proletarianization of the labor force, particularly the female labor force.

Omvedt's argument initially appeared to provide a compelling explanation for what she identified as a burgeoning women's movement with autonomous agrarian origins in the early 1970s. However, certain problems in her analysis have increasingly become apparent. First, given changes in census definitions of work, the decline in cultivators and growth of agricultural laborers is much less significant than Omvedt suggests.[36] Reacting against restrictive definitions of women workers in the 1951 census, the 1961 census included in the category of workers those who had performed wage labor for at least an hour a day in the agricultural working season. The 1971 census reverted to a much more restrictive definition: only those who described their "main activity" as economically productive work (determined by the time spent on the task) were considered workers. Thus, women who considered domestic work their principal responsibility were deemed nonworkers.

Second, although women are at the focus of Omvedt's analysis, she does not explain why proletarianization among men and women often differs within the same region. In West Bengal, for example, only 11 percent of rural women compared to 53 percent of rural men were classified as workers in 1961 (when the census employed a liberal definition of work). The 1981 census records 6 percent of rural women compared to 49 percent of rural men as workers.[37]

Omvedt is unable to explain differences in the wage labor of men and women because she does not adequately consider noneconomic, particularly social, influences. Thus, she does not emphasize the extent to which women's labor-force participation and political activism in Dhulia district, as in several other regions in which she identifies women's militance, is influenced by their *adivasi* identities and not simply by their class backgrounds.

Similarly in West Bengal, social norms restrict women's labor-force participation quite independently of economic influences. As the previous section described, the *bhadralok* distinguished itself from the *abhadra*, or common folk, by repudiating manual labor, particularly for women. Even today, employers hire women only after exhausting the supply of male labor and prefer hiring migrants to local female laborers.[38] Women perform those paddy cultivation tasks that are most closely linked with food processing and preparation—such as threshing, winnowing, drying, parboiling, and dehusking the paddy. Men alone plough and level the land, prepare the seedbed, spread fertilizer, and spray pesticides. Women's work is much more likely than men's work to be unremunerated; within sharecropping families, for example, the husband is designated a sharecropper and the wife his helper.

Particularly in cases in which capitalism has marginalized women from production—as an alternative to proletarianization rather than its accompaniment—Omvedt tends to ignore its debilitating consequences. An excellent example concerns women's displacement from paddy production in West Bengal, where rice mills have been taking over women's work dehusking rice. In southern India, many of women's agricultural tasks are now mechanized.[39] Personal observation suggests that mechanization has not significantly displaced female labor in Dhulia district; it seems plausible that women's resistance diminishes when mechanization renders their labor obsolete.

Clearly, few generalizations about the consequences of capitalist development hold for all of India; for example, although in Maharashtra the demand for female labor has increased with capitalist development, in West Bengal, female laborers are more numerous in economically backward than in advanced districts. However, once one takes into account the tenuous link between capitalism and the size of the female labor force, Omvedt's argument concerning the greater militance of women who are waged than those whose labor is unremunerated remains persuasive.

National Sample Survey figures, which are the most reliable source on the subject, indicate that in West Bengal women constituted 14 percent of the work force in 1977–78 and 11 percent in 1983, whereas in Maharashtra they constituted 48 percent and 47 percent during those same periods.[40] Not only are women's labor force participation rates consistently lower but they also suffered a much greater decline in West Bengal than in Maharashtra. Economic marginalization is likely to be associated with political demobilization.

The problems with these figures, however, is that they convey little sense of the actual resources that women's work places at their disposal. One might argue that in conditions of poverty, women's earnings scarcely empower them, for most of their earnings cover the family's subsistence, particularly because men often spend extravagantly on liquor, gambling, and cigarettes.[41] As Kay Johnson notes of China, women's relationship to the market is mediated by their husbands, who generally control the family income.[42]

These broad generalizations must be qualified in light of comparative evidence from Maharashtra and West Bengal. Even if women spend most of their income on family subsistence, they thereby achieve some protection against discrimination. Various studies show that women's subjection to malnutrition, illness, and abuse increases with their economic dependence.[43] Moreover, men's wasteful consumption, particularly on alcohol, has been a frequent catalyst to protest among female wage laborers. Questions of women's control over the family income are mediated by caste: whereas Bengali Hindu men generally control their wives' earnings, Bhil women

TABLE 10 *Real Wages of Female Agricultural Labor in West Bengal*

District	*1951/52–1953/54*	*1963/64–1965/66*	*1978/79–1980/81*
Bankura	1.92[a]	1.85	3.29
Birbhum	1.97	1.64	2.62
Burdwan	2.64	2.27	3.22
Cooch Behar	2.80	2.02	2.14
Darjeeling	2.71	2.08	2.91
Hooghly	2.94	2.41	3.34
Howrah	2.17	2.30	2.67
Jalpaiguri	3.54	2.25	2.88
Malda	—	1.69	1.55
Midnapur	2.14	1.92	2.81
Murshidabad	2.04	1.77	2.63
Nadia	1.75	1.64	2.22
Purulia	—	1.36	2.56
Twenty-four Parganas	2.40	1.96	2.86
West Dinajpur	2.43	1.86	1.96

[a]Rupees per hour.
Source: Data compiled and provided by Professor James Boyce, Department of Economics, University of Massachusetts at Amherst, April 1988.

retain their own incomes.[44] Thus the benefits women derive from wage labor are much greater for *adivasi* women in Maharashtra than for Hindu women in West Bengal.

One way in which Bengali women appear to occupy a more favorable position than Maharashtrian women is with respect to male-female wage inequalities. In 1977–78 female wage laborers earned 81 percent of male earnings in West Bengal but only 64 percent of male earnings in Maharashtra.[45] (See tables 10 and 11 for more detailed information at the district level.) However, while the differential in male-female wages has increased in West Bengal, it declined in Maharashtra between 1964–65 and 1974–75.[46]

Women and Property Rights

The sizable female labor force in Dhulia district, compared to any district in West Bengal, suggests a straightforward contrast between

TABLE 11 *Ratio of Female to Male Agricultural Laborers' Wages, West Bengal*

District	*1951–53*	*1963–65*	*1978–80*
Bankura	0.73	0.85	0.92
Birbhum	0.75	0.87	0.85
Burdwan	0.88	0.84	0.97
Cooch Behar	0.75	0.76	0.78
Darjeeling	0.81	0.82	0.85
Hooghly	0.92	0.87	0.98
Howrah	0.67	0.72	0.74
Jalpaiguri	0.82	0.75	0.89
Malda	—	0.74	0.76
Midnapur	0.78	0.81	0.84
Mushidabad	0.78	0.80	0.77
Nadia	0.66	0.67	0.88
Purulia	—	0.83	0.96
Twenty-four Parganas	0.81	0.78	0.80
West Dinajpur	0.79	0.77	0.78

Source: Data compiled and provided by Professor James Boyce, Department of Economics, University of Massachusetts at Amherst, April 1988.

women's freedom in the west and bondage in the east. However, by itself women's labor force participation cannot explain many facets of women's power and powerlessness. Women's lack of property rights provides an important key to this puzzle while also indicating certain common forms of women's subjugation in West Bengal and Maharashtra. The silences of both scholars and political activists on the question of women's property rights are in themselves noteworthy and informative.[47]

Bengali women and Hindu law. Two major forms of Hindu law, *mitakshara* and *dayabhaga*, determine rules of succession. According to *dayabhaga* (literally, "the partitioning of ancestral estates"), which prevails in West Bengal, the man has absolute ownership over all his property, whether ancestral or self-acquired, and can bequeath it to whomever he chooses. At the owner's death the property, if unbequeathed, is given in equal shares to his sons. Women, as daughters, wives, and widows, have no such claim to ancestral property; at best they have a right to maintenance but only if they remain in the family household. A widow who returns to her ancestral village thereby renounces all benefits from her husband's property.

Under the *dayabhaga* system, women's only property rights traditionally consisted of *stridhan*, the gifts which the bride's natal or marital family gave her either before or after marriage. *Stridhan*, which could amount to large sums, was considered a woman's personal property and was passed down the female line.[48] Today, the dowry bears little resemblance to inheritance, as it generally excludes income-generating property and is no longer under a woman's control.

The Hindu Succession Act of 1956 abolished differences between the *mitakshara* and *dayabhaga* schools and created equal rights of succession for male and female heirs in the same category—that is, sons and daughters or brothers and sisters. Under the act, the class one heirs of a man—his widow, mother, sons, and daughters—inherit property in equal shares as absolute owners. If there is a predeceased son, his widow and son get the share that he would have inherited; the same is true for a predeceased daughter. When a Hindu woman dies, all the property she has inherited from her parents, husband, or father-in-law devolves equally on her sons, daughters, and grandchildren. The Hindu Succession Act reduced but did not eliminate sexual discrimination; one of its most significant omissions is the devolution of tenancy rights, which it leaves to the discretion of state governments.[49] Tenancy laws in most regions deprive women of the most valuable asset in rural India.[50]

Even more significant in the agrarian context is the continued adherence to *dayabhaga* customary law. Dissatisfied female heirs rarely challenge property allocation in court. Only if women are infirm, widowed, or daughters in families without sons can they acquire property, and even in these cases they seldom do; harassment and intimidation by male relatives prevents most women who inherit land from retaining it. Daughters often willingly relinquish their share of ancestral property for fear of alienating brothers whose support they might later need.[51] The safer strategy, and an additional insurance, is for women to bear sons.

Certain structural conditions—village exogamy, long-distance marriage arrangements, and patrilocality—all prevent women from claiming and retaining their legal share of inheritance. Indeed, one important reason why villagers prefer to marry their daughters to a husband some distance away is precisely because they fear that endogamy will encourage women to provoke land disputes.[52] Women who live far from their natal families find it difficult to tend the ancestral land and can easily be cheated by male relatives. Thus there is a mutually reinforcing relationship between marriage rules and patrilineality.

Maharashtrian women and adivasi customary law. With the exception of a few communities in south and east India, most *adivasis* are patrilineal. However, even among patrilineal groups, succession practices vary significantly. K. S. Singh notes that among hunting and gathering communities, lineage and community-owned land has not yet supplanted private property ownership; men and women have relatively equal access to the land.[53] Until recently, even among settled agricultural communities, cattle, ornaments, and household goods constituted the major components of inheritance, for land was plentiful and it was unnecessary to identify its heirs.[54] As land has become a major part of inheritance, women have suffered a loss of inheritance rights, particularly of movable, income-generating property.

Among the Maharashtrian Bhils, only male descendants inherit the land. When direct heirs do not exist, the land goes to the deceased man's nephews (brothers' sons), cousins (father's brother's sons), and other male relatives. In their absence, the village *panch* determines how the land in question should be distributed.[55] A woman who leaves her husband loses all rights to their jointly owned land. If she is widowed or abandoned by her husband she has usufructory rights to the land and can pass it on to her children—her daughters can use but not own the land—but only if she does not remarry or develop romantic attachments. The *panch* scrutinizes her private relationships and accepts even the testimony of children who report that she has had nonmarital relationships and should thus lose land rights. Furthermore, the *panch* equates rape and consensual sexual relationships.[56]

In practice, land is sometimes given by fathers to elderly, infirm, and unmarried daughters and by brothers to divorced and widowed sisters. However, since tribal customary law makes no provision for women's property rights, women who are rendered destitute by fathers, brothers, and husbands have no recourse.[57] Moreover, women must pass on any property they receive from their fathers to their male agnates.

It is extremely difficult to determine the origins of Bhil patrilineality, because the British, with their preference for private and male-owned property, maintained the earliest written records on this question. Rather than assuming a matrilineal golden age of the past, it is safer to simply identify conditions that simultaneously reduced *adivasi* access to the land and accentuated gender inequalities. The most important factors include: increasing population pressure on the land, which was associated in turn with changes in cropping patterns and new forms of agricultural technology; state policies during both colonial and postcolonial periods of which forest enclosures provide the most important example; and the appropriation of *adivasi* land by outside traders, industrialists, and cultivators.[58]

The Correlates and Consequences of Patrilineality

Women's lack of inheritance rights significantly contributes to their economic dependence, which is associated in turn with a range of discriminatory practices. Whereas such dependence is to some extent mitigated among Maharashtrian Bhils by high levels of women's labor-force participation, it is reinforced among Bengali women by their marginalization from the labor force.

Still, notwithstanding this important difference between *adivasis* and Hindus, women's lack of property rights contributes to the compulsory character of marriage and forces women to tolerate oppressive marital situations. According to *adivasi* customary law, a married woman who leaves an abusive husband foregoes the right to return to her parents' home. The incidence of marital abuse is also likely to be greater when women's access to land is mediated through male relatives.[59]

Upon divorce the presumption in *adivasi* customary law is that the father will gain custody of the children. The preference for sons over daughters, although less marked among the Bhils than among Bengali Hindus, characterizes both communities. Indeed, even mothers may favor sons over daughters, for if widowed, their sons can provide them usufructory rights to the land. The one provision that the Bhils make for women's access to land after their husbands' death is widow remarriage, although widows too are denied ownership rights.

The threat posed to men by women who demand property rights is dramatized by the not uncommon persecution of widows. In Dhulia district, activists reported that widows, some of whom had demanded land from male agnates, were often deemed witches and forced to leave their villages. Similarly, stories abounded in several villages in West Bengal of "witches" causing disease and destruction.[60] The traditional village councils put these women through a cruel trial and expelled from the village those it considered guilty. In all four cases that I personally investigated, the accused women were widows; in two they had demanded property from male agnates. Witch hunts had become so prevalent that block officials in Bankura district had launched a campaign to stop them.

Why have Marxist movements largely failed to demand land rights for rural women when Marxists should be especially sensitive to the disabling consequences of propertylessness? Perhaps radical groups have assumed that the question is of scant significance to women from agricultural laborer households, who constitute their major constituency, for even their husbands own little property that they can pass on to their sons. Perhaps they also fear the conservatizing consequences of conferring land ownership rights on women with little or no land. However, this view ignores the much more extreme forms of economic dependence among women than men. Compared to men, women own smaller amounts of property—and less productive or income-generating property.

Perhaps Marxists have failed to demand women's land rights to appease men who have suffered increasing fragmentation and loss of their land holdings. Whereas the notion that the family owns land jointly mystifies gender inequality, the demand for women's land rights would highlight conflicts in the interests of rural women and men.

However, it is important not to lose sight of differences in the nature of women's landlessness among Bengali Hindu and Maharashtrian *adivasis*. Whereas the former is continuous with other forms of women's marginalization from economic production, the latter contradicts the relatively favorable position of *adivasi* women and may represent a specific response to the *adivasis'* massive dispossession from their land.

The conflict between two dispossessed groups—namely women and *adivasis*—presents a particular dilemma for male activists, one that they have generally resolved to women's detriment. Those who are sympathetic to the *adivasis'* plight often argue that conferring land rights on *adivasi* women would lead to the further alienation of *adivasi* land should these women marry outside their communities. Therefore, although husband and wife, or brother and sister, should be considered the joint owners of landed property, *adivasi* male agnates should have exclusive rights to dispose of property.[61] To some extent, this dilemma is more acute in theory than in practice. The incidence of *adivasi* women marrying caste Hindus appears to be relatively small in regions like Dhulia district in which *adivasis* have resisted assimilation.

Adivasis themselves have debated the most desirable means of increasing *adivasi* women's rights. For example, is it preferable for the official *panchayats* to supplant the *adivasi panchs*, when the latter, unlike the former, deny women political representation and inheritance rights but foster solidarity within the *adivasi* community? Similarly, should codified Hindu law supplant *adivasi* customary law and thereby provide women with succession rights, although the price paid may be the further assimilation of *adivasis* into caste Hindu society? By and large, *adivasi* women have chosen to work within the traditions of their own community—by seeking to reform the *adivasi panchs* and customary law—rather than rejecting them outright.

Conclusion

This chapter has sought to identify the economic conditions associated with the greater militance of the Shramik Sangathana in Dhulia district Maharashtra than of the CPI(M) in West Bengal. To what extent has capitalist development brought about the proletarianization and radicalization of the labor force? How do the forms of proletarianization and protest differ among women and men? To what extent is property ownership among the rural poor a conservatizing force?

Before we explore contrasts in the nature of economic development and social change in the two states, note that in both cases mobilization has been relatively extensive. With respect to similarities in their class structures, both states contain large proportions of agricultural laborers. At the upper end of the class hierarchy, the dominant classes have not played a hegemonic role in the political arena. In the case of Dhulia district, the situation might have been quite different if Marathas rather than Gujars had constituted the dominant class. In West Bengal, caste dynamics have also weakened the dominant classes in the rural areas; industrial capitalists are non-Bengalis who prefer to remain politically inactive.

At the lower end of the class hierarchy, both states contain significant proportions of agricultural laborers: according to the 1981 census, 33 percent of male workers and 49 percent of female workers in Maharashtra, and 27 percent of male workers and 50 percent of female workers in West Bengal. Studies have found that in many other regions of India, landlessness and agrarian radicalism are correlated.[62] Thus the four states that have experienced the most extensive agrarian radicalism contain the largest proportions of wage laborers: Andhra Pradesh (42 percent), Maharashtra (39 percent), Tamil Nadu (42 percent), and West Bengal (39 percent); Kerala (32 percent), which has also experienced a vibrant tradition of protest, does not lag far behind with respect to its agricultural laborer population.[63]

Within the context of this study, however, the contrasts between the two regions are more germane than the similarities. The most striking economic contrast concerns their differing levels of capitalist development. Ironically, ecological conditions, although more favorable in regions of wet cultivation like West Bengal than in regions of dry cultivation like Maharashtra, became associated with less commercialization in the former than the latter. However, the nature of state intervention, both before and after Independence, further contributed to a spiralling cycle of dynamic growth in Maharashtra and stagnation in West Bengal. A prime example is the different forms of tenancy legislation that state governments introduced in the two states, facilitating owner-cultivation in Maharashtra and discouraging it in West Bengal.

The agrarian class structures of the two regions thus differ significantly. At the upper end of the class hierarchy, the dominant classes are economically and politically weaker in West Bengal than in Maharashtra. As a result of the legacy of permanent settlement, absentee landlordism coupled with high levels of subinfeudation discouraged investment in the land and severed the political commitments of the dominant classes to the rural areas; the Bengali *bhadralok* repudiated agrarian entrepreneurship and manual labor. Political parties that explicitly represent Bengali capitalists have not survived. By contrast, the state has helped foster the growth of an entrepreneurial class of rich peasants in Dhulia district that has not subsequently migrated elsewhere. Rich peasants have consolidated their power both through economic institutions, such as cooperatives and banks, as well as political institutions, including the *panchayats* and political parties.

The contrasts persist at the lower end of the class hierarchy. In Dhulia district, agricultural laborers are largely landless or own insignificant amounts of land and earn their livelihood primarily through wage labor. Stark class disparities, judged by discrepancies in landownership, income, and consumption patterns, frequently ignite class conflict. By contrast, in West Bengal the rural poor consists of an agglomerate that includes sharecroppers and agricultural laborers, with and without land. Various factors inhibit class consciousness; poverty has contributed to the growth of the labor force while depressing the condition of rural employers—typically middle peasants—who can only provide limited wage increases. A further consequence of immisiration is the absence of the kind of glaring class disparities that characterize Dhulia district. Nor are the Bengali rural poor a unified class; sharecroppers are economically stratified while the interests of wealthier sharecroppers and wage laborers often conflict.

However, the political significance of differing levels of capitalist development in Maharashtra and West Bengal is not altogether straightforward. In the case of Dhulia district, capitalist development and agrarian radicalism indeed appear to be associated at the *taluka* and village levels, but Dhulia's experience cannot be generalized to other districts in Maharashtra. The absence of agrarian radicalism in districts of Maharashtra where capitalism has been at least as widespread as in Dhulia would otherwise be inexplicable. In the case of West Bengal, although comparative evidence from the district level could substantiate the links between capitalism and agrarian radicalism, some of the most economically backward regions within Midnapur district have experienced the most militant protest.

Relatedly, attending simply to the differing *extent* of protest among these regions neglects the more critical difference in its *forms*. Agrarian radicalism and class conflict are often equated, thereby undermining the significance of conflict along ethnic or gender lines. Because class and caste conflict are closely correlated in Dhulia district, both appear to have been instigated by capitalist development, when in fact conflicts between Hindus and *adivasis* may have autonomous sources.

The questions raised above can only be resolved by emphasizing social influences upon class formation and consciousness. Agrarian class structures are shaped and given meaning by caste dynamics. For example, Dhulia's experience of capitalist development only becomes comprehensible when one explores the dynamics of caste and "tribalism." Conversely, conflicts that appear to be rooted primarily in class differences may in fact have as much or more to do with caste relations and consciousness. Similarly, even if the existence of relatively large proportions of agricultural laborers has provided fertile terrain for political mobilization in Maharashtra and West Bengal, political organizations still choose whether or not to represent their interests. Whereas the Shramik Sangathana has heightened agricultural laborers' consciousness of their distinctive class interests, the CPI(M) has emphasized peasant unity.

In West Bengal, for a variety of reasons, women's class position is not the principal influence on their political radicalism. There is no clear link between capitalist development and women's proletarianization in West Bengal. Indeed, caste is often a more significant determinant than class of women's performance of paid manual labor.

The significance of wage labor is also quite different for women and men. The notion that wage labor confers a measure of economic independence must be qualified for most wage-earning women, who must relinquish their savings to their husbands. Furthermore, most women are forced into a position of economic dependence because aside from the wage, which mainly provides for family subsistence, they are denied rights to inherit land from their husbands and fathers.

Women are most apt to challenge exploitative practices when they can reap some of the benefits of performing wage labor. Whereas *adivasi* women routinely exercise control over their earnings, Hindu women do not. Thus, not only is women's labor-force participation much more extensive in Maharashtra than in West Bengal; its empowering consequences are also much greater.

Part Two

Structural Contours and Political Possibilities at the Village Level

Chapter Seven

Political Mobilization and Immobilism in Midnapur District

Introduction

The preceding chapters explored the distinct social, economic, and political influences on peasant radicalism; chapters 7 and 8 assess the interrelationships between these influences. These chapters could prove bewildering because of the range and complexity of the influences that they describe. For purposes of clarity, only one or two incidents of protest are described in each village, in narrative form. My focus is on protest that occurred around the time of my first visit in 1980; in the conclusion, more recent events are described.

In both Midnapur and Dhulia districts, the most militant protest among both men and women occurred in villages in which class cleavages overlaid by caste differences were pronounced, there was a significant *adivasi* population of subordinate class status alongside Hindus of higher-class backgrounds, and political organizations had represented the most underprivileged groups: *adivasis*, agricultural laborers, and women. In villages in which all these conditions were absent (that is, villagers are predominantly or exclusively landowning caste Hindu cultivators), radical protest had not occurred. However, political mobilization had occurred along reformist lines in the presence of some of these conditions.

Most studies have not illuminated the immense variations in the fortunes of political organizations under diverse socioeconomic conditions at the village level. For example, although the Shramik Sangathana is active throughout Dhulia district, it is much more successful in the plains of Shahada and Taloda *talukas* than in the hills of Nandurbar. Similarly, although the CPI(M) has become the dominant political party in Midnapur district, it is much weaker in Tamluk than in Debra. Thus, during my first visit I highlighted the influence of structural conditions on political protest. By 1985, however, my focus had shifted to the explicitly political sources of each movement's growth or decline. Whereas during the earlier phase, structural conditions appeared to decisively shape political strategy, the reverse seemed true by 1985.

Before I turn to each district, it may be useful to describe the methodology employed for village research and to discuss the basis for differentiating class and caste relationships within the agrarian context.

Methodology for Village Research

Classification of agrarian social classes. If a voluminous literature exists on peasants and peasant movements, much less has been written about class differentiation within the peasantry. Although Leninist analysis remains the point of departure for most Indian scholarship on the subject, which among the multiple criteria Lenin identified should receive most attention is still sharply disputed: peasants' role in the production process, their relationship to the means of production, their role in the social organization of labor, or their mode of acquiring social wealth and the amount of wealth they possess.[1] Scholars agree, however, that whatever other criteria are used, landownership is the most crucial determinant of peasants' status, power, and influence.[2]

In the context of this research, landownership provided only a crude means of specifying class location but a useful initial device for determining patterns of *economic* stratification within the villages I studied.[3] After a few visits to each village, in which I would informally discuss my project, I began to collect information about landholding patterns from *panchayat* members and *talathis*, who are responsible for keeping land records. I would then meet with groups of villagers with whom I would cross-check the information I had received and discuss employment patterns.

To further refine my initial approximations, I took account of a variety of factors that determine the value of the land: soil quality, the proximity to markets, and most important, whether the land was irrigated and by what means. Irrigated land permits peasants to grow two or more crops each year, whereas dry land, which is dependent on rainfall, permits only a single crop; canal irrigated land falls between the two. I then calculated that land seasonally irrigated from canals was double the value of unirrigated land; perennially irrigated land was worth three times as much.

I also had to decide whether to distinguish tenants from owner-cultivators. The question is complicated because often the same family, even the same individual, may simultaneously lease in and lease out land. Thus, in order to determine peasants' operational holdings, I added together the land peasants owned and the land they rented from which I subtracted the land they rented out. As in most other studies on the subject, I did not distinguish tenants from owner-cultivators in my sample.[4]

Determining the number of classes within a given village constituted a further methodological puzzle. Theorists who consider class conflict immanent tend to identify fewer social classes and more extensive class disparities, particularly between groups at the top and bottom of the class hierarchy. By contrast, those who are uninterested in class conflict and consider it unlikely identify more numerous social classes, distinguished by slighter gradations of wealth and power.[5]

My decision to identify four social classes—agricultural laborers, poor peasants, middle peasants, and rich peasants—reflects an attempt to avoid the possible biases of both approaches, but not simply to "split the difference."[6] The classification scheme corresponds to the class map that most activists employ. If using the terminology of CPI(M) and Shramik Sangathana activists resulted in some oversimplification, it provided me with an excellent "view from within."

A more difficult question concerned the extent to which these class categories reflected villagers' lived experiences. I decided against relying upon villagers' own judgments concerning their class positions because the disparate criteria they would have used might have impeded comparative analysis of villages and districts. Moreover, it would have been naive to anticipate authentic responses. Indeed, I came to expect that falsification of landholdings would increase as villagers' class position ascended. Although those who claimed to be agricultural laborers rarely falsified information, the dominant classes never represented themselves as such.

The amount of land that peasants own is a crucial determinant of whether they will retain a surplus over the needs of family and farm reproduction; the amount of the surplus is in turn an accurate gauge of the manner in which peasants use their labor. Rich peasants regularly have an annual surplus through their ownership of relatively large amounts of land. Although men cultivate their land themselves, they also hire laborers to work on their land. Middle peasants generally derive a sufficient income from their land to meet subsistence needs but have little remaining surplus. In lean years they must work for wages while in better years they can hire laborers to work on their land. Because poor peasants always have a deficit after the harvest, they must supplement their income by working for wages.

Agricultural laborers are generally but by no means inevitably landless. On the one hand, agricultural laborers may own small plots of land while, on the other hand, landless individuals or families may be prohibited by their caste position from performing agricultural labor. Consistent with the Rural Labor Enquiry (1974–75), I identify agricultural laborers as individuals or groups who derive over half of their income from wage labor.[7]

However, even the most sophisticated attempt to differentiate agrarian social classes on the basis of landownership patterns generally ignores two other crucial sources of peasants' status: their gender and caste. Men's landholdings scarcely confer upon their wives, sisters, and daughters the status and prestige that they themselves acquire. Furthermore, by virtue of their gender, women are often excluded from certain forms of employment, irrespective of the size of their husband's landholdings. Similarly, caste designations are crucial in determining occupations; they exclude *dalits* and *adivasis* from certain prestigious forms of employment and exclude landless men and women of upper caste backgrounds from performing wage labor.

To more adequately understand the sources of peasants' status, power, and influence, I could have redefined class to consider the influence of caste and gender. However, aside from operational difficulties, although this approach would have yielded a highly nuanced definition of class within a particular locality, it would have impeded comparisons between villages, districts, and states. For example, women from Hindu middle-peasant backgrounds are permitted to work for wages in Maharashtra but not in West Bengal. Moreover, it would be highly misleading to suggest that women from agricultural laborer and large landowning families suffer the same disabilities as a result of their gender identities. Thus, for the purpose of classification, I initially adopted a narrow understanding of class, based on landownership patterns, and then considered the distinct and interacting influences of class, caste, and gender.

Methodology for interviews. I interviewed a sample of approximately 5 percent of the population in each of the six villages that I studied, adjusting for significant differences in village size; in the smallest of the six villages, which had a population of 540, my sample was larger and in the largest, with a population of 2,000, it was slightly smaller. My samples were stratified to reflect the proportions of classes—based on landownership patterns—in each village. Women were overrepresented in my sample, particularly among agricultural laborers and poor peasants.

Given an atmosphere of class polarization and conflict, one of the greatest challenges was to establish the confidence of the rural poor without antagonizing the dominant classes. I rejected the possibility of focusing exclusively upon the rural poor. At a practical level, dominant groups were often the first to approach me and ask what I was doing there; in one of my first such encounters I antagonized the questioner with a brusque response and risked his making me leave the village. More important, I wanted to learn from dominant groups even when this meant displeasing the village poor. I sadly recall offending an *adivasi* agricultural laborer who was my host in Madhyampur village, Dhulia district, by asking her to leave the room while I interviewed a wealthy village *sarpanch*.

However, when I was unable to straddle the fence, which was more often than not the case, I chose to identify with the poorest groups in the village by contacting them first upon arrival, staying in their homes, voicing my sympathy for their concerns, and at times openly siding with them in their conflicts with the rural rich. Particularly in Dhulia district, with political parties and the state machinery arrayed against them, agricultural laborers would never risk honesty with people they could not trust. Conversely, they gained clarity and strength when their views found support.

My rejection of a value-neutral stance made it especially imperative to cross-check the information I received. Sometimes I would share information that was not confidential with a small group of people. Returning to the same village several times seemed to establish my seriousness; I was generally welcomed back more warmly with each visit and made privy to further information. Although these methods by no means ensured the authenticity of respondents' views or wholly demarcated them from my own, they multiplied the number of voices I heard at the village level.

Midnapur District

The Political Context

Midnapur has experienced a greater range of political movements than any other district in West Bengal. The so-called terrorist movements during the partition of Bengal in 1905 and again in 1928–33 were active in the district. *Adivasi* protest against the economic dislocation that Bengal experienced between 1914 and 1918 occurred quite independently of middle-class leadership.[8]

Midnapur subsequently became one of the principal centers of Congress-sponsored nationalist activity in West Bengal, particularly during the Quit India movement, which followed nationalists' demand for unconditional independence in August 1942. Party militants helped Tamluk and Contai subdivisions to establish parallel governments with their own police, military, and judiciary and prevented the British government from regaining control of these regions for years. Midnapur was also traditionally a center of communist activity and, as previously described, a strong base of the Tebhaga movement (1946–47).

It is difficult to assess the extent of women's activism, for popular accounts glorify their roles in the 1919 and 1930 civil disobedience movements and particularly in the Quit India movement. Matungini Hazra, an elderly peasant woman who was killed by police while leading a demonstration to occupy a police station in Tamluk, has become a legendary symbol of women's courage and martyrdom. Upon closer inspection, however, it seems that the upper-caste, upper-class women whose participation is most exalted played secondary and supportive roles. An elderly woman in Tamluk who had earlier been a prostitute recalled, in the course of an interview, that on several occasions when the state exercised repression against men, their wives were helpless onlookers, for they were prohibited from leaving their homes. In one such instance, when a number of men lay injured on the streets, a group of prostitutes took them buckets of water so that they could quench their thirst and clean their wounds.

As a result of this rich legacy, a range of political parties are active in Midnapur district today. Congress and the CPI are stronger in Midnapur than elsewhere in West Bengal. The influence of the extra-parliamentary radical Left is still evident as a result of CPI(M-L)'s activities in the Debra and Gopiballavpur regions in 1968. Today, splinter leftist, "communal," and *adivasi* parties organize oppositional movements.

CPI(M) influence, though of relatively recent origins, greatly increased following the Left Front government's creation. The CPI(M) fared better in the 1978 *panchayat* elections in Midnapur than in most other districts. The CPI(M) won 60 to 85 percent of the seats, above the state average, in the *gram panchayat* (village level), *panchayat samiti* (block level), and the *zilla parishad* (district level) *panchayat* elections in both districts.[9]

The Socioeconomic Context

Midnapur forms a rectangle that is bordered by Bankura and Hooghly on the north, Purulia on the northwest, and the Hooghly river on the east. Western Midnapur adjoins Orissa and southern Midnapur borders the Bay of Bengal. Midnapur comprises five subdivisions: Sadar north and south (which are sometimes considered separate subdivisions), Tamluk, Contai, Jhargram, and Ghatal. The district headquarters are in Midnapur town in Sadar subdivision.[10] My criteria for selecting villages in Midnapur district were twofold. I was interested in studying villages that were characterized by diverse class and caste compositions and levels of economic development. I also wanted to compare villages in which the extent and forms of protest had varied. The subdivisions that I selected—Tamluk, Debra, and Jhargram—satisfied both criteria, for they differ considerably from one another both along socioeconomic and political lines.

As the second largest and second most populous district in West Bengal, Midnapur mirrors the ecological, demographic, and socioeconomic characteristics of the state as a whole. Eastern Midnapur, where Tamluk is located, resembles the economically advanced, contiguous districts of Birbhum, Burdwan, and Hooghly. Western Midnapur, where Jhargram is located, is characterized by infertile, drought-prone land and isolation from metropolitan markets and facilities. Central Midnapur, where Debra is located, is a paddy cultivating region characterized by an intermediate level of economic development. The caste and class compositions of subdivisions within Midnapur differ along with their levels of economic development. The more developed paddy growing eastern regions are densely populated, mainly by small and medium Hindu peasant cultivators. The underdeveloped hilly jungle regions in western Midnapur are thinly populated and contain substantial *adivasi* populations; central Midnapur shares characteristics of east and west.

Paanagar, Anjalinagar, and Lodhanagar Villages

Within Tamluk subdivision I selected Paanagar village.[11] Judged by its relative prosperity through betel-leaf cultivation, its large Mahishya population, and its preponderance of small landowners, it was fairly typical of the region. Paanagar provided an opportunity to examine the likelihood of protest in a region that was characterized by relative class and caste homogeneity. A practical consideration was its accessibility by bus from the town of Tamluk, where I was staying. The CADP rural development agency, which included this village in its ambit, provided me with a wealth of relevant socioeconomic information.

A large, sprawling village composed of more heterogeneous castes and classes, Anjalinagar differed considerably from Paanagar in both size and composition. As a paddy growing region, its political economy was more typical of delta villages, particularly with respect to women's employment. Although Anjalinagar was not conveniently situated, my decision was solidified when I learned that the CPI(M) *kisan sabha* had been active around wage demands, including equal wages for men and women, in this village.

I decided to study Lodhanagar village within Jhargram subdivision for a variety of reasons. A poor, arid, drought-prone village that included a significant *adivasi* population, Lodhanagar was quite typical of Jhargram as a whole. I was particularly interested to learn more about the Lodhas in this village; like the Bhils they had earlier been classified as a "criminal tribe." Lodhas were less assimilated into caste Hindu society than most other *adivasis*. Access to Lodhanagar and background information about it was easily available through the Rural Development Program (RDP), which had worked there for some years.

My initial contact with the three villages occurred in different ways. Not wanting to be associated with any political party or organization, I naively went to Paanagar without introductions. Only after several trips back (including one with my bona fide Bengali father) did villagers' suspicions abate. Although their distrust was ultimately very informative, I decided to tap more direct sources of information in Anjalinagar. Thus armed with letters of introduction from senior CPI(M) officials in Calcutta, I went to see Sukumar Sen Gupta, the chair of the CPI(M) for Midnapur district, who introduced me to party officials in Debra subdivision.[12] Maujam Hussein, CPI(M) Member of the Legislative Assembly (MLA) from Debra and Sibsadan Bhattacharya, head of the *panchayat samiti*, who were especially helpful, introduced me to *gram panchayat* members in Anjalinagar. Similarly, the RDP provided introductions to its village workers in Lodhanagar. Given these less than neutral initial contacts, the views that villagers' expressed toward the CPI(M) in Anjalinagar and the RDP in Lodhanagar may have been skewed in a favorable direction; the critical comments they expressed about the CPI(M) and RDP respectively are thus especially significant.

Paanagar Village: The Politics of Privilege

> *I used to vote for Congress. Then I saw that the jotedars [landlords] voted for Congress so I started voting for the CPI. Later I realized that it didn't make any difference which party I voted for; they are all the same.*
>
> A Mahishya poor peasant

The Socioeconomic Context

Paanagar village is a mile southwest of the town of Tamluk. Once an important seaport and cultural center, Tamluk is at present the subdivisional headquarters. Paanagar is connected by a direct bus to the town of Tamluk; a tea shop by the bus stop provides a central meeting place where village men can relax and socialize. The main road connects with a narrow dirt path that runs through the village; smaller paths lead into the *paras* (residential neighborhoods). Ponds, paddy fields, and huts in which betel leaves are grown intersperse the densely populated village. On the outskirts, large date palm, banyan, and tamarind trees create a shady resting place from the blazing sun. Paanagar contains 630 people (324 men and 306 women), who live in three *paras* of the village.[13] Wealthier families live in mud houses that are built around private courtyards; poorer families live in smaller huts constructed of mud, wood, and bamboo.

Socioeconomic conditions have contributed to political quiescence. Paanagar is wealthier, class differences are less marked, and agricultural laborers are fewer in number than in most other regions of Midnapur. Moreover, disparities in status are virtually nonexistent, for with the exception of three Goala families, Paanagar is composed of the Mahishya cultivating caste. Members of an upwardly mobile, enterprising community, Mahishyas are apparently uninterested in challenging the status quo.

Agrarian capitalist development might well be expected to contribute to class differentiation and political protest. Most of Paanagar's land—210 out of 245 acres—is cultivated. Betel leaf, a cash crop, is sown in June and harvested the following summer. It is then exported to other parts of India to be rolled into *paan* (a betel leaf that contains betel nut, spices, and sometimes tobacco). However, betel-leaf cultivation has only given rise to petty capitalist production. In contrast to IADP "green revolution" districts, the state has not intervened to provide cultivators with facilities for capitalist development in Midnapur. Thus Paanagar lacks controlled irrigation facilities; the single tube well in the village supplies drinking water. Although cultivators must borrow extensively to meet the high costs of betel-leaf cultivation, they lack access to low-interest institutional loans.

Furthermore, although betel-leaf cultivation is profitable, it is expensive and risky. Twenty decimals (one-fifth of an acre) of betel-leaf land generally yield an annual revenue of two thousand to three thousand rupees. However, betel-leaf prices are contingent upon unpredictable weather and market conditions. The average price for one thousand betel or *paan* leaves is about forty rupees, but prices range between twelve and one hundred rupees. Nor does capital investment ensure a profit, because betel leaves are extremely fragile and their production is highly labor intensive.

In order to determine the rough distribution of social classes in Paanagar, different numerical values were assigned to the betel leaf and the paddy land that each family owned. The value of betel-leaf land, which was found only in this region, was three times that of paddy land. On the basis of these calculations it appeared that of the 128 families in the village, approximately 29 percent (35 families) were agricultural laborers who owned up to .29 acres of land; 48 percent (62 families) were poor peasants who owned between .30 and 1.99 acres; 18 percent (24 families, including three Goala families) were middle peasants who owned 2.00 to 3.99 acres; and 5 percent (7 families) were rich peasants who owned over 4 acres of land. (See figure 1.)

Wage strikes in Paanagar have been short and infrequent. Agricultural laborers and poor peasants derive some income throughout the year both from their land and from nonagricultural employment.[14] Several laborers explained that most of their employers were middle peasants who could not afford to pay higher wages. Others said that because there was a labor shortage in the region, employers immediately granted their demands.[15] Although seemingly contradictory, both comments may be partially correct; agricultural laborers have hesitated to demand higher wages, but when they have done so, middle peasants have quickly conceded.

Women have had even fewer incentives and opportunities to organize than men. Women rarely work for wages, for Mahishyas and Goalas regard women's performance of paid manual labor as degrading. Employers thus hire migrant men in preference to Mahishya women. Poor peasant women work on their own paddy and betel-leaf land. Although they also work with their husbands on leased land, only the male head of household is considered a sharecropper and thereby remunerated. A poor peasant woman commented, "If we help our husband in doing this work the whole family profits. But it is unfair that the employer profits even more when we work for free." Although many Mahishya women agreed, most Mahishya men described their wives as "helpers" rather than sharecroppers in their own right.

Women's cultivation of betel leaves is so demanding that it leaves little time for other activities. In fact, most interviews with women in

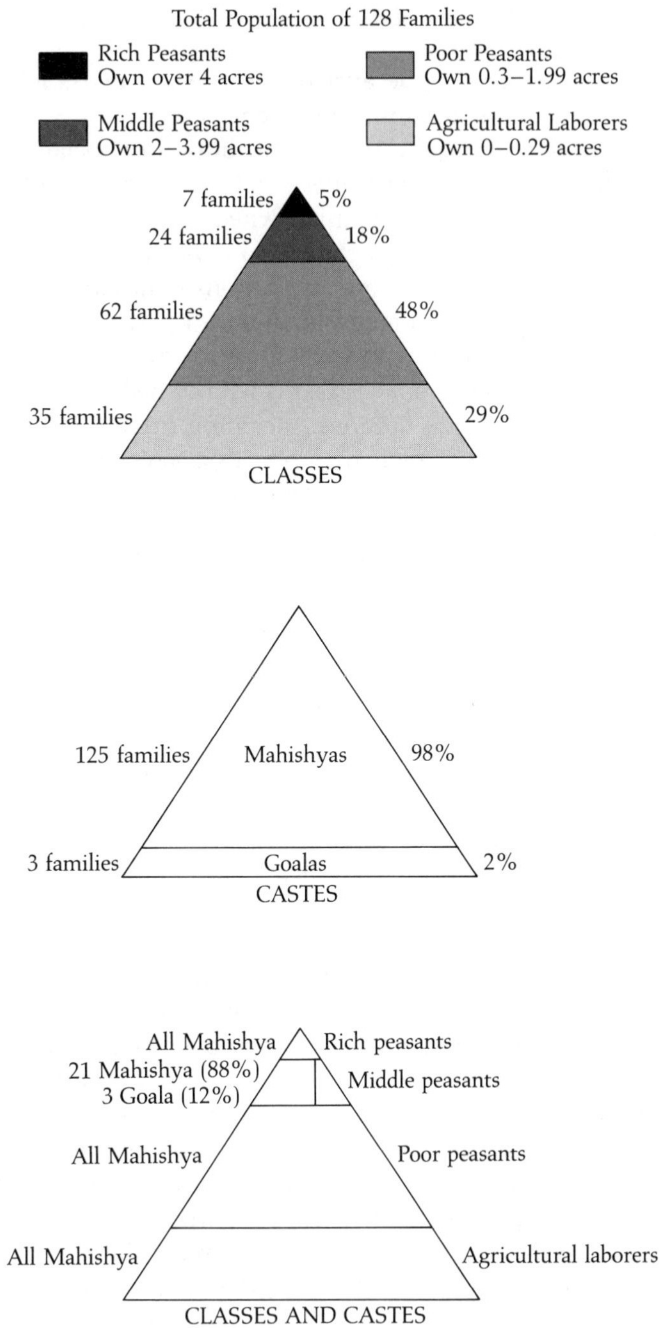

Figure 1. Demography of Paanagar Village, Tamluk *thana*

Paanagar had to be conducted in the fields while they pruned, weeded, and irrigated betel leaves. Furthermore, betel-leaf cultivation does not lend itself to collective organizing, for women tend betel leaves in isolation, and as "helpers" rather than wage laborers.

Mahishya Women and the Politics of Family Life

Mahishyas have adopted many upper-caste Hindu traditions concerning marriage and the family. In Paanagar, girls generally marry around age twelve so that they can easily adapt to their in-laws' homes. Married girls continue to live with their parents until puberty, when their family consults an astrologer about the advisability of consummating the marriage and performing a ritual second marriage. Mahishyas believe that without the astrologer's consent, sexual relations can endanger the husband's livelihood and even physical safety. Innumerable superstitions about female reproduction indicate the sanctity and fear that surround women's attainment of motherhood. Mahishyas believe that women's seclusion and subordination ensure harmonious relations within the family and in the larger society. Thus, a woman is expected to show modesty and deference before her husband and in-laws by avoiding eye contact, touch, conversation, and the use of her husband's name. When asked their (married) surnames in the course of interviews, Mahishya women would ask children to respond.

The Mahishya community doubly penalizes women, first by prohibiting them from working and owning property and then by punishing them for their economic dependence. This pattern is most evident in the workings of the dowry system. The dowry is extremely high among most Mahishyas: in 1980 it ranged from fifteen hundred to three thousand rupees among poor peasants, three thousand to five thousand rupees among middle peasants, and up to ten thousand rupees among rich peasants. In addition to cash, the dowry also included utensils, gold ornaments, and household goods. The growth of the dowry has been accompanied by increasing harassment of new brides by in-laws, who claim that the dowry is insufficient. During my stay in Paanagar, a young mother of a year-old baby allegedly committed suicide by swallowing pesticides. The women's friends claimed that her in-laws had murdered her because the dowry was inadequate.

The murder of the first wife so that her husband can remarry and collect another dowry helps cultivators meet high cultivation costs and repay their debts. Since women are prohibited from working for wages, they cannot otherwise contribute to the income. Within the joint family, which is prevalent in Paanagar, the dowry is of tremendous significance. Moreover, the notion that the bride's family should give the groom's family continual, unreciprocated gifts legitimates in-laws' harassment of young brides.

Mahishya women freely criticized the dowry system, the low age of marriage for girls, and polygamy—which is quite common and motivated in part by the desire for additional dowries. Women reported in interviews that polygamy led to frequent conflicts between wives, involving the tendency for the first wife to dominate the second, and for the husband to prefer the second wife (especially if she was younger and bore him a son). But women rejected the possibility of openly challenging polygamy, the dowry, and other abuses.

One important explanation for women's quiescence is their economic dependence. On the subject of men's alcoholism and battering, for example, which several women complained of, one woman commented, "When I try to stop him from drinking he says, 'Since I earn the money in this house, who are you to tell me how to spend it?' " Furthermore, Mahishyas have a strong sense of privacy about domestic matters. Several women reported that their husbands would be outraged if they learned that women discussed their husbands' drinking. Notions of male superiority are also deeply internalized: "It is important for us to control our husbands when they drink. But at the same time we must show respect for them. After all, men are *boro*" [older, bigger, wiser, more experienced].

Women's feelings of ignorance and dependence on men became even more evident when they were asked about the conventional political arena, which they considered men's domain. A woman nominated to the seat reserved for women in the *gram panchayat* described her political apathy:

> I told my husband that I did not want to become involved in politics because it would interfere with my housework. He said, "You won't even know that you are a member. You only have to put your thumb print on some papers

every few weeks." He was right. I have never had to go to a meeting or do anything else. I still do not understand what work the *gram panchayat* does.

Men view women as ignorant partly because women are more apt to be illiterate, and Mahishyas value educational attainments.[16]

However, along with their misgivings about their own abilities to discuss political affairs, many women criticize political parties for ignoring women: "How can we know about these things? When men from the SUC [Socialist Unity Centre] come to the house they only talk to my husband. They don't believe that we can understand politics." Another woman commented: "Political parties promise many things before the elections. But power damages their memories. They forget all their promises afterwards." Her views were widely shared.

Political Factionalism in Paanagar

Tamluk's preponderance of landowning peasants seems to have influenced the constituencies and demands of political parties. Not only Congress but even the communist parties, which became increasingly influential in the 1960s, were primarily composed of middle peasants. The familial connections between Congress and the CPI in Tamluk are graphically illustrated by the fact that Ajoy Mukherjee, Congress party leader and former chief minister of West Bengal, and Bishwanath Mukherjee, CPI leader and secretary of the Midnapur district committee, are brothers.[17]

The 1978 *panchayat* elections transformed political arrangements in Paanagar. Until then the *gram panchayat* and the village council, which performed complementary functions, supported the Congress party. Men who were distinguished by age and wealth were represented on both bodies. Radhanath Quila, who inherited from his nationalist parents a commitment to Congress, headed the *gram panchayat* and the village council.

When Quila ran for the *gram panchayat* elections on a Congress ticket in 1978, he was defeated by Santosh Jena, a young candidate from the Socialist Unity Centre (SUC) a breakaway faction of the Revolutionary Socialist Party. The SUC won eight seats and the Independents two seats in the *gram panchayat* election. The SUC's victory is particularly noteworthy, for it did not gain control of any other *gram panchayat* in Tamluk. The party's victory had less to do with its stated platform than with its immersion in a factional village dispute. As a close observer of Midnapur politics suggests, the pervasiveness of factionalism in Tamluk is related to the dispersal of economic and political power.[18] Thus the residents of two *paras* in Paanagar became fiercely divided over whether a Sitala goddess temple should be built in Dokhinpara or Uttarpara. The SUC candidate, Santosh Jena, promised Dokhinpara funds for the temple. Since Dokhinpara was larger than Uttarpara, the SUC was elected.

To Quila, the SUC victory represented the tendency for youth, though lacking in age and experience, to challenge the authority of their elders. Quila touted the reliability of the village council and bemoaned its demise. Unlike the *gram panchayat*, the village council provided the opportunity for redress and appeal and enforced a strict code of ethics. Quila argued that problems like excessive drinking and crime had greatly increased because the *gram panchayat* did not exercise moral authority. However, to many young people in Paanagar, the village council was a paternalistic, undemocratic organization. Many people questioned why village council membership should be lifelong and hereditary. Although several wanted greater opportunities for political participation themselves, others simply wanted the democratization of procedures governing village affairs.

The residents of Uttarpara and most older and wealthier villagers continued to regard Quila as their leader, whereas Dokhinpara and the younger generation generally supported Jena. Yet, as one man noted, villagers' support for the SUC was conditional: "We will not support the SUC just because we voted for it. We will first see what it does and then decide."

People expressed keen disillusionment with political parties, which they viewed as corrupt, dishonest, and self-interested. The unpopularity of parties is evident from the significant number of spoiled ballots and the high incidence of split-ticket voting. Several people commented that they felt greater confidence in state than local leaders. Thus they would vote for Congress, CPI, or the CPI(M) in the Legislative Assembly elections but not in the *panchayat* elections.

Villagers' most serious criticism of the CPI(M) was that it did not sufficiently represent landowning cultivators. Although agricultural laborers, in regions where they are numerous, criticize the CPI(M) for catering to middle peasants, villagers in Paanagar regard the CPI(M) as an agricultural laborers' party. A middle peasant commented:

Agricultural laborers are well off here. They get plenty of work and high wages. Rich peasants aren't affected by price increases because they make profits from moneylending and hoarding. We are in the most difficult position. We have to pay high prices and high wages to laborers and we never have a steady income from our *paan* leaves. We will support whichever party understands these problems.

In addition to the many negative reasons why people voted for the SUC, an important positive reason was that the SUC explicitly represents middle-peasant interests. Its main demands have been for subsidized loans, irrigation facilities, higher prices for agricultural commodities, and lower prices for fertilizers and pesticides. Many villagers complained that the CPI(M) had been inattentive to these demands. They were relatively indifferent about the party's attempts at registering sharecroppers, increasing wages, and achieving land redistribution.[19]

The SUC has capitalized on people's disillusionment with the CPI(M). It has organized opposition to CPI(M)-dominated *panchayats* on grounds that they are corrupt. It has also organized several mass demonstrations in Calcutta protesting "the anti-people policies of the leftist government." In Calcutta, as in Paanagar, these have mainly attracted young people. SUC strength in Tamluk is a significant barometer of villagers' discontent with the CPI(M).

The views of Mahishyas provide a corrective to the common assumption that the CPI(M)'s attention to the grass-roots level would bring about its radicalization. To the contrary, in villages like Paanagar, the CPI(M) faces pressures to be more responsive to middle peasants and less responsive to agricultural laborers. Several villagers agreed that radical opposition to capitalist development would serve neither them nor the party well. Simply to criticize the CPI(M)'s reformism without hearing these voices in Paanagar would do a grave injustice both to the party and to its Mahishya critics.

Anjalinagar Village: Reformist Mobilization

A child does not get attention until it cries out. You must learn to cry out or you will never be heard.

Anjali Das, *mahila samiti* secretary and *gram panchayat pradhan*

A vote is like an appeal. We vote because we need help from the Left Front government.

a female agricultural laborer

The Socioeconomic Context

Anjalinagar is located about twenty miles northwest of Paanagar in Debra p.s.[20] The distance is magnified by a long, strenuous trip involving two changes of bus. To reach Anjalinagar from Balichak, which is the nearest town, one must travel by train to a neighboring village and walk through three miles of paddy fields.

Anjalinagar is a large, sprawling village with a population of 2,005 (1,013 men and 992 women). There are at least four small shops and five temples in the village. Numerous ponds provide fish for local consumption. Houses are closely clustered within each of Anjalinagar's eight dispersed *paras*. Differences in living standards are more marked than in Paanagar. Several landlords inhabit double- and triple-story concrete houses surrounded by high boundary walls. Adjoining huts shelter cows, buffaloes, and goats. At the other end of the class spectrum, agricultural laborers live in huts constructed of mud and bamboo in which a single room generally houses the entire family. In several *paras, dalit* families have built their huts around a common courtyard that provides a shared cooking and recreational space.

Anjalinagar initially appears to be more agriculturally developed than Paanagar. Out of 1,100 acres in the village 670 are irrigated (620 by the Midnapur dam, 20 acres by tanks, and 30 from shallow tube wells.) However, only 79 percent of its land is cultivated and most of this land is monocropped.[21] Poor and middle peasants are unable to grow cash crops because their land is not assured irrigation throughout the year. Rich peasants, who own most of the irrigated land, grow small amounts of sugar cane, jute, and high-yielding varieties of rice but invest little in cash crops, because they make greater profits from moneylending. Poor peasants and agricultural laborers are forced to borrow large sums from their employers because of the dearth of employment opportunities.[22] They must frequently sell their land and work for extremely low wages to repay their debts.[23]

Class disparities are much greater in Anjalinagar than in Paanagar. Of the 387 families in the village, 62 percent (234 families) are agricultural laborers; among them 65 families are landless and 169 families own less than an acre of land. Twenty-seven percent (106 families) are poor peasants who own between 1 and 2.4 acres of land; 4 percent (18 families) are middle peasants and own 2.5 to 4.9 acres; and 7 percent (29 families) are rich peasants and own more than 5 acres of land.

Anjalinagar contains a large number of castes: Brahmins, followed by Khotriyos (Kshatriyas), are at the top of the caste hierarchy. Next are the Mahishyas and a number of Nabasakha castes including Kamars, Napits, and Tantis. *Dalits* constitute 29 percent of Anjalinagar's population (114 families). There are many different *dalits* in the village including the Bhumij, Dhobas, Doms, Namasudras, and Chamars. Four percent (16 families) of Anjalinagar's population are Santals (*adivasis*). Although there is some overlap between class and caste categories, the intermediary castes are the village's largest landowners whereas most Brahmins engage in traditional priestly duties. Middle and poor peasants are Mahishyas, Kamars, Napits, and Tantis. Half of all agricultural laborers are *dalits*, 6 percent are *adivasis*, and the remainder are Hindus. Most *adivasis* (save for 14 percent, who are middle peasants) are poor peasants and agricultural laborers. (See figure 2.)

Women's labor-force participation is greater in Anjalinagar than in Paanagar and Lodhanagar because of its larger population of agricultural laborers. Women are primarily responsible for rice transplantation and share with men the tasks of weeding, harvesting, boiling, and drying the paddy. Often sharecroppers' wives perform these tasks in their employers' homes to repay an outstanding debt. Despite their work on the family land, women from sharecropping families lose all rights to the land when their husbands die or abandon them. Some *dalit* women work as domestic servants for five to ten rupees a month; wages for domestic work have risen very little in recent years.

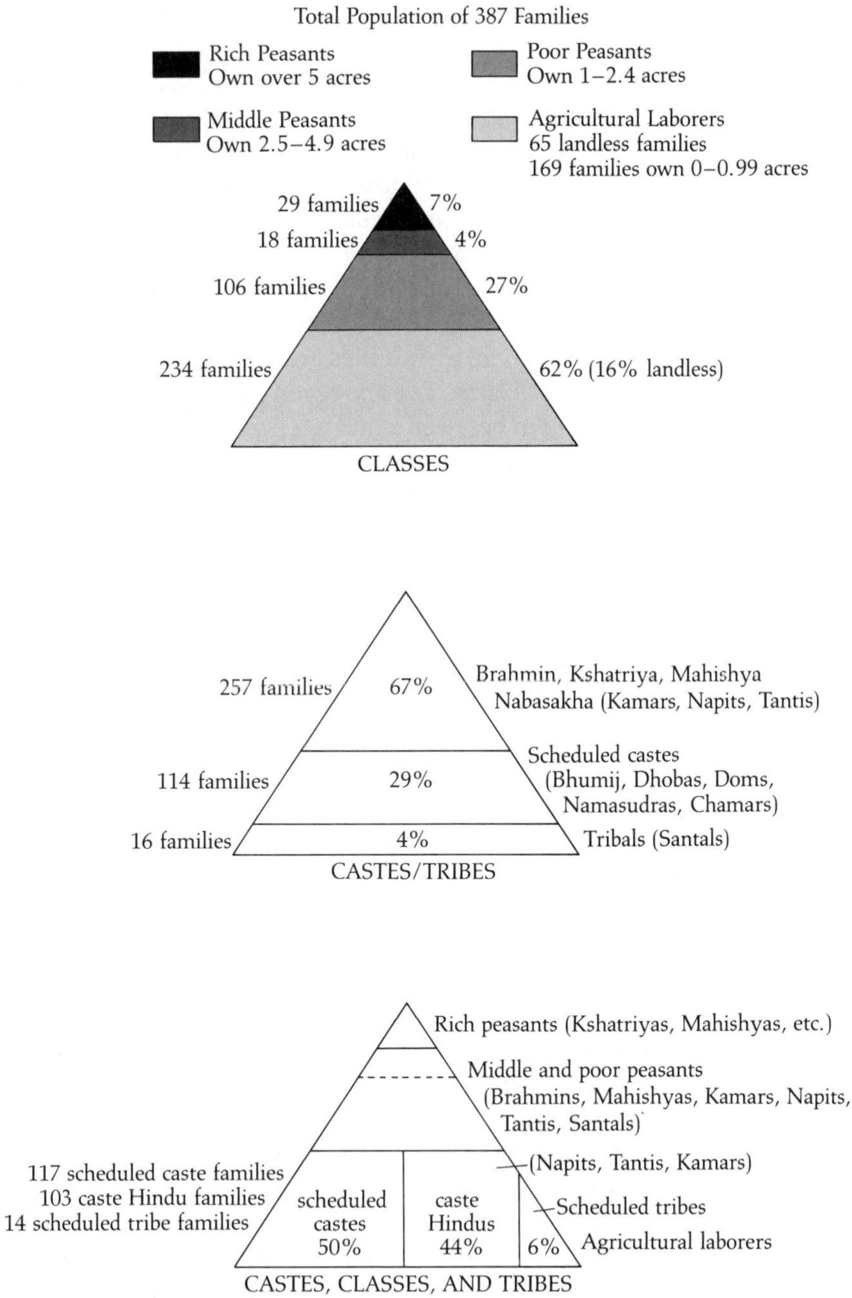

Figure 2. Demography of Anjalinagar Village, Debra *thana*

The CPI(M) in Anjalinagar

Villagers trace the CPI(M)'s presence in Debra back to the period when the second United Front government occupied office. Many peasants were radicalized by the repression they experienced after Congress dismissed the leftist government. Peasants claimed that landlords brought false charges against them, forced them to return land, and denied them employment. Women reported being brutalized by landlords and the police.

CPI(M) strength in Debra has steadily grown. The CPI(M), Independents, Congress, and Janata each won a single seat in the 1977 Legislative Assembly elections in Debra. In the *panchayat samiti* elections, the CPI(M) won twenty-four out of thirty-five seats, whereas Congress (I) and the Independents won the remainder. In elections to the *gram panchayat,* which includes Anjalinagar and eight other villages, the CPI(M) won eight and Congress two seats. Anjali Das was elected head of the *gram panchayat* and also secretary of the block-level women's organization.

The CPI(M)'s *mahila samiti* and *kisan sabha* as well as the CPI(M)-dominated *gram panchayat* jointly seek to achieve reform through institutional channels and political mobilization. As Sibsadhan Bhattacharya noted, the *gram panchayat* cannot become directly involved in political agitation because it represents the government and therefore must assume responsibility for village welfare. Because the *kisan sabha* is linked to the party and considers itself an advocate for the poor, it must organize confrontations within the village and against the government. However, the *gram panchayat* provides the *mahila samiti* and the *kisan sabha* with legitimacy and support.

The mahila samiti. Nando Rani Daal, secretary of the CPI(M) women's organization for Midnapur, visited Debra in 1972 and appointed Anjali Das to the Midnapur district *mahila samiti.* She also persuaded Anjali Das and another woman to start a women's organization in Debra. The organization that they formed is active in twenty-eight villages and in 1980 claimed a membership of five hundred women. It organizes meetings at least once every two weeks. The *mahila samiti* also designates a few women to organize meetings in their own villages.

The activities of the women's organization accord with the CPI(M)'s dual emphasis on institutional reform and political mobilization. Its social welfare, or "constructive," activities include a maternity center, an income-generating project, and adult literacy classes for women. It has also mobilized women to participate in movements protesting inflation, demanding greater employment opportunities, and, most important, demanding equal wages for male and female agricultural laborers.

The *mahila samiti* has devoted greater attention to social welfare activities than to organizing agitational movements. Gita Hui, a forty-five-year-old widow who is active in the Anjalinagar women's organization, explained the rationale: "Kamars, Tantis, Santals, and the Mahishyas all have different marriage practices. But constructive activities and demands for relief concern women from all castes."

However, the *mahila samiti*'s social welfare activities have not had as universal an appeal as Gita Hui suggests. Most of the women involved in these activities, including *mahila samiti* leaders, are middle peasants. Sewing lessons, nutritional programs, and adult literacy classes are luxuries that female poor peasants and agricultural laborers cannot afford. Moreover, the *mahila samiti* has inadvertently perpetuated gender inequality by organizing activities that reinforce women's sex-linked roles.

Even when organizing agitational activities, the *mahila samiti* minimizes differences in the interests of women and men. For example, at one *mahila samiti* meeting with female agricultural laborers, Anjali Das argued that men and women should receive equal wages because the whole family would thereby benefit. Several women questioned this interpretation: a female agricultural laborer noted that her husband did not believe that women worked as hard as men. Another woman said her husband preferred to earn more to demonstrate that he was the household head. But the *mahila samiti* refused to recognize male laborers' opposition and continued to depict the struggle as directed solely against employers.

The *mahila samiti* is immeasurably weakened by its relatively small size and dearth of qualified leadership. The block-level *mahila samiti* is too small to organize in twenty-eight villages and few women are active in the Anjalinagar *mahila samiti*. Maujam Hussein noted that most *mahila samiti* leaders were "auxiliary" rather than full party members and thus lacked the skill to effectively mobilize peasant women. When asked why the CPI(M) had not involved full party members in the women's organization, Hussein responded, "The *mahila samiti* is only temporarily necessary to help peasant women to achieve the same level of political consciousness as men. Once it has achieved this goal there will no longer be a need for a separate women's organization." Hussein not only underestimates the obstacles to organizing rural women but also implies that the problems of men and women are ultimately the same. Most important, his comment reflects the CPI(M)'s tendency to trivialize the women's organization.

The kisan sabha. The *kisan sabha* resembles the *mahila samiti* in its moderate, consensual approach and its middle-class composition. However, because the *kisan sabha* is responsible for implementing the CPI(M)'s agrarian mobilization program, it has more resources, more qualified leaders, and more support from the CPI(M). The *kisan sabha* claimed a membership of thirty thousand in Debra p.s. and five hundred in Anjalinagar village in 1980. Although membership is open to anyone who pays the twenty-five paise fee, its membership is almost entirely male. According to the *kisan sabha,* half its members are agricultural laborers; most of the remainder are poor peasants, middle peasants, and sharecroppers. Several rich peasants are also *kisan sabha* members.

Kisan sabha leaders in Debra describe land redistribution as their major long-term goal. However, the amount of surplus land that the government has vested and redistributed in the area has actually declined since the Left Front government was elected.[24] The constitutional protection of property has enabled landlords to block land redistribution through the courts and the *kisan sabha* now opposes the earlier "land grab" movement. "Operation Barga" has also been hampered by land scarcity and by tenants' dependence on landlords for employment and loans. Moreover, many sharecroppers who were interviewed feared registering because they had vivid memories of landlord retaliation after the fall of the second United Front government. The *kisan sabha*'s major immediate demand has thus been for higher wages.

The *kisan sabha* organized strikes in each block for the minimum daily wage of 8.10 rupees for agricultural laborers in 1980. The most militant strikes took place in block eleven, where Anjalinagar is located. Strikes generally occur in the winter harvesting season when there is a labor deficit. The *kisan sabha* has lessened migration to Anjalinagar in the harvesting and transplanting seasons and persuaded migrant laborers not to accept lower wages than local laborers. But overall the frequency and duration of wage strikes have decreased since the Left Front government took office. In the past, strikes sometimes spanned most of the harvesting season; they presently last only two or three days. Sibsadhan Bhattacharya regards this as an achievement: "There is less need for strikes than in the past because the government is no longer an enemy but an ally. As a result, landlords concede much more quickly to our demands."

In 1980, the *kisan sabha* had yet to achieve the minimum wage of 8.10 rupees although, by its own estimate, this wage barely meets the subsistence needs of a family of three.[25] Moreover, Surya Mishra, the *subadipati* of the Midnapur *zilla parishad,* argued that CPI(M)-organized strikes were the single most important determinant of wage rates in the district.[26] Once again, the CPI(M) seemed willing to abdicate agitational methods in order to preserve class harmony. A *dalit* laborer commented: "The *kisan sabha* decides when to meet with landlords and reach an agreement. It always ends strikes before our demands have been met. Often we would like to continue the strike but we have no choice."

When the possibilities for CPI(M) intervention are examined, it is clear that the scope for reform is most restricted in the economic sphere. Although additional wage increases are quite feasible, further progress in land redistribution and sharecropper registration are impossible in the absence of legal and constitutional reform. But the CPI(M) has barely explored the arenas in which change is much more feasible: namely, in caste and gender relations. This failure is especially striking in Anjalinagar, where 62 percent of the population are agricultural laborers; over half of them are *dalits* and *adivasis*, who are much more sexually emancipated than are caste Hindus.

Far from stemming the tide of Sanskritization, the CPI(M) *mahila samiti* has actually socialized poor rural women into *bhadralok* values by tacitly accepting inequalities between male and female worlds. With respect to women's employment, it has simply demanded public provision of income-generating projects for women and scarcely questioned women's marginalization from economic production. It thereby implicitly upholds the *bhadralok* disdain for manual labor and reinforces the notion that women's work should be restricted to low-paying, home-based jobs. Within the sphere of family life, the *mahila samiti* has ignored village women's bitter complaints about the dowry system, although reducing the dowry would have salutary consequences for the lives of both women and men.

Lodhanagar Village: *Adivasi* Militancy

The British called us thieves because they wanted our forests. Then the Mahatos came to our village and called us thieves because they wanted our land.

A Lodha agricultural laborer

Our conditions have improved in the past few years. But we have only achieved progress when we have fought for it ourselves. We should never forget the past.

A Lodha poor peasant woman

The Socioeconomic Context

Lodhanagar village is located nine miles south of the town of Jhargram.[27] It is a mile's walk from the bus stop along a windy, dusty, unpaved road. Lodhanagar is thinly vegetated and even more thinly populated—by 541 people (283 men and 258 women). There are few facilities in the village; the nearest post office is over one mile away, the nearest hospital, over seven miles away, and the nearest high school and college are in Jhargram town.

There are marked differences between the living conditions of the Hindu Mahatos and Lodha *adivasis*. Mahato homes usually have several rooms, including a kitchen, bedrooms, and cow sheds. The wealthier Mahatos have large courtyards and granaries; nine Mahato homes have electricity. Most Lodhas live in one- or two-room mud huts that contain few personal belongings. Lodhas were said to have deliberately constructed small dark rooms to conceal their crimes.[28]

Lodhas traditionally had few opportunities to forge collective identifications as a result of high levels of out-migration. Agricultural productivity is extremely low in Lodhanagar because the soil is infertile. Of 319 acres, 179 are forests and only 50 are cultivated. (Of these, 34 acres are irrigated from natural sources; there is no controlled irrigation in the village.) Paddy is the major crop; there are small amounts of wheat, maize, and potatoes but no cash crops are grown. There is no mechanization in the village.

Male and female agricultural laborers who do not have young children spend most of the year in more economically developed regions, for agricultural employment is only available in the vicinity about six weeks annually.[29] Villagers rely heavily on the government's Food for Work program for employment in the lean season.[30] Jhargram's large *adivasi* population also depends on the forests—the second largest forest in West Bengal—for their subsistence. *Adivasis* consume the *sal* trees' fruit and the *mohwa* trees' flowers. They make eating utensils of *sal* tree leaves and agricultural implements from its wood.

Like most other villages in Jhargram, Lodhanagar is composed of numerous small landowners, a smaller number of agricultural laborers, and a handful of large landowners. Of 118 families, agricultural laborers constitute 33 percent (39 families) and own less than an acre of land; poor peasants constitute 48 percent (57 families) and own 1 to 2.99 acres; middle peasants constitute 14 percent (16 families) and own 3 to 5.99 acres; rich peasants constitute 5 percent (6 families) and own over 6 acres of land. (See figure 3.) *Adivasis* constitute a majority of Lodhanagar's population and Hindu cultivators a minority. Lodhas are 63 percent, Santals 5 percent, and Mahatos 32 percent of Lodhanagar's population. Lodhas are concentrated at the lower end, Santals in the middle, and Mahatos at the upper end of the class hierarchy. Agricultural laborers are 97 percent Lodhas and rich peasants are all Mahatos.

Exploitation by both the dominant classes and the state has been the major source of Lodhas' radicalization. For the past twenty years the West Bengal Forest Department had been auctioning the forests to private industrialists who replaced many of the *sal*, *mohwa*, and *kendu* trees with commercial trees for paper manufacture, thereby depriving Lodhas of the forest products on which they had traditionally subsisted. Once the Rural Development Project (RDP) began providing them employment and subsidized loans, many Lodhas began to remain in the village during the lean seasons.[31] The RDP highlighted the responsibility of both the Mahatos and the government in restricting Lodhas' access to the forests.

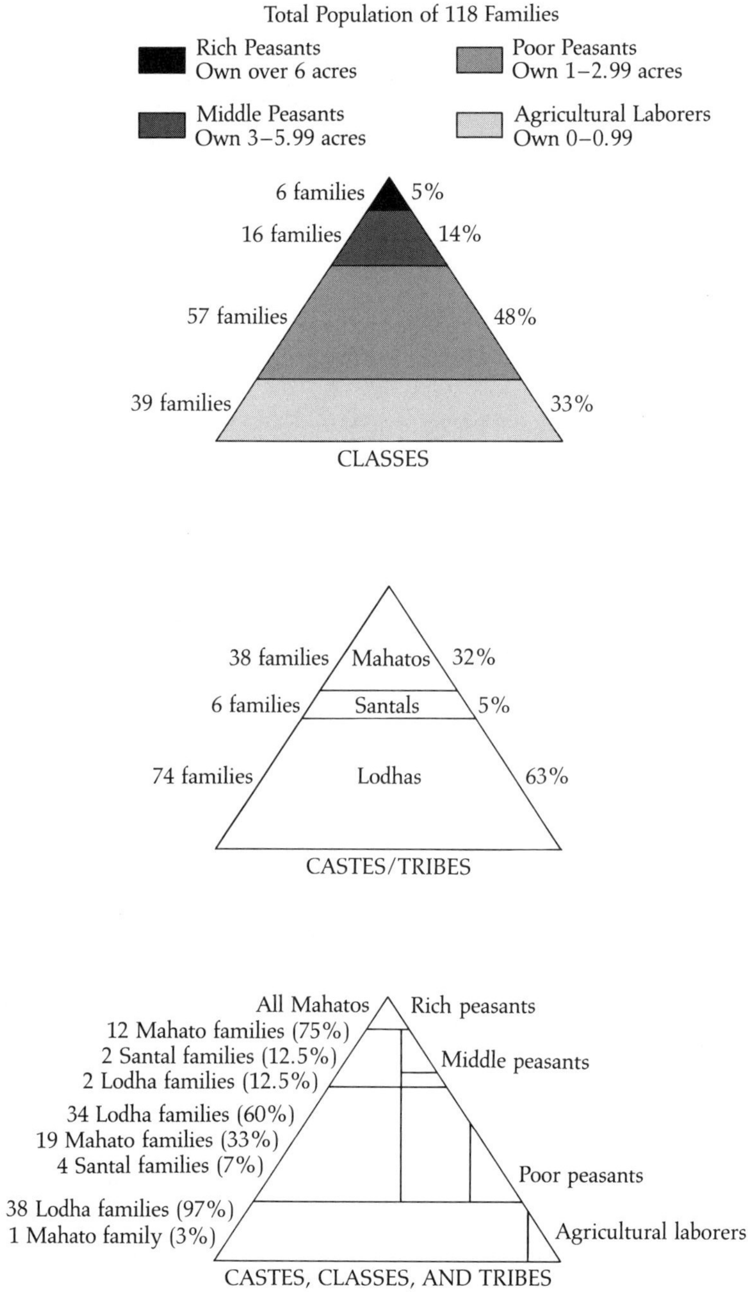

Figure 3. Demography of Lodhanagar Village, Jhargram *thana*

Lodha Criminality

The history of the Lodhas illuminates the manner in which a marginal group begins to assert its rights, an internalized sense of inferiority becomes politicized, and perhaps most remarkably, the very sources of cultural oppression become tools of resistance. Lodhas consider themselves descendants of the Savaras and frequently attach "Savara" to their names, for they take great pride in their ancestry. Savaras are a mythical forest-dwelling community who feature in the Hindu epic literature.[32] Lodhas have a strong and exclusive sense of community identity: they observe strict rules of endogamy and have their own caste priests; they do not dine or celebrate festivals with other *adivasis* or with caste Hindus; in the past they even refused employment from caste Hindus.

Lodhas were among two hundred Indian "tribes" whom the British branded criminals. In October 1871 the British passed the Criminal Tribes Act, which empowered government officials to designate any caste that systematically engaged in nonbailable offenses as criminals. An amendment in 1911 stipulated that criminal tribes had to keep the police routinely informed of their whereabouts. From 1916, when they were classified as a criminal tribe, until 1952, when the law was repealed, the Lodhas were punished on the mere suspicion of crime.[33] Indeed, a Bengali expression quipped, "When a crime occurs, search the Lodhas." Lodhas could be arrested if found on the streets after the 6 P.M. curfew that was imposed on them.

The Lodhas doubtless acquired their reputation in part because they engaged in theft. Deprived of their livelihood from forest and agricultural lands, they lacked the skills and opportunities to earn an income. But another possible reason why the British branded the Lodhas a criminal tribe was that they feared a recurrence of early nineteenth-century *adivasi* revolts. The British may also have considered the Lodhas barbaric; a hunting and gathering community, Lodhas did not readily take to settled cultivation. Lodha men and women killed and ate wild animals and reptiles from the jungles. One of their traditional skills was to catch and skin live snakes.

Lodhas' conditions deteriorated further after Independence. Lodhas had traditionally enjoyed unrestricted rights to *zamindars'* forests in exchange for providing *zamindars* with their services for a short period each year. After the government gained control of the forests, it greatly restricted the Lodhas' use of forest produce. Moreover, the Mahatos, who migrated from Orissa and Bihar to Jhargram, exploited the Lodhas through usury. Many Lodhas reported that the Mahatos paid them to steal small sums; Mahatos would then sell the stolen goods and turn Lodhas over to the police. When Mahatos and the police hounded the Lodhas, men hid in the forests while the women remained at home with the children and bore the worst brunt of police repression.

P. K. Bhowmick's study of the Lodhas provides one of the few available estimates of the number of Lodhas convicted for crime. The five major categories of crime that Bhowmick lists are, in descending order of gravity: murder, dacoity, robbery, burglary, and theft. Bhowmick found that in 1953 no Lodha was convicted for murder or robbery. They were convicted for only 5.5 percent of all dacoities, 8 percent of all burglaries, and 7 percent of all thefts. Lodhas' motivations for theft are evident from the fact that 82 percent of those convicted were landless and 12 percent owned less than an acre of land; the majority had large families.[34]

Lodha Resistance

Like other foreign-financed development organizations, the RDP's major objectives were to increase agricultural productivity by creating irrigation facilities, improving cultivation techniques, and providing peasants with credit. It also hoped to develop health care, communications, and sanitation facilities in the village. Less typical, however, was the director of the RDP's Jhargram office.

Dhiren Chattopadhyay, who had previously been a CPI(M) member, had become a severe critic by the late 1970s. Dhiren was outraged by the indifference of the government, development organizations, and political parties toward this exploited and impoverished *adivasi* community. He felt that the meager assistance that the government granted the Lodhas simply perpetuated their isolation and dependence. The key to improving Lodhas' material conditions, he believed, lay in restoring their sense of dignity.

Of the twenty-five villages in which the RDP was active, Lodhanagar had the largest proportion of *adivasis*. Dhiren was especially drawn to Lodhanagar by Hitesh, a young man whom he met upon his first visit in February 1975. With a ninth-grade education, he was among the most educated Lodhas in Jhargram. Upon Dhiren's suggestion, Hitesh decided to give up his job as a contract laborer in Howrah to work for the RDP. After several months in which they discussed the needs of the Lodha community, Dhiren and Hitesh persuaded Lodha men to revive the traditional *solo ana* (village council). After attending its meetings for a few months, Dhiren gradually withdrew and his influence over the Lodha council declined. For example, the Lodhas did not heed his suggestion that they include poor Mahatos in their deliberations.

One of the council's first objectives was to curtail police intervention in village affairs by controlling theft. Hitesh claimed that in its first year of existence, people from Lodhanagar and neighboring villages brought about thirty cases of alleged theft before the council each week. The council would render a verdict and, if necessary, mete out punishments. Its most common penalty was social boycott, whereby the entire village would isolate the offender. The council also fined culprits. On one occasion Hitesh beat two Lodha boys whom the police had caught stealing in another village. An observer reported, "At the meeting that night we scolded Hitesh and made him understand that he should never have used force."

Shortly after creating the village council, Dhiren organized biweekly literacy classes, which were designed to politicize the Lodhas.[35] Within a few months, up to forty Lodhas were attending. The students learned to read and write familiar words and then discussed their meanings. One of the first words they studied was *dadar*, a loan from moneylenders at exorbitant interest rates. A skit on *dadar* portrayed a Mahato moneylender confronting a woman alone in her home and demanding her *mangalsutra* (the necklace married women wear), thereby signifying both material and sexual exploitation. When the Lodhas first enacted this skit, the moneylender took the woman's necklace; in a later version, the woman forced him to leave without it. After performing the skit, the Lodhas would explore various means of regaining their possessions from moneylenders. They decided against using force because they could not defend themselves.

One of the few issues that provoked Lodhas to resort to violence was rape. In May 1979 the Lodhas marched to the Mahato *para* armed with bows and arrows to avenge a Mahato's rape of a Lodha woman. Hitesh intervened and prevented a violent clash. The Lodhas fined the culprit three hundred rupees and placed him under social boycott. Dhiren initiated a discussion of rape in literacy classes shortly thereafter. He noted that although they opposed Mahato men's violence against women, Lodha men sometimes forced women to have sexual relations. For example, during an annual festival when many prohibitions were relaxed, Lodha men could abduct and forcibly marry women. Hitesh later commented, "In the past we had no respect for women because we had no self-respect. We treated our women the way Mahato men treated us."

In keeping with past traditions, the village council excluded women from its deliberations and ignored the issues that most concerned them. Although this generated some discontent among women, they did not confront the council until two years after the council was formed. In June 1977 three men who were active in the village council got drunk and beat their wives. About thirty women dragged the men to the village square, tied them to a tree, and beat them. Several of these women attended the village council meeting that evening. One woman asked how the men could imagine changing conditions in the village without first changing their own behavior in the family. The women demanded that the council fine men who drank heavily and resolved to ensure that it did so by attending council meetings themselves.

However, two years later, women were only attending the council meetings sporadically when a particularly grave problem arose. At a council meeting in June 1979 several women complained of being excluded. Hitesh's wife, Renu, said she rarely attended council meetings because she felt self-conscious and ignorant in front of men; moreover, she could not leave her children in the evenings. Several women expressed an interest in creating a separate women's organization where they could discuss their own concerns. But they later admitted that they did not have the time to create such an organization. They also felt handicapped by the lack of female leadership. Dhiren also contributed to women's quiescence. While encouraging them to participate in the village council, he opposed women's expression of their own interests on the grounds that this would weaken the still vulnerable Lodha community.

That Lodha women have been politically active at all is testimony to the respect they command within the Lodha community. That their roles have been secondary to those of men reflects the Lodhas' patriarchal character. Indeed, in certain respects gender inequality may have increased among the Lodhas with the upward class mobility they have experienced. As the following incidents suggest, women have often restrained, prompted, and influenced men rather than asserting their own interests.

In April 1979 the village council petitioned the government to build another primary school in the village, because the Mahatos who attended the existing school made the Lodha children extremely uncomfortable. The government refused but offered instead to place thirty *adivasi* children from Lodhanagar in a nearby *adivasi* hostel, where they would receive free tuition, board, and lodging. Several women adamantly opposed the proposal at the village council meeting. They argued that the school would alienate their children from the community by entitling them to special privileges. One of the women said:

> I have five children. How will the others feel if one of their brothers comes home with good clothes and he knows how to read and write while they spend their day working in the fields? How will we feel when he forgets his family's problems and goes to work in the cities? I would rather that all my children were equally poor.

Upon the women's insistence, the village council wrote to the Tribal Commissioner rejecting the scheme because it would further isolate and segregate the Lodha community.

Consider another incident that occurred a few months later: the RDP employed about eighty men to construct a road between the village and the bus stop. Many men complained that they received higher hourly wages from the public Food for Work Program than from the RDP. Women reported that some outside agitators, presumably CPI(M-L) members, had urged male workers to slow down their pace of work. A few days later, these women passed by the construction site and saw the men sitting and chatting. When their husbands returned home that evening they found that their wives had not cooked dinner but were sitting outside, talking and laughing. One woman described the incident:

> When they asked us why, we said, "This is what would happen if we all decided not to work. You are not building that road for the RDP but for the village. When any one of us is lazy, we all suffer."

In both incidents, one can discern the impact of prevailing social values on women's consciousness. Lodha mothers, who were responsible for feeding their children each day, were more skeptical than men of charity. Their injunctions to abide by "the rules of the game" could be interpreted as a sign of their conservatism. Conversely, their rejection of individual material rewards reflected their stronger sense of collective identity (better education for a larger number; a road for the village). Without attempting to resolve the contradiction between these two possibilities, it is noteworthy that women's roles after the RDP's formation were entirely consistent with their past history.

Wary of the patronizing quality of government "rehabilitation programs" among the Lodhas, the RDP initiated development projects that challenged exploitation, generated self-sufficiency, and drew upon Lodhas' traditional skills. For example, the RDP provided a number of families with loans with which to manufacture plates from *sal* leaves, baskets from rope, and medicines from herbs. It arranged for them to bypass exploitative intermediaries and gain direct access to local markets. It also encouraged the village council to revive the Bengali practice of *anradhan*, a community grain bank. In the first year of its existence, the Lodhas collected seventy pounds of rice, which they lent out in the lean season at 5 percent annual interest. The bank's holdings increased the following year. *Anradhan* provided Lodhas with low-interest loans and helped to foster cooperative methods.

The RDP and the CPI(M)

After 1977 the Left Front government became increasingly responsive to Lodhas' demands. Two CPI(M) leaders from Jhargram informed the village council of the forthcoming *gram panchayat* elections and encouraged Hitesh to run on a CPI(M) ticket. Hitesh was elected to the predominantly CPI(M)-controlled *gram panchayat*, thereby defeating Sidhu Mahato, Lodhanagar's largest landlord, who ran as a Congress party candidate.

The *gram panchayat*'s first responsibility was to distribute land that had been vested in Lodhanagar. A few months after receiving land, thirty Lodha families returned it to Mahato cultivators. Some feared that Mahatos might retaliate by denying them loans and employment whereas others could not afford the costs of cultivation.

The village council fined the Lodhas and helped them to secure loans for cultivation.

With the CPI(M)'s support, the villagers organized a strike in the harvesting season of 1978 to demand equal wages for all agricultural laborers, for Mahato employers were paying one rupee more a day to Mahatos than to Lodhas. After three weeks, several Lodhas accepted bribes from Mahatos and returned to work. When some Lodha women discovered this, they forced the men to return the bribes and continue the strike. Mahato landlords retaliated by refusing to allow Lodhas to traverse their land or purchase goods from their shops. The Lodhas in turn denied Mahatos access to their land, which connected the Mahato *para* to the main road. The Mahatos eventually withdrew their threats and conceded to the one-rupee wage increase.

Unlike Hitesh, Dhiren was extremely critical of the role that the CPI(M) and the *gram panchayat* were playing in Lodhanagar:

> Where has the CPI(M) been all these years? After Hitesh was elected on the CPI(M) ticket—no thanks to the Party—and after the CPI(M) saw the Lodhas' progress, it decided to take an interest in Lodhanagar. This is just another example of its opportunism.

Dhiren did not recognize, as Hitesh and other villagers did, that the *gram panchayat* provided the village council with resources, legitimacy, and institutional support. Moreover, it created linkages between Lodhanagar and the surrounding villages. Although the RDP created village councils in eight other villages, they were unable to replicate their achievements in Lodhanagar.

Furthermore, Dhiren's idealism blinded him to the contradictions that were implicit in sponsoring radical reform through a development organization. Because it was the wealthiest organization and often the largest employer in the village, many Lodhas resented the RDP. The incident described earlier, in which male laborers demanded higher wages for road construction, indicated that many Lodhas saw Dhiren as an employer. One of the laborers explained,

> The camp [RDP] tells us to demand higher wages from the landlords and the government. We say, "But you are paying us less than the Food for Work Program pays." They say, "This is not a wage; you are doing this work to build your own road. The government only gives you work for six weeks. We give you work all year." I do not understand the difference, we should get the same wage from all employers.

The RDP found itself involved in a series of conflicts because it was trying to achieve contradictory goals. The Lodhas criticized the RDP for not doing enough while the RDP head office criticized it for doing too much. In 1982 Dhiren resigned from the RDP because of mounting pressures that he discontinue political organizing. The RDP thus reached a stage when it could no longer simultaneously engage in development activities that were ostensibly designed to benefit the entire village while actually inciting the Lodhas to resist Mahato domination.

Midnapur Revisited

Between 1979 and 1985 there was a marked decline in Lodhas' consciousness and activism. Although Lodhas reported that they occasionally attended CPI(M) meetings and demonstrations in the town of Jhargram, they did so as spectators. Village council meetings had become infrequent and villagers were less active in the CPI(M)-dominated *gram panchayat*.

Clearly the Lodhas had less to protest about: the Mahatos no longer subjected them to abusive treatment, police raids had ceased, and the Left Front government had invested more resources in this arid, impoverished *adivasi* region. Under the state and central governments' jointly financed Integrated Tribal Development Program, villagers could buy rice at the subsidized rate of 1.80 rupees per kilo and wheat at 1.50 rupees per kilo, almost half the market price. The government had provided several landless *adivasi* women with loans for income generation, particularly through the manufacture and sale of forest produce. Like the RDP in the past, the government encouraged women to manufacture and sell minor forest produce. Furthermore, the government's economic reforms were being implemented: 97 of Lodhanagar's 131 sharecroppers had been registered, fifty acres of land had been distributed to fifty-five families, and agricultural wage rates had increased. Men and women were now receiving the same wage: five to six rupees in the lean season and eight rupees in the harvesting season.

However, in other respects Lodhas' conditions had deteriorated. Lodhas' powerful sense of collective identity diminished as divisions set in between beneficiaries and those who were denied public support. Government provision of agricultural loans, homestead land,

and funds for income generation were limited and selectively distributed. Since Lodhas were no longer active in designing and implementing these programs, their sense of self-sufficiency also declined. Theft, alcoholism, and intercommunity strife had all increased; the RDP's demise created a vacuum that increased CPI(M) visibility was unable to fill. An old man commented bitterly, "When the village is so backward, these short-term programs do not help much."

Elsewhere in Midnapur, as in Lodhanagar village, there had been a striking growth in the CPI(M) and its affiliated organizations by 1985. According to Surya Mishra, the district's *kisan sabha* comprised a million members in 1985. Since the 1983 *panchayat* elections, the CPI(M) controlled all but ten of fifty-four *panchayats*. Moreover, CPI(M) influence was much more uniform throughout the district than it had formerly been. When asked to explain the party's growth, Mishra replied, "The CPI(M) has persisted in class struggle by allying with the oppressed." In fact, quite to the contrary, the CPI(M)'s growth had more to do with its progressive deradicalization.

In May 1987 the most recent strike that villagers in Anjalinagar and Paanangar could identify had occurred over two years earlier—and this "strike" had been a two-day symbolic work stoppage throughout West Bengal. Surya Mishra attributed diminished class conflict to the administration's preventive measures. He explained that the *panchayats*, bureaucracy, and police would meet before each sowing and harvesting season to forestall conflicts. They would refer particularly sensitive problems to a higher-ranking crisis management committee that was formed for this purpose. Testimony to the success of the approach is that the most serious conflicts involved clashes between political parties, which in only some cases were underlaid by class conflicts.

A decade after the Left Front government had been elected, the fruits of its efforts with respect to sharecropper registration and increased agricultural wages were evident. By 1987 all 182 sharecroppers in Anjalinagar had been registered. Although agricultural laborers were not receiving the minimum wage rate, which had been 14.91 rupees per day since 1984–85, wages had significantly increased. Men were receiving 8 rupees in the lean season and 10 rupees in the harvesting season in Paanagar. Moreover, men and women were receiving equal wages in Anjalinagar village—9 rupees in the harvesting season and 6 rupees in the lean season.

Given the CPI(M)'s economistic bent coupled with its reformist goals, it is not surprising that it had been most successful in achieving redistributive reform in the villages. As a result of a government directive to link employment generation to the creation of durable assets, the *panchayats* had supervised the construction of roads, canals, and schools. By 1987 Anjalinagar had a paved road that connected it to Balichak, electricity in two *paras*, and most symbolic of modernity, a video parlor!

With central government assistance, the Left Front government was administering various economic programs for women. The most important was a program of subsidized loans for a poultry scheme, sewing, and needlework. Other programs that were still at the experimental stage included mobile creches (child care centers) for *adivasi* women, adult literacy programs, and a nutrition program for lactating mothers.[36] But rather than further politicizing women who had achieved wages equal to those of men, the *mahila samiti* had become less active in Debra since attaining this demand. Nor had women's political representation increased at the local level; few women served on the *gram panchayats* in the three villages and those who did had been nominated rather than elected. Local *mahila samiti* leaders spoke of the need to fight "atrocities against women" as a rather abstract, long-term objective.

The CPI(M)'s economic reforms did not begin to challenge the sexual division of labor. The best example concerns the distribution of land titles to largely male household heads in the course of Operation Barga. Those villagers who favored joint titles demonstrated a sophisticated understanding of their significance. Consider the following comments from Anjalinagar: "If men own the land, then women have no security after their husbands die"; "If women and men are equal, as the Party says, they must own the land jointly." Many people felt that the CPI(M) *mahila samiti* could do much more to attain joint titles for husbands and wives. Why had it not directed the *panchayats* to distribute joint *puttas*, organized delegations to confront government officials, or joined hands with the *kisan sabha* in struggles around the issue?[37]

In most respects, the balance sheet of progress with respect to the CPI(M)'s performance in Midnapur was more favorable in 1987 than it had been in 1980. The CPI(M) had not only held ground but had become electorally and organizationally stronger. A key to its success seems to lie in its creation of a rural machine that rewarded its supporters; unlike Congress, however, the Left Front government maintained its redistributive thrust in the process. Agricultural laborers, who might have favored a more radical approach, constitute a minority of the electorate. By contrast, Mahishya cultivators in Tamluk, who had been beneficiaries of irrigation facilities, a new road, and poultry for income generation, expressed relief that the CPI(M) was not simply a party of the poor.

Paanagar, Anjalinagar, and Lodhanagar: Comparative Perspectives

The striking differences among Paanagar, Anjalinagar, and Lodhanagar provide an opportunity to explore the range of structural and political conditions associated with protest at the village level. To what extent is capitalist development associated with the growth of the agricultural laborer force and in turn with political protest? How significant are large *dalit* and *adivasi* populations to agrarian radicalism, particularly women's radicalism? To what extent have political organizations shaped patterns of political mobilization at the village level?

None of the villages that were analyzed in this study have experienced extensive capitalist development within the Indian context. Even within the context of West Bengal, Midnapur is characterized by an intermediate level of development compared to the more capitalist districts of Burdwan and Hooghly, where perennial irrigation is more extensive, mechanization is widely used, and landholdings are less fragmented. However, the extent of capitalist development varies significantly within the district and sharply decreases as one moves westward from Paanagar to Lodhanagar.

The contrasting experiences of Lodhanagar and Anjalinagar disprove the common identification of agrarian capitalism with class polarization and conflict within West Bengal. The agricultural laborer population is small and class disparities are slight in Paanagar partly because its most significant source of income is from betel leaves that families grow themselves; paddy, by contrast, requires greater use of wage labor. Conversely, in the impoverished village of Lodhanagar, the agricultural laborer population is larger and protest has been more extensive. Nor do these village studies suggest that regions containing larger agricultural laborer populations necessarily experience greater political protest. Although the absence of class conflict in Paanagar seems to accord with its small proportion of agricultural laborers (29 percent of its population), Anjalinagar contains more than double the proportion of agricultural laborers compared to Lodhanagar (62 percent and 33 percent, respectively) but has not experienced greater political protest.

Nor has capitalist development in Midnapur brought about the proletarianization of women. Indeed, confirming the findings of Bardhan and Rudra about West Bengal as a whole, my research suggests that women's *marginalization* from the labor force increases with economic advancement; thus, of the three regions in Midnapur under study, women's labor-force participation rates are lowest in Tamluk and highest in Jhargram. In 1981 women constituted 3 percent of the rural population who are main workers in Tamluk, 16 percent in Debra, and 19 percent in Jhargram. Furthermore, in all three *thanas*, womens' labor-force participation had declined rather than increased between 1961 and 1981 from 6 percent to 3 percent in Tamluk, 17 to 16 percent in Debra, and 35 percent to 19 percent in Jhargram.[38]

However, simply comparing the *extent* of political protest across villages conceals far more striking differences in its *character*. The focus on economic-wage demands in Anjalinagar may have been strongly influenced by its large agricultural laborer population. Conversely, questions of human dignity were more salient in Lodhanagar because two-thirds of its population is *adivasi*. Furthermore, the extent to which class and ethnic cleavages are mutually reinforcing is a critical determinant of the intensity of conflict. (See figures 1, 2, and 3.) Mahishyas' attainment of upward caste and class mobility are closely linked and both contribute to Mahishyas's unwillingness to participate in leftist movements. Conversely, polarization along ethnic and class lines has been an important catalyst to political radicalism in Lodhanagar, where all rich peasants are Mahatos and 97 percent of agricultural laborers are Lodhas.

Anjalinagar's caste structure, which of the three villages is most typical of West Bengal as a whole, consists of numerous castes that vie for economic dominance at the upper end of the caste hierarchy and several lower caste groups at the lower end. Militant opposition to the dominant castes is less likely in Anjalinagar than in Lodhanagar for a variety of reasons: its upper castes use less repression against subordinate castes than the Mahatos traditionally exercised against *adivasis* in Lodhanagar; a third of Anjalinagar's population is *dalit*, whereas over two-thirds of Lodhanagar's population is *adivasi;* and traditions of political radicalism are stronger among *adivasis* than *dalits* in West Bengal. (See figures 1, 2, and 3.)

Political organizations have been strongly influenced by these structural conditions. The Congress party traditionally owed its strength in Tamluk largely to Mahishya cultivators' support.[39] Mahishyas' conservatism has made it more difficult for the CPI(M) to create a base in Tamluk than in most other parts of the district. With the erosion of the Congress party base in Tamluk, most villagers express distrust of political parties. The SUC only gained support in the *gram panchayat* by becoming involved in a factional village conflict.

For quite different reasons, namely its lack of interest in organizing *adivasis* in a peripheral jungle region, the CPI(M) was traditionally inactive in Lodhanagar. The very features of the region that repelled the CPI(M) attracted an independent grass-roots organization. The militant but short-lived radicalism that the RDP inspired was entirely consistent with earlier traditions of *adivasi* radicalism. Structural conditions in Anjalinagar are more typical than in Paanagar and Lodhanagar of regions in which the CPI(M) has been active. Anjalinagar's class and caste structure have enabled the CPI(M) to mobilize without concerted opposition from the dominant castes. However, the absence of class and caste polarization have been more conducive to reformism than to a radical approach.

Women, like men, have been more active in protest in Anjalinagar and Lodhanagar than in Paanagar; their protest has been reformist along class and gender lines in Anjalinagar and more militant in both respects in Lodhanagar. In villages like Paanagar, which are characterized by class and caste homogeneity, the principal forms of subordination women experience emanate from within their own community. Once again the contrasts between Paanagar and Lodhanagar are stark: Lodha women's experience of sexual and class exploitation has politicized them against the Mahatos. In the process they have also become increasingly conscious of inequalities within their own community.

Of much greater significance than economic influences in determining the levels of women's labor-force participation are women's caste identities. Among the three villages, Mahishya women in Paanagar are the most secluded from economic and political life, whereas *adivasi* women in Lodhanagar are the most active; women's labor-force participation in Anjalinagar varies according to their caste backgrounds.

This chapter illuminates the ways in which socioeconomic conditions constrain political radicalism at the village level. The best example is provided by Paanagar village, where the relatively small proportions of agricultural laborers and sharecroppers and the dearth of surplus land present major obstacles to CPI(M) organizing. Conditions in Paanagar are only a more extreme version of the problems that confront the CPI(M) in West Bengal as a whole.[40]

However, attention to socioeconomic constraints should not detract attention from strategic choices. The RDP, for example, typifies both the strengths and weaknesses of grass-roots political organizations. The RDP suffered at once from inadequate structure and yet also a tendency to unselfconsciously endorse external political leadership, male domination, and even the welfare mentality that it decried.

Similarly, many of the CPI(M)'s weaknesses in Anjalinagar typify both the strengths and weaknesses of parliamentary communism. In contrast to the RDP, the CPI(M) enacted reforms that had a lasting impact. But the CPI(M) failed to push the limits of reformism, especially outside the economic domain. Its neglect to challenge both gender and caste inequality, especially among *adivasis*, most vividly demonstrates the political constraints imposed by a parliamentary approach.

Chapter Eight

Political Quiescence and Resistance in Dhulia District

The red flag of the revolution has come,
Let us hail it
(Chorus) It resounds from village to village
It has come in the form of the landless
Who is joined by the poor peasant
(Chorus) It resounds from village to village
It begins with strikes and marches
Landlords, moneylenders, the police are terrified
(Chorus) It resounds from village to village
The rich know their deceit must end
The landless are telling you to organize
For there is no other way
(Chorus) It resounds from village to village

Shramik Sangathana song

Introduction

Gaining the confidence of Shramik Sangathana activists was not an easy task. By 1979 the movement had received so much attention from middle-class sympathizers that it was becoming a must on the circuit of grass-roots organizations in western India. The activists worried about making the Shramik Sangathana "success story" a blueprint for change elsewhere.

When by January 1979 my numerous letters to the Shramik Sangathana from Calcutta and New Delhi remained unanswered, I traveled to Shahada to seek authorization for my research. After several discussions with Dinanath Manohar, Kumar Shiralkar, and Vijay Kanhare, the activists agreed to my spending several months in Dhulia district and subsequently returning there for follow-up visits. They also helped me to select three villages that I could study in some detail and gave me introductions to the villagers.[1]

The activists' willingness to assist me was indicative of their interest in the issues that I was addressing: although *adivasi* women had displayed considerable militance, there were no women activists in Shahada at the time and the male activists were anxious to discuss women's role in the movement. They were also interested in my work on West Bengal, for they were debating among themselves the trade-offs between parliamentary communism and autonomous grass-roots movements.

I accepted the activists' suggestions as to the three *talukas* to study and myself selected particular villages within these localities. According to the activists, in the first *taluka*, Shahada, the movement was relatively weak, even though it was powerful in the Shahada plains. The second locality, the plains of Taloda—where class conflict was acute—exemplified the movement at its strongest. The third *taluka*, Nandurbar, had not been a principal site of activists' involvement but had witnessed women's militancy around a range of issues. (See map 2, p. 8.)

If certain biases entered into my analysis because of my reliance upon the activists for introductions, interviews with villagers would have been impossible without the activists' authorization. On balance these biases were relatively slight, and they diminished over time as I was exposed to a great diversity of perspectives. I also interviewed activists from the Gram Swarajya Samiti and the Satya Shodhak Communist party, to gain contrasting perspectives from those of the Shramik Sangathana. Finally, I talked to members of the dominant classes, although I cannot claim to have gained their confidence.

But it would be disingenuous to exaggerate my distance from the Shramik Sangathana and thereby to imply that I possessed a critical perspective that the activists lacked. I discovered a great deal from the Shramik Sangathana and, far from anticipating the movement's demise, learned with them about its dilemmas and weaknesses. Scholars, however, can reap the rewards of hindsight where activists can merely reflect on their errors of judgment.

The Topography of Dhulia District

Dhulia district is divided into two administrative subdivisions and ten *talukas*, including Shahada, Taloda, and Nandurbar—the *talukas* in which the Shramik Sangathana is most active. Of its population, 84 percent is rural and inhabits over 1,360 villages. Shahada contains 180 villages, Nandurbar 125, and Taloda 86, the smallest number of villages of any *taluka* in the district.[2] In 1987 the Shramik Sangathana was active in approximately twenty-five villages in Shahada, eighteen villages in Taloda, and eight villages in Nandurbar.

Dhulia district as a whole, as well as Shahada, Taloda, and (to a lesser extent) Nandurbar, comprises two distinct geographic regions: the underdeveloped mountainous forests and the more affluent central plains. The forests in Dhulia district are the largest in the state.[3] The Shramik Sangathana has not been very active in the mountainous forest region because class and caste disparities are slight: most of the population consists of *adivasi* poor peasants. By contrast, the Shramik Sangathana has been extremely active in the plains villages of Shahada, Taloda, and Nandurbar. A small proportion of the population has accumulated large tracts of land while 54 percent of the working population of Shahada, 42 percent of Taloda, and 39 percent of Nandurbar are landless agricultural laborers.[4] Class disparities are overlaid by caste inequalities. Rich peasants are Marathas, Gujars, and Rajputs, whereas agricultural laborers are mainly *adivasis*. Laborers' sense of discontent is acute; their impoverishment has increased as these regions have prospered.

At the broadest level of analysis, it is possible to identify the nexus of socioeconomic and political conditions associated with different expressions of resistance in the three villages. In each case, the nature of Shramik Sangathana activity has been influenced by the proportions of *adivasis* and agricultural laborers, the relationship between caste and class cleavages, and the extent of agrarian capitalist development. Udaspur village, located in the impoverished northwestern Shahada hills, has been relatively politically quiescent; it is composed almost exclusively of *adivasi* small landowners.[5] In the absence of marked class cleavages among villagers, the Shramik Sangathana has not organized class struggles. It has instead channeled villagers' energies into social reform and opposition to corruption in public employment.

Daulatpur village, located in the agriculturally developed Taloda plains, has been the site of numerous militant wage strikes. Agrarian capitalist development has exacerbated inequalities and conflicts between agricultural laborers and rich peasants. Class and caste cleavages are mutually reinforcing: most agricultural laborers are *adivasis* and most rich peasants are upper-caste Hindus. The class structure of Madhyampur is less polarized than that of Daulatpur. Protest has also been relatively extensive in Madhyampur village, but in contrast to Daulatpur it has centered on nonmaterial issues.

Most of the conditions described above have had the same implications for protest among men and women. The extent of women's roles in paid production, which varies considerably between villages, is a particularly important determinant of women's militancy. Women have been least politically active in Udaspur, where their labor-force participation is limited, and at the other end of the spectrum, organized separately from men in Madhyampur, where their labor is extensive. Daulatpur can be situated midway on the continuum: women are moderately active in the labor force, although male laborers outnumber female laborers; men have been more politically radical than women.

The more difficult question, which will be addressed after recording the stories of the three villages, involves differentiating the relative significance of the conditions identified above. Is class a more important determinant than ethnicity of *adivasi* laborers' militancy? Do men and women express different commitments to their ethnic and class identities? To what extent is the Shramik Sangathana ultimately captive to existing ethnic and class structures or, conversely, responsible for heightening certain forms of identity while rejecting others?

Udaspur Village: The Obstacles to Political Mobilization

> *It is much more difficult to organize people who are oppressed than people who are exploited. Poor peasants in Udaspur are oppressed.*
>
> Gulab, a Shramik Sangathana activist

The Socioeconomic Context

Udaspur village is located in the hilly jungle region of northwestern Shahada *taluka*, fourteen miles from Shahada town. The distance is magnified by poor bus connections and roads. The bus stops frequently along the way so that women can give the drivers bundles of firewood and kindling to sell for them in the town. The bus stop is a mile from an outlying section of the village; the center of the village is another mile's walk through thick fields of *dadar* and *jowar*. Udaspur is separated by large tracts of arid land from other villages and access to public amenities. There are no banks, cooperatives, or development schemes near the village.

Not only is Udaspur isolated from other villages but, as reflected in its dispersed residential arrangements, villagers in Udaspur are extremely isolated from one another. One hundred and forty-five families live in six sections of the village, three of which are almost a mile apart. Each of the six sections is inhabited by Bhils and Pawras of different class backgrounds. Most families live in one-room mud houses that open onto small courtyards. They generally own a few chickens; about twenty families own goats. Two grocery stores in the village sell staples, often on credit at exorbitant interest rates.

Udaspur's agricultural land is extremely unproductive. Half of its 1,250 acres are covered by forests and only 510 acres are cultivated. Agricultural productivity is low because the soil is infertile and chronic floods destroy half the crop annually. *Jowar*, rice, and lentils, the main crops, are grown primarily for consumption. Even vegetables must be imported from other villages.

Agricultural employment is available only for about four months annually.[6] Thus, poor peasants and agricultural laborers must construct roads, raise and sell animals, and collect firewood to supplement their income. Men from Udaspur seek work in the plains but return frequently to Udaspur to cultivate their small plots of land and see their families (whom they are reluctant to take along because they distrust plains' people). This employment pattern impedes the emergence of class-based loyalties among men both in Udaspur and in the plains. Nor do women from landowning families tend either to perform wage labor or to engage in collective organizing.

The absence of pronounced class and ethnic cleavages poses an even bigger obstacle to class-based movements. Udaspur is primarily a poor peasant economy, composed entirely of *adivasis*. There are two *adivasi* communities in the village: the Bhils, who constitute 83 percent of the population; and the slightly higher status, wealthier Pawras, who comprise 17 percent of the population. Of the 145 families in Udaspur, 31 percent are landless agricultural laborers and the remainder are poor and middle peasants; there are no rich peasants in the village. Seventy-five percent of agricultural laborers are Bhils and 25 percent are Pawras. Eighty-nine percent of poor peasants are Bhils and 11 percent are Pawras. Eighty percent of middle peasants are Bhils and 20 percent are Pawras. (See figure 4.)

A complex system of cultivation known as reverse tenancy has developed because poor peasants lack the collateral to secure low interest loans from either banks or *adivasi* welfare programs in the area. Thus they rent out their land to middle peasants and declare themselves landless or land poor. Although they are thereby granted loans, they must pay the crushing annual interest rate of 75 percent, frequently by selling their cattle and utensils. The reverse tenancy system has not generated class conflicts because disparities in poor and middle peasants' landholdings are relatively slight. Furthermore, *adivasi* poor peasants in Udaspur, unlike those in the plains' villages, rarely lose their land to lessors. Poor peasants find reverse tenancy more profitable than leaving their land uncultivated.

Udaspur's class and caste composition limits the likelihood of political conflict within the village in several ways. In the absence of caste Hindus, Bhils are less likely to attribute their poverty to an identifiable class in Udaspur than in the plains' villages. Moreover, class and status differences between Bhils and Pawras have inhibited them from organizing jointly against outside forces. In the past, Pawras claimed that they were of Rajput descent (which Rajputs denied). Although

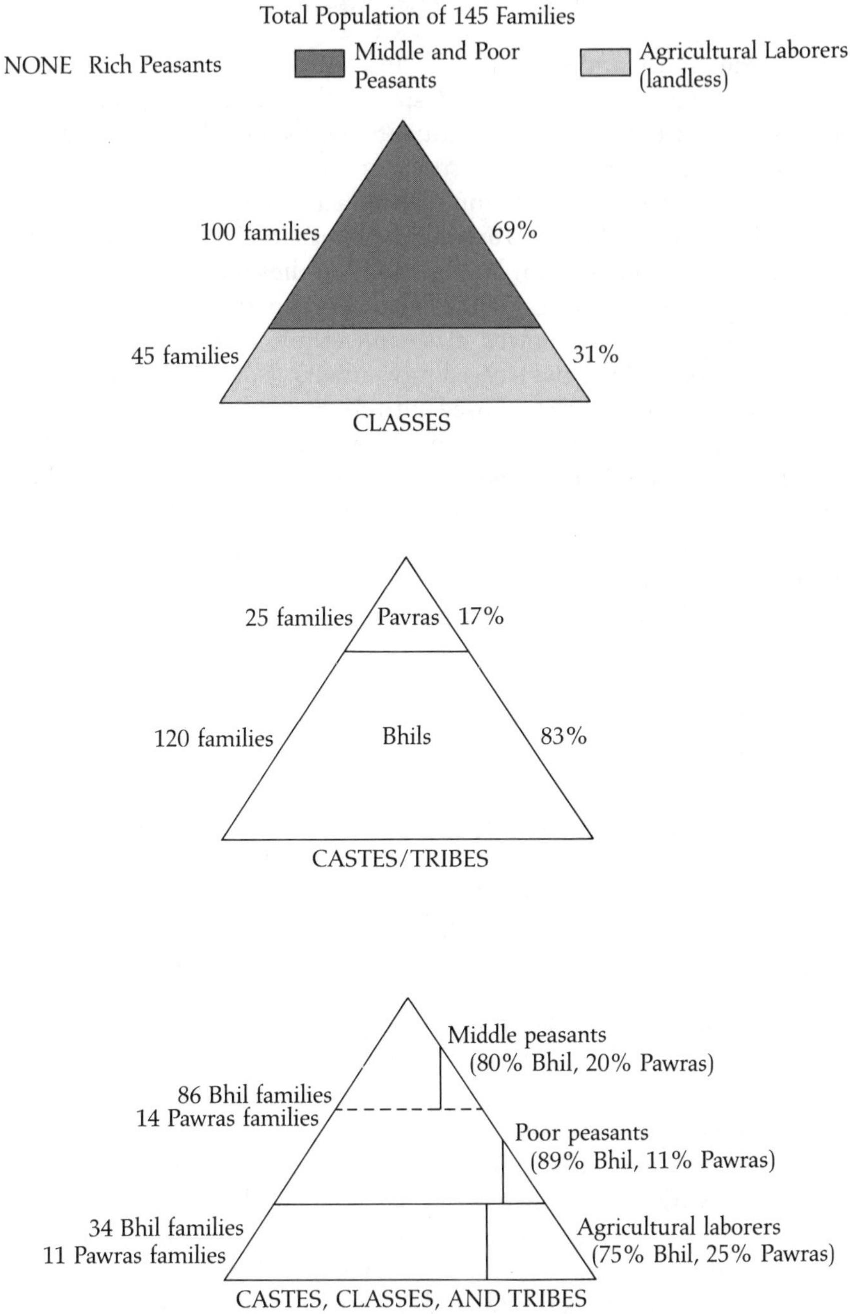

Figure 4. Demography of Udaspur Village, Shahada *taluka*

today most Pawras acknowledge *adivasi* status to obtain benefits designed for scheduled tribes, they are highly Sanskritized. Although Pawra poor peasants resent middle peasants, they retain a strong caste identity. A Pawra agricultural laborer commented, "Ours is a small community and we want to preserve it." Thus Pawras have been politically inactive.

Women from the hill region occasionally organized against sexual harassment that they encountered in the plains' villages. For example, in January 1979 a rich peasant from central Shahada raped an *adivasi* woman from the northern hills. A group of women from Udaspur and the surrounding villages marched to his home and publicly humiliated him. However, it was more difficult for them to challenge men's practice of abducting women and forcing them into polygamous arrangements. The Shramik Sangathana activists were also more reluctant to oppose sexual exploitation by *adivasis* than by caste Hindus.

Interviews revealed that *adivasi* men tended to discourage women from making sustained political commitments on grounds of women's supposed ignorance. A Bhil man commented, "Men go to meetings to take part seriously. Women go as spectators to giggle and gossip." A Bhil woman provided a different interpretation:

> How can we go to meetings when we do not understand what they are discussing and we do not even have good clothes to wear? Naturally then men will say that we are stupid.

A frequently advanced explanation for why men did not encourage their wives to accompany them to meetings was: "She has too much housework. And she will understand what happened at the meeting better if I explain it to her when I return." However, another common view, in the words of a Bhil man was: "She belongs to me for I paid a bride price for her. So she should listen to what I say." Men in Udaspur regard women as economic liabilities, for despite their arduous labor on their own land, they do not work for wages.

Political Struggles in Udaspur

For years the Shramik Sangathana was relatively inactive in the hilly region of Shahada. The activists were reluctant to organize a predominantly poor peasant population for both practical and ideological reasons. They could not include Udaspur and the surrounding villages in their major struggle in the plains: to regain *adivasi* land from Hindu rich peasants. Furthermore, the activists were more committed to organizing the "rural proletariat" in the capitalist plains than to organizing peasants over whom, they believed, the waves of "progress" were about to roll.[7]

The Shramik Sangathana sought to include Udaspur in several strikes in the early 1970s. But these failed because agricultural laborers were few in number and relied more heavily on the Employment Guarantee Scheme than wage labor for their subsistence. Given the obstacles to class-based mobilization, the Shramik Sangathana encouraged villagers to undertake social reform and to challenge corruption in public-sector employment.

Gulab and Chander, the two Shramik Sangathana activists who were active in northern Shahada during my first trip to Dhulia, felt that crime, violence, and corruption were partly responsible for villagers' low self-esteem. The Bhils often borrowed money from Pawras, which they squandered on drinking and gambling. Fights would ensue when the Pawras refused them further loans. Many villagers claimed that the corruption of the Bhils' *panch* further exacerbated these conflicts. By 1976 the activists had encouraged the villagers to form a youth committee, which met weekly. The youth committee exposed the corruption of the *gram panchayat*, which had siphoned off government funds designed for road construction, appropriated village land by altering official records, and irrigated land with water intended for public use. After a series of confrontations, the *gram panchayat* and the *panch* decided to cooperate with the youth committee. Police intervention to quell conflicts between the Bhils and Pawras declined.

The activists described their efforts to reform Bhil social practices and eliminate petty corruption as creating the groundwork for politicizing villagers about public corruption. With this objective in mind, the youth committee decided, in consultation with the full-time activists, to demand fallow forest land for cultivation and higher wages for road construction. Both demands were directed at the government, the largest employer in Udaspur, through the Forest Department and the Employment Guarantee Scheme. Although the Shramik Sangathana succeeded in pressuring the Forest Department to abolish forced labor, it was less successful in gaining *adivasis'* rights to cultivate fallow forest land, because the state derived a handsome revenue from commercialization of the forests.

The largest political struggle involving Udaspur was directed against the Building and Construction (B & C) department, the government agency responsible for constructing administrative buildings, major roads, and irrigation schemes. Years earlier the department had hired contractors to build a road to Udaspur, which had still not been completed. Although the government set 5.50 rupees as the daily wage, it paid most of the five hundred laborers it hired less than 3 rupees a day. Laborers reported that working conditions were hazardous and they were often injured but did not receive medical attention.

In December 1978 the Shramik Sangathana publicly charged that B & C contractors and supervisors were stealing government funds. The activists, supported by workers, bureaucrats, and the press, demanded the deputy engineer's suspension and the back wages owed to workers. When B & C did not respond, about 250 people from Udaspur and a neighboring village occupied its office in Shahada in May 1979. Two weeks later the contractors agreed to return seventeen thousand rupees of back pay. However, the demonstrators agreed to leave the building only after the chief minister of Maharashtra transferred the deputy engineer and ordered an investigation of his alleged corruption.

Struggles against the Forest Department and B & C, despite their ambitious intent, only curtailed the petty corruption of low-ranking contractors and forest officials. But these struggles represented the high watermark of political organizing in the region. Udaspur's impoverishment, *adivasi* composition, and class homogeneity made it unlikely that villagers would experience the sense of injustice that fueled *adivasi* militance in the plains. In the absence of Hindu rich peasants in Udaspur, *adivasis* tended to attribute their poverty to circumstance rather than past injustice.

The Shramik Sangathana responded by following the path of least resistance. For example, rather than attempting to abolish the reverse tenancy system, it simply dissuaded middle peasants from taking more than half the crop from poor peasants. It found ample justification in the fact that Pawra middle peasants were relatively impoverished themselves. It would have been inexpedient to reject middle-peasant support in a region in which the Shramik Sangathana lacked an agricultural laborer base.

Daulatpur Village: The Maturation of Class Conflict

All the other groups in the village have some organization. Adivasis *have the Shramik Sangathana, rich peasants have the Crop Protection Societies and the* panchayats. *But there is no unity and no organization to help small landowning farmers like us.*

A Rajput middle peasant

We cannot organize effectively because there are few of us and we have no leaders. In Gujarat the government provides protection for farmers; our government even opposed our Crop Protection Society. The Shramik Sangathana is stronger than any political party in the area so the government is afraid of the Shramik Sangathana.

A Gujar rich peasant

We have strength in our unity and in our organization—the Shramik Sangathana. Now maldars *[landlords] are afraid of us. The times have changed.*

An *adivasi* agricultural laborer

The Socioeconomic Context

Daulatpur village is located twelve miles southwest of Udaspur, in eastern Taloda *taluka*, eleven miles north of Taloda town. With a population of 1,460, Daulatpur is larger than Udaspur. It also has more public amenities within the village, including a post office, primary school, and family-planning center. There is a secondary school in the neighboring village.

Differences in wealth and status are more marked in Daulatpur than in Udaspur. Agricultural laborers live in small, one-room mud huts, middle peasants in semipermanent homes, and rich peasants in two-story cement homes that have electricity. Although the wealthier cultivating classes live on the village periphery, agricultural laborers' homes are in the interior section. *Adivasis* homes in Daulatpur are crammed into a much smaller space than those of any other caste community. Most *adivasis'* huts consist of a single room in which the family cooks, eats, and sleeps (although on warm nights they usually sleep outside); they often share their huts with domestic animals. The injustice of such crowded living conditions is heightened by the fact that *adivasis'* homes are surrounded by vacant government land that rich peasants use for processing the harvested grain.

In Daulatpur, as in the Taloda plains as a whole, there has been extensive commercialization of agriculture. All but 50 of Daulatpur's 750 acres of land are cultivated. Rich peasants own the irrigated land—about 20 percent of all cultivated land; they use tractors, electric pumps, and threshers to cultivate cash crops. Small landowners generally grow staple food crops without mechanized equipment.

Agricultural employment opportunities are much greater in Daulatpur than in Udaspur because the irrigated, double-cropped land yields a *rabi* winter crop in January in addition to the monsoon *kharif* crop. Laborers are hired in quick succession to sow, reap, and harvest the crops and plow the land. According to villagers, four hundred to five hundred people migrate to Daulatpur from other areas in the harvesting season. Although migrant laborers previously performed labor-intensive jobs at lower wages than local laborers, the villagers have stopped this practice. In the lean season, a few poor peasant and agricultural laborer families migrate to Gujarat for agricultural work; others are employed in road construction and in the Shahada sugar factory.

Extensive class disparities, rich peasant prosperity, and the heavy demand for wage labor have all contributed to laborers' radicalism. Forty-three percent of the population are landless agricultural laborers and 6 percent are rich peasants, who own an average of 70 to 80 acres of land. Five families own well over a hundred acres each. Daulatpur's largest landlord owns 168 acres of agricultural land. Over half the villagers are poor and middle peasants. Economic disparities are overlaid by ethnic distinctions between Gujar and Maratha rich peasants and *adivasi* agricultural laborers. Gujars comprise 70 percent, Marathas 24 percent, and Marwaris 6 percent of all rich peasants. Bhil *adivasis* are 92 percent of all agricultural laborers. (The remainder are caste Hindus, including Kolis, Sutars, Navis, and Marathas.) The Bhils comprise 53 percent, Marathas 25 percent, and Gujars 22 percent of the population. (See figure 5.)

Non-*adivasi* agricultural laborers (except for Maratha laborers) are

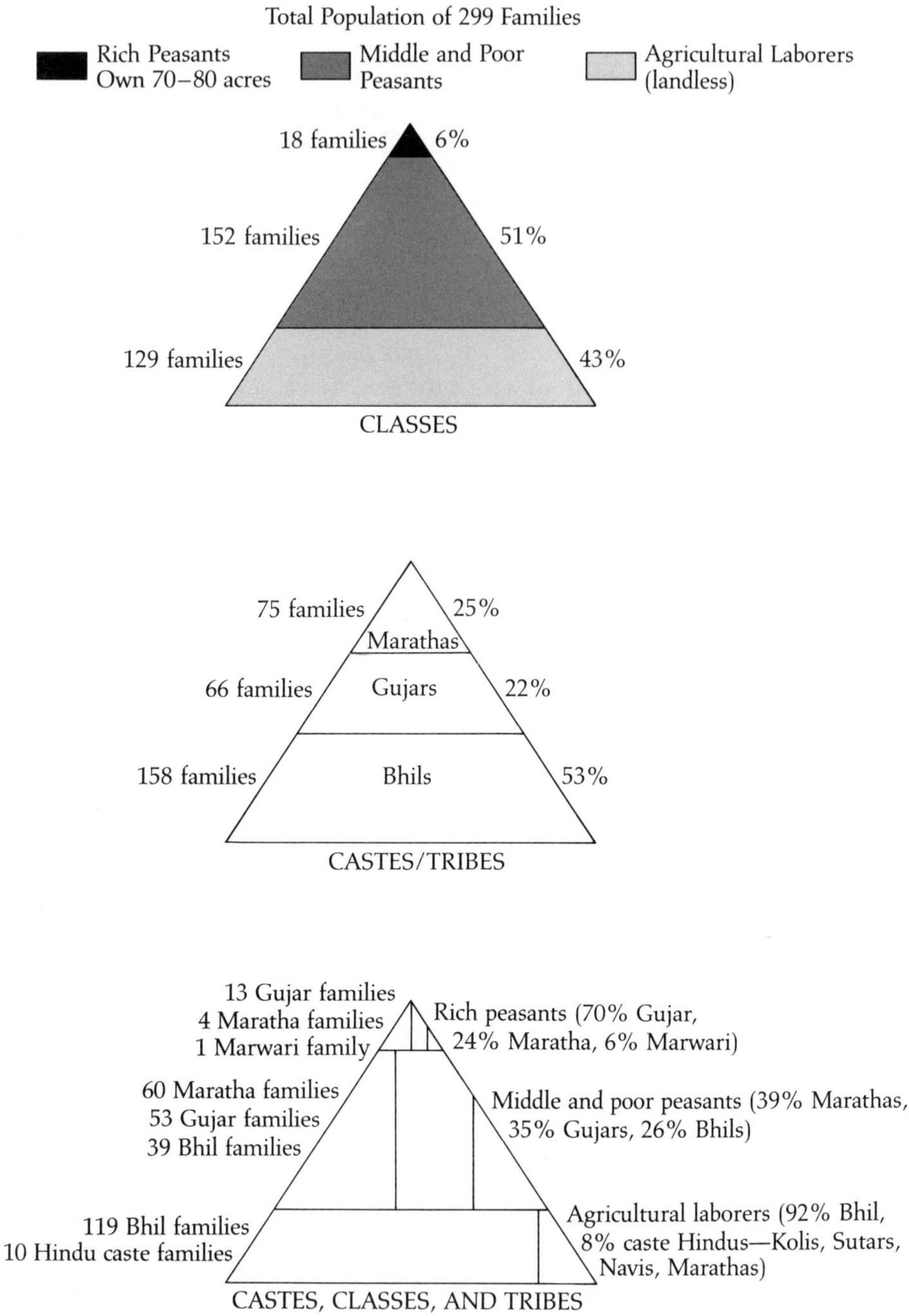

Figure 5. Demography of Daulatpur Village, Taloda *taluka*

isolated; they are few in number and divided by caste barriers from each other and from *adivasis*. Although rich peasants are less divided by caste than poor and middle peasants, they lack the unity to defend their common interests against the Shramik Sangathana. Given their large numbers and shared ethnic and class position, *adivasi* laborers are more unified than any other group in the village.

Political Struggles in Daulatpur

In 1973, Shramik Sangathana activists began organizing in Daulatpur and adjoining villages. In characteristic sequence, the activists proceeded from social reform issues to class-based organizing; as a first step in this direction they encouraged *adivasi* laborers to protest the *gram panchayat*'s appropriation of over sixteen acres of *adivasis'* land. Despite the *panchayat*'s opposition, *adivasis* cultivated the land for two years. When a court case that the Shramik Sangathana filed was settled two years later in favor of the thirty landless families who had been cultivating the land, conflicts arose over how it should be allocated. The activists organized a meeting where they suggested that the recipients should farm the land collectively for three years and then reconsider the matter. The laborers consented.

From 1975 to 1978, the activists organized *adivasis* to reclaim land that rich peasants had appropriated and to demand fallow forest land for cultivation. However, the activists gave priority to wage gains over land redistribution, for they believed that landownership would conservatize *adivasis*. Moreover, socioeconomic conditions in eastern Taloda were highly propitious for strikes.

The activists Prakash and Ravi helped organize a series of wage movements in eastern Taloda from 1978. Newly formed laborers' committees demanded higher wages, shorter working hours, equal wages for men and women, and compensation to workers who had previously received subminimum wages. The first strike in Daulatpur in July 1979 was followed three months later by a longer and more important strike, which reflected an underlying tension between class and caste bases of mobilization: whereas the activists attempted to polarize villagers along class lines, both dominant and subordinate groups within the village expressed greater caste or "tribal" loyalties.

Rich peasants hired a group of night watchmen to guard the village and perform certain agricultural tasks. The watchmen worked irregular hours and received 1.50 to 2 rupees a day; they did not realize that this was far below the minimum-wage rate. The laborers' committee demanded that the government consider these watchmen agricultural laborers so that they would be legally entitled to the minimum wage of 150 rupees a month. It also asked employers to compensate the watchmen who had been paid subminimum wages that year. The Block Development Officer (BDO) and Minimum Wage Inspector agreed that watchmen were entitled to minimum wages and employers should pay them retroactively by 28 September. When the date passed unheeded, the laborers' committee began planning a strike.

Prakash organized a series of meetings, which rich peasants refused to attend. He argued that middle and rich peasants, whom he differentiated by the size of their landholdings and consumption patterns, should pay according to their means. His proposal foundered on villagers' caste loyalties. Maratha middle peasants wanted their wealthy kin to be permitted to pay the lower wage rate; *adivasi* agricultural laborers contended that both Maratha and Gujar rich peasants should pay the higher rate. Prakash tried to convince middle peasants that despite their shared caste identity with rich peasants, the interests of the two groups differed.

By the third day of the negotiations, rich peasants still refused to concede but most middle peasants agreed to provide 25 to 50 percent of the wages owed to workers for the past six months. They also agreed henceforth to pay watchmen minimum wages. A Maratha middle peasant commented, "At first we did not want to return the money. But we realized that if we did not reach a settlement then, we would have to pay a much larger amount later." Middle peasants recognized that they lacked the political clout of both rich peasants and agricultural laborers.

On 11 October, the BDO, *tehsildar*, and Minimum Wage Inspector met at the *panchayat* office but failed to reach agreement. That day, agricultural laborers and watchmen organized a strike directed solely against rich peasants. In a fight that ensued a week later, a Gujar rich peasant grabbed a young *adivasi* boy and held him hostage. When *adivasis* retaliated, injuring fourteen people, Gujars called the police and filed a case against the laborers for looting and stealing. The following day the police searched *adivasis'* homes but were unable to find any stolen goods. They arrested twenty-five *adivasi* men and women for instigating violence.

Under increased pressure from the BDO and *tehsildar*, rich peasants finally agreed to pay minimum wages and the eight thousand rupees in back pay that they owed laborers for the previous six months. The laborers returned to work. The strike achieved moderately substantial material gains. More important, from the activists' perspective, it served to politicize laborers. Prakash noted that had the case gone to court it could have dragged on for years. Even if workers ultimately received higher wages, they would have forgotten that this was the outcome of their struggle.

The Shramik Sangathana contributed in large measure to the success of the strike by exploiting middle peasants' resentment of rich peasants. For example, both groups competed over leasing land from poor peasants, but middle peasants were also sometimes forced to lease out their own land to rich peasants. More important, increasing deterioration in middle peasants' economic conditions in the wake of capitalist development had exacerbated their resentment of rich peasants. Although previously, middle peasants rarely had to work for wages, now they were increasingly forced to do so during periods of scarcity. The activists believed that the interests of middle and poor peasants converged because demands for higher wages indirectly benefited middle peasants. Hindu laborers were less active in the strike than *adivasi* laborers, because they derived their income principally from traditional artisanal caste occupations rather than wage labor. Thus, although Hindu laborers tended to be isolated from one another and from the exchange economy, *adivasi* laborers had ample opportunity to organize collectively against class exploitation.

A few *adivasi* women became extremely active in the strike and participated in all phases—from negotiations with government officials and middle peasants to violent clashes with rich peasants. However, most female agricultural laborers were less politically active than male laborers, in part because they were fewer in number. Furthermore, the strikers' demands were not directly relevant to women, for the "watchmen" were all men whose work was defined by their gender.

In the absence of female leadership and democratically organized women's groups, *adivasi* women did not articulate their own grievances and demands. The activists in turn, oblivious of the extent to which the struggle primarily served the interests of male workers, did not make equal wages for male and female laborers a central aspect of their demands. Nor did they attempt to organize women around other issues that concerned them.

The most striking feature of the Daulatpur strike is the manner in which the Shramik Sangathana created a class conflict out of a more fluid, indeterminate series of conflicts based on caste, gender, and class. Although the activists ultimately succeeded, their attempts met with significant resistance. "Middle peasants" considered themselves and were identified by subordinate groups according to their caste rather than class identity. Even Pitabai, despite her leading role in the movement, bitterly rejected the notion of a class alliance between middle peasants and agricultural laborers when she commented, "They are afraid of the Shramik Sangathana but they put on a different face with us. We do not consider them our allies." Although class conflict appeared to emerge organically from Daulatpur's social structure, the activists played a critical role in determining its form.

Madhyampur Village: The Revolt of Women

Tribals in this village are thieves. They have become more and more brazen in stealing our crops.

A Gujar rich peasant

In the past we would go secretly to the fields at night and take some peanuts and chillis. The maldars *called us thieves and we believed it. Now we go openly during the day and we no longer consider this theft. We say it is our right.*

An *adivasi* agricultural laborer

The Socioeconomic Context

Madhyampur is on the main bus route, fourteen miles southwest of Nandurbar town. A large, sprawling village, it contains a post office and a government primary school, which 180 children attend; a secondary school is two miles away. The nearest hospital, college, and railway station are in Nandurbar town.

Madhyampur is densely populated, with 1,590 people of different caste backgrounds. Although laborers' homes are closely clustered in three sections of the village, wealthy cultivators live in large, spacious homes, often two or three stories high. The largest Gujar landowner, who lives in an enormous house on the outskirts of the village, was deputy chairman of the *panchayat samiti* from 1962 to 1967, a *panchayat samiti* member from 1967 to 1971, and the *sarpanch* of the village *panchayat* after 1977. He was also chairman of the Cooperative Credit Society and a Janata party member. The largest Maratha landowner in the village owns a three-story, spacious cement house. He was a village *panchayat sarpanch* from 1971 to 1976, as well as a member of the District Cooperative Bank, Cooperative Engineer Owners' Association, Credit Society, and Congress (I).

Rich peasants have introduced capitalist agriculture to Madhyampur. They own all the irrigated land in the village—which represents a sixth of all cultivated land. They grow a variety of cash crops, including sugarcane, corn, peanuts, chillis, and wheat. They own seventy-five electric pumps, fifteen diesel engines, and fifteen tractors. They also own two flour mills and a rice mill. They have ready access to credit through a Credit Cooperative Society and several banks.

Following a successful strike in 1978, male laborers' wages increased to 4 to 4.50 rupees depending upon the tasks. Discrimination against female laborers took the form of paying them 2 to 2.50 rupees for what employers described as a half-day's work, which was in fact six hours long. Given the large number of female laborers in Madhyampur, women's low wages substantially inflate employers' profits.

Madhyampur is more occupationally diversified than Udaspur or Daulatpur. Although most of the population earns its livelihood from agriculture, many also work in small-scale industry, construction, and trade. Laborers supplement their income through a public dairy program and the Employment Guarantee Scheme in the lean season; about forty or fifty families migrate to Gujarat annually.

The proportions of agricultural laborers and rich peasants are larger in Madhyampur than in Daulatpur. Agricultural laborers, who are completely landless, comprise approximately 45 percent and rich peasants 10 percent of the population. Rich peasants own an average of 70 to 80 acres of largely irrigated land. The seven wealthiest families in the village each own between 100 and 180 acres of land.

Adivasis constitute 29 percent of the population of Madhyampur compared to over half of Daulatpur's population. Thus, agricultural laborers are more ethnically divided in Madhyampur than in Daulatpur. Fifty-eight percent of all agricultural laborers in Madhyampur compared to 92 percent in Daulatpur are *adivasis*. Other agricultural laborers in this village are Gujar (18 percent) and Marathas, Harijans, Kumbars, and Navis (6 percent each).

Class and caste divisions cross-cut in Madhyampur to a greater extent than in Daulatpur. Gujars, the largest caste (excluding *adivasis*) in Madhyampur, are found among all classes. They are 56 percent of all poor peasants, 67 percent of middle peasants, and 50 percent of rich peasants. The third largest caste in Madhyampur are Marathas, who form 20 percent of the total population (22 percent of poor peasants, 33 percent of middle peasants, and 50 percent of rich peasants). Five percent of the population are *dalits*. (See figure 6.)

Caste prejudice and conflicts are greater in Madhyampur than in either Udaspur or Daulatpur. Until recently, caste Hindus, *dalits*, and *adivasis* were completely socially segregated. Gujars and Marathas prevented *adivasis* from drawing water from their wells, entering their homes, attending their festivals, and sitting with them. Hindu women were particularly anxious to maintain social distance from *adivasis*. A frequently related incident that occurred some years earlier is revealing: a Kunbi Patil woman drank water from a pitcher that an *adivasi* had drawn from a well. The woman's relatives locked her in a hut, which they set on fire. They only extinguished the flames when she burst out of the hut, her clothes ablaze. The fire was designed both as punishment and to cleanse her of polluting contact with *adivasis*.

A Kunbi Patil female laborer explained Hindus' repudiation of contact with *adivasis* as follows:

> It is a matter of honor. People in my community would say, "Look at the way she mixes with *adivasis*"; then no one would marry my daughters. It is different for my husband. He doesn't have to worry so much about these things.

To demonstrate their social superiority, Hindu women would express extreme caste prejudice. In their view, *adivasis* were not only dishonest but also dirty, uncouth, and immoral. *Adivasi* women's sexual freedom further fueled their prejudices.

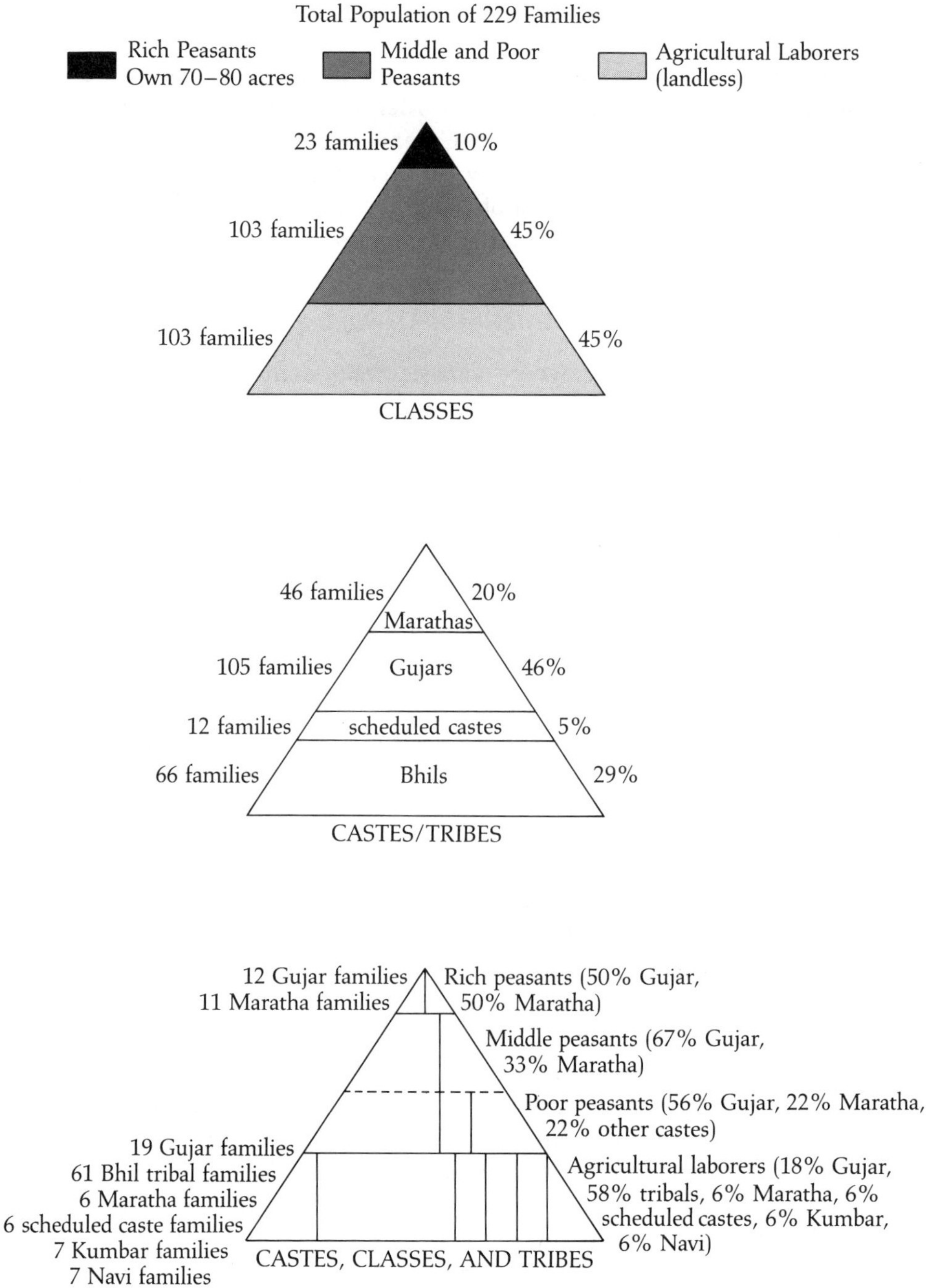

Figure 6. Demography of Madhyampur Village, Nandurbar *taluka*

Caste consciousness also finds expression in rivalries between Gujar and Maratha rich peasants. The Marathas own more land and enjoy a higher caste status than Gujars; however, Gujars are the more enterprising farmers and wield greater political power in the village. Gujars gained control of the *gram panchayat* by supporting the Janata party in the 1977 national elections.

Political Struggles in Madhyampur

In contrast to Daulatpur, where *adivasis'* major demand was for wage gains, protest in Madhyampur centered on *adivasis'* struggles to retain a sense of dignity in the face of attempts by the dominant castes to keep them suppressed. An important instance of this conflict concerned rich peasants' allegation that *adivasis* habitually steal. *Adivasi* resistance to degradation is also critical to understanding women's militancy.

A chain of events surrounding the issue of theft began to unfold in 1973, when *adivasis* forcibly harvested crops on land that rich peasants had appropriated from them. Rich peasants contended that *adivasis* were stealing their crops and began to deduct a portion of *adivasi* laborers' wages as compensation. They also created a village Crop Protection Society (CPS) to curtail theft. They required all landowning Hindu peasants to pay the CPS thirteen rupees a month to hire watchmen, who guarded their fields and fined *adivasis* for possession of chillis and peanuts. The CPS executive body consisted of six Maratha and eleven Gujar rich peasants. Most CPS members belonged to the *gram panchayat* and the two organizations shared the same office. Not surprisingly, *adivasis* considered local administrators indistinguishable from the dominant classes.

A major conflict around the issue of theft erupted in 1979. A Maratha rich peasant recalled his version of the incident: wealthy farmers found that twenty *adivasi* families were each hoarding about eighty kilos of stolen grain. Although the farmers were willing to settle the matter amicably, the Shramik Sangathana inexplicably intervened, harassed the CPS chairman, and forced him to resign.

Adivasis recounted a different version of the incident: it was customary for employers to give laborers some chillis each harvesting season. But on this occasion, they severely beat *adivasis* when they found chillis drying outside the *adivasis'* huts. A group of *adivasis* and *dalits* demanded to see the CPS chairman and the *sarpanch*. Within hours they forced the chairman to return six hundred rupees in fines and to resign from the CPS. The crowd insisted that corrupt government officials, *gram panchayat* members, the police, and village workers repay the fines they had fraudulently charged. *Adivasis* collected several hundred rupees over the next few weeks.

After this incident, rich peasants from several contiguous villages, including Daulatpur, met to devise more effective means of preventing theft. They decided to replace the local watchmen with thirty trained, armed guards from Rajasthan. They collected twelve hundred rupees for this purpose. A Hindu poor peasant, whom wealthy cultivators had made CPS chairman, described a meeting at which the Marathas and Gujars disagreed over how they should prevent theft. The Marathas wanted to completely prohibit *adivasis* from trespassing their land. The Gujars, who prevailed, decided that they would issue laborers who owned cows passes to collect grass from their fields and punish laborers who were caught without passes.

Adivasis were increasingly politicized by growing repression. Earlier, rich peasants had attempted to subdue *adivasi* radicalism by denying them employment; now, by restricting their access to grass, *adivasis* felt that rich peasants were trying to deprive them of income from the dairy program. From defending themselves against allegations that they had stolen crops, *adivasis* increasingly questioned the very notion of theft. An *adivasi* woman commented:

> We go to the fields to sow chillis in the rain and cold when *maldars* would not dirty their hands. We cannot afford two meals a day from our wages. Don't we even have the right to a handful of chillis. Is this stealing?

Adivasis' resistance to allegations of theft crystallized their opposition to the spread of capitalist relations. Earlier, landlords had allowed laborers to take grass, chillis, and vegetables from their fields; chillis constituted a particularly important part of *adivasis'* otherwise bland diet of lentils and *roti*. Landlords' introduction of the passes symbolized the replacement of a system of reciprocity with one involving strict regulation. That rich peasants and watchmen invaded *adivasis'* homes and subjected *adivasi* women to body searches for stolen goods further extended this new system of control. Chillis and peanuts, the cash crops that had brought prosperity to Madhyampur as a result of *adivasis'* labor, became symbols of exploitation.

Adivasi Women's Militancy

The most significant incident of protest involving *adivasi* women from Madhyampur was the one with which this study opened. A Gujar rich peasant in a neighboring village habitually threw his garbage in front of an *adivasi* woman's home. When she complained one day, he became enraged, grabbed her by her hair, and dragged her twenty feet. He tore off her blouse, threw her on the ground, and beat her severely. Several villagers witnessed the incident and two *adivasi* women helped free her.

The woman went to the Shramik Sangathana office, where the activists suggested that she notify the police. Despite promises, the police did not conduct an investigation. Accompanied by the activist Prakash, the woman visited the surrounding villages to confer with other women. They decided to organize a demonstration outside the rich peasant's home. Nearly 300 women and 150 men from about twelve villages assembled one morning. The activists persuaded the men to remain in the background. The women unsuccessfully appealed to the *sarpanch* and the police *patil* to publicly reprimand the culprit. The women then surrounded the man's house. They offered him a chance to justify his actions but he remained silent.

The women shouted slogans like, "Men will not give us justice so we will obtain it ourselves," "If men oppress us, we will fight back," and "Women are not inferior." The women then seated the man on a donkey, which they found in a nearby field, blackened his face with cow dung, and garlanded his neck with slippers. They paraded him through the villages, where women mocked him and beat him with their slippers. Three days later the police arrested sixteen women and three Shramik Sangathana activists. The police dropped the case when two hundred women told the police that they were prepared to be arrested and one thousand people offered to pay the bail.

The incident attracted widespread publicity. Of three local newspaper editorials, one condemned the breakdown of law and order; a second argued that as long as the official legal machinery failed to produce justice, the poor could only take the law into their own hands; and the third, entitled "The Story of Justice," observed:

> Although we talk a lot about democratic rights, molestations of poor women by the rich and powerful occur everywhere and are ignored. . . . But if a woman from a rich and respectable family is harassed . . . police execute

their rights efficiently and promptly. Unfortunately justice can only be obtained in the courts. But when beatings and molestations occur, how is it possible to reach the courts without the help of the police? A poor man only sees a court when he is arrested. . . . It is different for those who wield power.

Yet the editorial went on to condemn the women's actions:

These women must have been instigated to act in this manner. In so doing, they disregarded the law. . . . This is a threat to democracy and even if the threat was initially caused by a bully, we cannot eradicate all bullies. Who can be responsible? The Communists wouldn't do something like this. Could the incident have been provoked by the Naxalites or the Indira supporters? We cannot say. But the Maharashtrian government must attend to this incident, protest the breakdown of law and order and officially clarify what happened.[8]

As the last editorial notes, this was not a spontaneous incident of protest; nor, however, as the editorial implies, was it engineered. If it is difficult for poor men to obtain justice in the courts, the challenge is even greater for women. Thus, women saw no alternative to taking the law into their own hands. Through inaction they would have passively accepted personal degradation. The manner in which the women chose to act is especially noteworthy. Women humiliated the landlord, inflicting on him the kind of indignity he had inflicted on an *adivasi* woman. But unlike the landlord they did not use brute force.

Women's actions gain added significance when situated in a broader context. McKim Marriott describes the Holi festival in northern India as providing villagers an opportunity to resolve disputes and redress injustice by abandoning restrictive social norms.[9] The "Fourth Estate of Shudras," and, one might add, "Women's Estate," organized this festival. Marriott recalls young people seating a village landlord backwards on a donkey, women rushing out of their homes to attack men with canes, and villagers garlanding the foreign anthropologist with slippers and making him dance in the village square. Marriott observes:

Aside from the Holi festival, each of the other thirteen major festivals of the year seemed to express and support the power structures of patriarchy and gerontocracy in the family, of relatively stratified relations between castes and of dominance by landowners in the village. . . . The idiom of Holi thus differs from that of ordinary life in giving explicit dramatization to specific sexual relationships that would otherwise not be expressed at all in reversing the differences of power conventionally prevailing between husbands and wives.[10]

Marriott suggests that spring festivals that sanctioned riotous social behavior ultimately strengthened established social relationships.

Each actor playfully takes the roles of others in relation to his own usual self. Each may thereby learn to play his own roles afresh, surely with renewed understanding, possibly with greater grace and perhaps with a reciprocating love.[11]

By contrast, *adivasi* women's defiance was neither confined to annual village rituals nor functional to maintaining the prevailing social order.

The landlord and the donkey incident can also be understood in cross-cultural perspective. There are surprising parallels between the actions of *adivasi* women in northwestern Maharashtra in 1978 and in southeastern Nigeria during the Igbo Women's War of 1929. In both cases, "tribal" women's experience of relative sexual egalitarianism, coupled with their exclusion from full participation in political life, led them to develop their own political networks. Through these networks they could contact and assemble large numbers of women to redress their grievances.

The "Aba Riots," or "Igbo Women's War," followed rumors that the British were planning to tax women. After several confrontations with British officials, thousands of Igbo women from the Calabar and Owerri provinces converged in the native administrative centers. The women, who had smeared their faces with cow dung and ashes, chanted, danced, and ridiculed the officials. Judith Van Allen explains the significance of the "war":

The word "war" in this context is derived from the pidgin English expression "making war," an institutionalized form of punishment employed by Igbo women and also known as "sitting on a man." To "sit on" or "make war on" a man involved gathering at his compound at a previously agreed-upon time, dancing, singing scurrilous songs detailing the women's grievances against him (and often insulting him along the way by calling his manhood into question), banging on his hut (which usually meant pulling the roof off). This might be done to a man who particularly mistreated his wife, who violated the women's market rules, or who persistently let his cows eat the women's crops. The women would stay at his hut all night and day, if necessary, until he repented and promised to mend his ways.[12]

To many outside observers, Igbo women in the 1920s, like Bhil women in the 1970s, appeared to be acting in an anarchic, irrational manner. However, women's seemingly illogical acts conformed to a well-developed code of behavior. This code was not simply permissive; the use of humorous, satirical forms restricted the use of violence.

Similarly, the unusual forms of women's defiance in Dhulia district only appear to be strange when judged by dominant standards of rationality. Yet it might be considered irrational that politically active women elsewhere have not devised forms of struggle that result from their experience of oppression and traditions of resistance. Why, for example, do women who attend CPI(M) demonstrations in West Bengal passively listen to the speeches of party leaders rather than singing and dancing?

Conclusion

To return to the questions with which this chapter opened, is class a more important determinant than ethnicity of *adivasi* laborers' militancy? Do men and women express different commitments to their ethnic and class identities? To what extent is the Shramik Sangathana captive to given ethnic and class structures or, conversely, responsible for heightening certain forms of identity while rejecting others?

There is significant evidence for emphasizing socioeconomic factors in explaining the greater incidence of protest in Madhyampur and Daulatpur than in Udaspur and in explaining differences in its character in the three villages. In the absence of an exploitative dominant class in Udaspur, protest was mainly directed against the government. Whereas protest in Daulatpur primarily concerned an economic, class-based demand—higher wages for agricultural laborers—protest in Madhyampur was concerned less with material gains than with preserving *adivasis'* sense of dignity.

First, the extent to which the three villages have experienced capitalist development and the different proportions of agricultural laborers they each contain have important implications for the character of protest. As a result of its economic impoverishment, Udaspur is characterized by a relatively small wage-labor force, limited employment opportunities, high rates of out-migration, and little collective organizing. Poor and middle peasants have been inactive in wage movements, for they derive their income primarily from their own land and from employment in the plains. Movements for land redistribution have not occurred, for landownership patterns are relatively egalitarian and *adivasis* have not lost their land to Hindu cultivators within the village.

In Daulatpur, by contrast, agrarian capitalist development has increased the demand for laborers' services. Less agrarian employment is available and agricultural laborers are fewer in Madhyampur than in Daulatpur, partly because agrarian capitalist development is less extensive. Whereas agricultural laborers represent 313 out of 1,463 people in Daulatpur, they constitute only 144 out of 1,591 people in Madhyampur. Agricultural laborers have been much more politically active in Daulatpur than in Madhyampur, where they have sporadically demanded greater employment in dairy production.

Villages in which class and ethnic cleavages coincide have experienced the most protest. Udaspur's entirely *adivasi*, largely poor peasant composition has precluded class conflict and channeled antagonisms within the village into animosity between the Bhils and Pawras. Traditional distrust among the less assimilated *adivasis* who inhabit the hill regions has made them receptive to Shramik Sangathana struggles against the government. *Adivasis* are more radical in Madhyampur and Daulatpur than in Udaspur because they are mostly agricultural laborers. However, the relationship between ethnic and class cleavages differs in these two villages. Agricultural laborers are more divided by caste and fewer of them are *adivasis* in Madhyampur than in Daulatpur. Caste divisions have prevented agricultural laborers from organizing around class demands in Madhyampur; instead, *adivasis* have been more concerned with challenging caste prejudice. (See figures 4, 5, and 6.)

In keeping with this argument, the Shramik Sangathana's actions might appear to be wholly determined by conditions at the village level. The Shramik Sangathana invested relatively little time and energy organizing in Udaspur because landowning peasants were less amenable than agricultural laborers to collective organizing; ideologically, the Shramik Sangathana was less committed to ameliorating their conditions than those of landless laborers. By contrast, it invested greater resources in Madhyampur and Daulatpur, where it could obtain greater political and organizational dividends.

However, this analysis ignores the Shramik Sangathana's initiative in shaping conditions in accordance with its own predispositions. An important instance concerns its tendency to ultimately privilege class over gender and ethnicity. This tendency was initially obscured by the fact that the Shramik Sangathana believed that it was responding to "objective conditions" in viewing agricultural laborers as the vanguard in struggles against class inequality. Thus the activists characterized Daulatpur as having experienced the most militant protest of the three villages because it had witnessed the most class-based organizing. By contrast, they only mentioned Madhyampur when asked about the sites of women's protest.

It seems likely that the Shramik Sangathana devoted more attention to Daulatpur than to the two other villages because Daulatpur had experienced the most extensive capitalist development and contained the largest wage-labor force. What the Shramik Sangathana did not recognize was the extent to which its own leadership heightened *adivasis'* class rather than gender or ethnic allegiances. Conversely, *adivasis* expressed a stronger sense of their ethnic identities in Udaspur and Madhyampur, where the activists provided less leadership and direction. For example, despite their resentment toward wealthier caste members, Pawras of subordinate class backgrounds felt greater caste than class allegiances.

Even within Daulatpur, although the Shramik Sangathana ultimately succeeded in organizing a strike along class lines, both dominant and subordinate groups expressed powerful ethnic identifications. When asked about a distinction that the Shramik Sangathana considered highly significant, between rich and middle peasants, *adivasis* often responded by substituting the language of caste for the language of class. For example, they were more conscious of differences in the way they were treated by Gujars, Marathas, and Rajputs than in the way rich as opposed to middle peasants treated them. Similarly, they were far more skeptical than the activists that middle peasants could form allies of agricultural laborers, because they insisted upon the preeminence of middle peasants' caste identities.

Similarly, far from expressing a transcendent form of class identity, Hindu *saldars* and agricultural laborers maintained superiority to *adivasis* by affirming caste allegiances. But more than status considerations were involved in their caste allegiances. The dominant classes often provided Gujar and Maratha agricultural laborers loans, employment on a favorable basis, and protection from repression by village watchmen, the police, and the state machinery. Rich peasants also maintained their caste members' loyalties by hiring them to perform domestic work. Thus, even if *adivasis* are most apt to be militant when class and ethnic cleavages coincide and they are concentrated at the lowest rungs of the class hierarchy, the grievances they express often pertain to their *adivasi* identities.

Women's Militancy

In all three villages women formed a minority of *tarun mandal* members and only a small group of women were generally active in political struggles. Structural constraints upon women's articulation of their grievances and demands are overwhelming. With the exception of a relatively small number of women whose fathers leave them property (often because they are disabled), *adivasi* women are propertyless. Marriage severs women's ties to their natal villages and thus to the nexus of women with whom they may have identified.[13]

If *adivasi* women's labor-force participation partially frees them from economic dependence on men, it also subjects them to the "double burden." *Adivasi* women reported that they were often unable to attend Shramik Sangathana meetings because their crushing burdens of cooking, cleaning, and child care left them no time to do so. As a result, the most politically active women in all three villages are single or divorced; the least active are married women with children.

Notwithstanding these constraints that all women experience, there are striking differences in the extent of women's protest in the three villages. Women were the most politically quiescent in Udaspur, more active in Daulatpur, and most militant in Madhyampur. Women have been most militant when they experience sexual exploitation by the dominant class but their own cultural traditions foster egalitarianism. Women had less contact with the dominant class, and *adivasi* men exhibited more restrictive attitudes toward women in Udaspur than in the two other villages. By contrast, women experienced sexual and class-based exploitation but found support from men in their own communities in Daulatpur and particularly in Madhyampur. Differences in women's labor-force participation in the three villages have also influenced women's protest. The proportion of female agricultural laborers is smallest in Udaspur, larger in Daulatpur, and largest in Madhyampur. Women's protest follows remarkably similar lines: women were least active in protest in Udaspur followed by Daulatpur and most active in Madhyampur.

However, a fuller account of the differences in women's participation in the three villages must consider the following puzzle: whereas *adivasi* women were more active in Madhyampur than in Daulatpur, the reverse was true with respect to the Shramik Sangathana's role in the two villages. Why was it that although the successful wage strike in Daulatpur was made possible by active Shramik Sangathana negotiation, activists played a minor role during the landlord and the donkey incident?

One explanation might be that the issues that *adivasi* women and the male Shramik Sangathana activists considered most significant diverged, for where the activists accorded centrality to class, *adivasi* women were more moved to act by the exploitation they experienced as *adivasis* and as women. Thus *adivasi* women's limited participation in the watchmen's strike in Daulatpur may be partly explained by the Shramik Sangathana's focus on an issue that did not concern them directly. By contrast, in Madhyampur village, where the Shramik Sangathana was less active and gave less preeminence to class, *adivasi* women more forcefully raised their own grievances and demands.

With the formation of the SSMS in 1982, women's participation briefly surged and then receded. By organizing regular *taluka* level meetings, the SSMS enabled the relatively small number of militant women from each village to form a critical mass. Several women described the self-affirmation they experienced in attending these meetings. In a parallel fashion to the role urban male activists had played earlier among *adivasi* men, feminists from Bombay legitimated Bhil women's political struggles. They also broadened *adivasi* women's purview from opposition to violence against women to their legal and political rights, the unequal sexual division of labor, and discriminatory social practices. Why were *adivasi* women excluded from deliberations of the *panch*? Why were they denied inheritance rights? Why were women primarily responsible for housework and child care? Why were women socially segregated during menstruation?

However, by the summer of 1985, SSMS meetings had become infrequent. Despite its attempts to safeguard autonomy from the Shramik Sangathana, the SSMS could not protect itself from the crisis that affected the movement as a whole. Splits between pro- and anti-CPI(M) factions of the Shramik Sangathana inevitably created rifts among *adivasi* women. One of the most serious consequences was the recurrence of past forms of sexual abuse, most notably men's alcoholism and wife-beating. Several women said they had confronted their husbands individually but were unable to curtail liquor production and consumption without broad-based support.

Political Quiescence in Udaspur, Daulatpur, and Madhyampur

By 1985 the movement as a whole had reached a low ebb. Although the youth committees would contact the activists if a serious problem arose, they were no longer taking new initiatives. In all three villages, declining employment opportunities crippled *adivasis'* radicalism. Rich peasants were increasingly cultivating cash crops like sugarcane and bananas, which required little labor, because wage rates had increased. At the same time the Employment Guarantee Scheme was providing less lean-season employment; a *tarun mandal* member in Udaspur attributed this to reduced Shramik Sangathana pressure on the government. Moreover, government restrictions on *adivasis'* use of forest land had grown; the Special Reserve Police now routinely employed force against *adivasi* "encroachers."

As a result of growing unemployment and hunger, agricultural laborers and poor peasants were increasingly preoccupied with questions of survival. Declining employment opportunities also lessened class antagonisms in Madhyampur and Daulatpur, for agricultural laborers found less opportunity than in the past to demand higher wages and improved working conditions. Instead, like hill villagers, they came to depend on public employment. For example, an animal husbandry scheme that the government introduced segregated villagers from one another and from the dominant classes while also exacerbating the sexual division of labor by according men responsibility for market transactions.

However, the more significant source of *adivasis'* growing quiescence was political rather than economic. Although structural conditions had clearly changed in the intervening years, the Shramik Sangathana no longer possessed a coherent leadership, ideology, and organization and was thus ill-equipped to confront changes in the agrarian political economy. Seen from the perspective of many villagers, the major source of the movement's decline was the split between the CPI(M) and the Shramik Mukti Daal. The split weakened the movement as a whole, eroded its democratic character, and created deep divisions among *adivasis*. Even many Shramik Sangathana members who supported the CPI(M) were extremely critical of the party's lack of interest in sustaining *adivasi* radicalism. In 1987 Kesar Singh, a committed *tarun mandal* member and a CPI(M) member from Dhara village, commented:

> The only activities the CPI(M) has taken up since the split are the May day celebrations, *morcha* to the *tehsildar*'s for demanding EGS work, and the *adivasi parishad*. In the past eight months it has not coordinated with the SMD although it keeps saying that both sides should work together. We informed party leaders that we wanted to work on the Dhara dam project. They did not respond and are now blaming us for not consulting with them and going against the party. I am very angry and have written many letters to CPI(M) activists—but no response.

The movement also declined because factional conflicts permeated the village level. Although most villages in Taloda and Nandurbar expressed allegiance to the CPI(M) faction, Shahada and Akkalkuwa villages generally did not. Lacking an opportunity to evaluate contending ideological perspectives, villagers' identifications were shaped by their personal loyalties to particular activists.

As a result of the Shramik Sangathana's diminished strength, repression against the movement increased. At the district level, rich peasants allied with the communal organization, the Patit Pawan Sangathana, which attacked *adivasi* villages on several occasions. In Daulatpur and Madhyampur, rich peasants hired armed guards who intimidated *adivasis* by searching their homes for stolen goods, prohibiting them from feeding cattle with hay from cultivators' land, and molesting *adivasi* women. Rather than denying the existence of Crop Protection Socities, as they had in the past, rich peasants proudly asserted that the societies would foster efficient agricultural growth, maintain law and order, and curtail *adivasi* crime. Villagers were intimidated by massacres of *adivasis* in neighboring villages.

In 1985 *adivasis* expressed fear at dominant-class repression but still asserted that their struggle would continue. The Shramik Sangathana movement had provided them with reservoirs of strength, solidarity, and self-esteem. It had enabled them to match repression with countervailing ideological and organizational force. But as dominant groups overpowered the Shramik Sangathana, a culture of fear had begun to supplant *adivasis*' culture of resistance.

Chapter Nine

Conclusion

My comparison of the CPI(M) and Shramik Sangathana has sought to identify both the striking contrasts in their approaches as well as the dilemmas that they both experience in reconciling diverse and contradictory objectives. Explanations for differences in the character of the movements they have each organized were sought in their divergent strategies and in the caste and class systems of Dhulia district, Maharashtra, on the one hand, and Midnapur district, West Bengal, on the other. Two questions remain to be explored below: What is the relative significance of what have been broadly termed structural constraints as opposed to the strategic choices of the CPI(M) and Shramik Sangathana in explaining differences in their approaches to political organizing, particularly with respect to women? And what emerge as the major achievements and weaknesses of each organization, particularly when viewed from women's vantage point?

Structural Constraints as the Only Possibility

The very weakness of grass-roots movements in West Bengal and of the CPI(M) in Maharashtra suggests that each may emerge from distinctive structural conditions. As its attitude to the Kashtakari Sangathana in Thana district, Maharashtra, testifies, the CPI(M) has often been openly hostile to independent left movements. However, although the CPI(M) may attempt to co-opt, thwart, or repress growing leftist movements, it is unlikely that it has obstructed their emergence. For example, given its cordial relations with Sachetana, one of the few independent feminist organizations in Calcutta, social and economic constraints probably weigh more heavily on feminist activism in West Bengal.

Further evidence of the overwhelming influence of what might be loosely termed structure upon the trajectory of political conflict derives from my research at the village level. My exploration of six villages in two states suggests that certain conditions systematically deter protest in both Maharashtra and West Bengal. In particular, there is a lower propensity to protest in villages where class and caste or ethnic distinctions are relatively slight. Thus, although Paanagar and Udaspur differ in striking respects—the former is upper-caste Hindu, the latter *adivasi;* the former is relatively prosperous, the latter quite poor; the former encourages female seclusion, the latter women's independence—protest has been negligible in both villages.

The absence of class and caste polarization has inhibited protest in Udaspur and Paanagar in a number of ways. On the one hand, the predominance of small landowners indicates the greater incidence of self-exploitation than of class exploitation within the village. The absence of caste disparities further contributes to the sense that the village resembles an extended family. On the other hand, the idiom of the family mystifies the exploitation that occurs within these villages: subordinate groups have failed to resist both the reverse tenancy system in Udaspur and usury in Paanagar.

If proximity on the class and caste spectrum deters protest among men, it creates an even more serious deterrent to women's protest. As the women's movement has emphasized, sexual exploitation is most difficult to substantiate and challenge when it occurs primarily within the family. As Mahishya women in Paanagar revealed, it is here that women are most likely to internalize their oppression. By contrast, *adivasi* women who experience and challenge sexual exploitation by men of dominant class and status are more apt to subsequently oppose sexual exploitation within their own families.

Conversely, the villages in both Maharashtra and West Bengal in which the most militant protest occurred were characterized by class and caste polarization and contained sizable *adivasi* populations. In Lodhanagar village, Midnapur district, and Daulatpur and Madhyampur villages, Dhulia district, inequalities are cumulative in a dual sense: they have increased through time and they coincide at both the top and bottom of the class hierarchies. At the upper end, the dominant classes not only own large amounts of land but also monopolize political power. Thus, it is not coincidental that in all three villages, *adivasi* laborers sought not only to improve their material conditions through land and wages but also to wrest power from the *panchayats* and the *panchs*. Another distinguishing feature of the villages that experienced militant protest is that in all cases exploiters are sharply distinguished from the exploited. Whereas middle peasants who engage in exploitative practices in Paanagar and Udaspur are part of a nameless, faceless mass, every *adivasi* knows the name of Sidhu Mahato in Lodhanagar or of P. K. Patil in the villages of Dhulia district. In the latter villages, dominant groups were also easily identified and challenged because they are outsiders to the state: the Mahatos in Lodhanagar are originally from Orissa and the Gujars in Madhyampur and Daulatpur are from Gujarat. In this respect, protest among *adivasis*, who pride themselves on being indigenous people, takes on the form of nationalist activity against colonizing forces. To those who suffer exploitation, the fact that it is perpetrated by outsiders not only makes it more unjust but also more amenable to solution than when it occurs within the community.

Thus far the discussion has not distinguished between the economic and social dimensions of "structural causes." Within the social domain, agrarian movements have emerged in West Bengal as a result of the unorthodox nature of its caste system compared with that of northern India. If the lack of caste rigidity permitted the growth of the communist movement, it also contributed to the communists' reformism. However, given the links between upward caste mobility and female seclusion, the Bengali Hindu caste system has had conservatizing implications for women.

In Dhulia district, Maharashtra, on the one hand, the relative weakness of the Marathas at the upper end of the class and caste hierarchies enabled a radical movement to emerge. On the other hand, the strength of the caste system precluded the possibilities for upward caste mobility that existed in West Bengal and forced subordinate groups to confront caste inequality more radically.

But in this context the key element in explaining differences in the extent and forms of protest in Midnapur and Dhulia districts concerns their *adivasi* populations. Although protest in Lodhanagar village in Midnapur and in Madhyampur and Daulatpur villages in Dhulia district is remarkably similar, Dhulia has experienced more militant protest overall because its *adivasi* population is much larger than that of Midnapur district. *Adivasis'* experience of exploitation contributes to their relatively egalitarian social structure and sense of community solidarity. Low levels of social stratification among most *adivasis* are linked in turn to their radicalism along gender and class lines. *Adivasi* militance is especially striking with respect to women and women's issues. In the mixed-caste villages containing substantial *adivasi* populations of both Maharashtra and West Bengal, only among *adivasis* did women challenge sexual oppression, notably men's drinking and wife-beating, women's underrepresentation on political bodies, and the unequal sexual division of labor.

Within the economic domain, at first glance it appears that agrarian radicalism in Dhulia district is a product of intensive capitalist development whereas communist reformism emerges from conditions of agrarian stagnation in West Bengal. However, although partially accurate, this argument is limited in its applicability. The experiences of Dhulia district cannot be generalized to Maharashtra as a whole, where many capitalist districts have been politically quiescent. Similarly, within West Bengal the so-called red district of Burdwan has experienced relatively high levels of capitalist development compared to Midnapur and West Bengal. Nor is protest in economically backward villages like Lodhanagar always reformist in character.

However, there may be a more consistent link between the class composition of political movements in Midnapur and Dhulia districts and the extent of their radicalism. Wage laborers, who form the base of the Shramik Sangathana movement, have engaged in shorter-lived but more militant protest than the landowning peasantry in Midnapur district, which forms the base of the CPI(M). Differences in the extent of capitalist development provide a partial explanation but are intertwined with the history of caste and ethnicity in the two regions. Agricultural laborers in West Bengal do not represent a rural proletariat created by capitalist development. Rather, population density, land scarcity, and economic stagnation have contributed to downward social mobility. The class divide between agricultural laborers and their employers, who tend to be impoverished middle peasants, is much less than in situations of dynamic capitalist growth. Thus, agrarian class formation in West Bengal creates greater tendencies toward the formation of multiclass coalitions than toward militant class struggles under the leadership of the rural proletariat.

By contrast, in Dhulia district the agricultural labor force and the peasantry are more clearly differentiated from one another. Agricultural laborers tend to be completely landless, for the dominant classes have continuously appropriated their land. Over the years, landless *adivasis* have regained small amounts of land only through political struggle, because state-sponsored land reform has been limited in Maharashtra. Furthermore, differences in income, landholdings, and consumption patterns between agricultural laborers on the one hand and poor and middle peasants on the other are more marked in Dhulia than in Midnapur district. Additionally, there are fewer nonagricultural pursuits from which agricultural laborers can derive an income in Dhulia than in Midnapur district. Thus, whereas in Dhulia district agricultural laborers' income derives almost exclusively from wage labor and public off-season employment, in Midnapur district it additionally derives from artisanal production, home-based industries, and sharecropping.

These arguments are even more germane to women than to men. Both the labor-force participation and political activism of women have been more limited than that of men from agricultural laborer families in West Bengal. The demand for women's services is limited both by economic stagnation and by cultural taboos against women's performance of manual labor. By contrast, the most politically active women in Midnapur district and West Bengal as a whole, albeit the most reformist with respect to gender and class, are from middle-class backgrounds. In Dhulia district, however, women's performance of wage labor exceeds that of men, and female agricultural laborers have often militantly challenged the nexus of class and gender inequality.

To sum up the argument thus far, my village research shows that certain structural arrangements are associated with the likelihood of protest, quite independently of the influence of political organizations. Most strikingly, multiclass, multicaste villages in which class and caste cleavages coincide are much more likely to experience protest than villages in which such cleavages are either negligible or cross-cutting. When the respective influences of class and caste are analyzed separately, two factors stand out: *adivasis* tend to be the most militant participants in protest in multicaste regions in which they comprise a substantial segment of the population. Agricultural laborers are more apt to display short-lived militance, whereas middle-peasant participation is both more durable and more reformist in character. Dhulia district's substantial *adivasi* population coupled with its experience of capitalist development help explain the short-lived radicalism of the 1970s; by contrast, West Bengal's smaller *adivasi* population but fluid caste and class structures help explain the durable reformism of political movements from the 1970s to the present.

Structural Constraints as the Path of Least Resistance

To what extent do political organizations have latitude in challenging dominant social and economic arrangements? To what extent is the path of least resistance the only feasible path? Although focusing on structural constraints is helpful in tempering our understanding of political possibilities, it may also be misleading, for the causal arrows do not simply point from the economic base to the political superstructure. Not only is the very distinction between base and superstructure questionable, but political organizations construct their strategies by selectively appropriating from a range of social and material conditions. This fact is masked because political organizations often appropriate unreflectively. Moreover, even ostensibly radical organizations often mirror and help reproduce dominant patterns. Those instances in which the CPI(M) and Shramik Sangathana have confronted and reshaped social and economic conditions suggest a greater latitude for political intervention than is usually recognized.

The CPI(M) often implies that it has little choice but to adopt the path of least resistance and compromise more ambitious social change goals. By accepting given constraints as inevitable, it actually solidifies inequalities and makes them more intractable. Consider the Left Front government's approach to agrarian reform. Whereas many states in India (including Maharashtra) have abolished tenancy outright, the present West Bengal government has further entrenched the *bargadar* (sharecropping) system by giving sharecroppers permanent rights to the land. Similarly, by bestowing land titles on male household heads, it has aggravated gender inequality within the family.

The CPI(M) often justifies its failure to enact more far-reaching reform by highlighting its close relationship to indigenous traditions. However, the CPI(M) can potentially derive a certain latitude from the fact that cultural traditions are generally not monolithic but diverse and contradictory. The critical question is whether it chooses to appropriate progressive or regressive aspects. Thus, when the CPI(M) asserts that Bengali society is patriarchal, it affirms *bhadralok* values against the conflicting traditions of *adivasis* and *dalits*. Similarly, in assuming that cooperatives violate peasants' individualism, the CPI(M) overlooks indigenous traditions that affirm community solidarity and challenge materialistic values.

In rejecting revolution, the CPI(M) has settled for pallid reformism without seriously considering a more feasible strategy of radical reformism. Once again its approach to women's issues is symptomatic of this larger tendency. Given the fact that Bengali Hindu women have traditionally been excluded from political life, the CPI(M) could take steps to ensure their better representation in the *panchayats* and at higher levels of political office. It could increase women's economic independence by increasing employment opportunities that challenge traditional gender-linked roles. It could foster women's solidarity and consciousness by inventing new forms of ritual and celebration.

The Shramik Sangathana's tendency to conform is less evident than that of the CPI(M) because the *adivasi* cultural traditions to which it appeals are more radical than those of the Bengali *bhadralok*. But the Shramik Sangathana has lacked inventiveness in some of the same respects as the CPI(M). Despite its radical rhetoric, it has tacitly rejected producer cooperatives and accepted private ownership and control over land. Rather than building upon prior traditions of women's independence to demand women's land rights, it has supported the patriarchal practices of the Bhil community.

The CPI(M) and the Shramik Sangathana have benefited from exaggerating the weight of "objective" constraints at some points but not others. By doing so, Marxist organizations may justify inaction; recall the many occasions on which the CPI(M) claimed that "objective" conditions favor neither class struggle nor women's liberation. Alternatively, leftist organizations may seek "scientific justification" for what might be considered a questionable course of action. For example, by depicting the movement it had generated primarily as a class struggle that was fostered by capitalist development in Dhulia district, the Shramik Sangathana implicitly sought to refute the charge that this was a marginal movement of scant relevance to non-*adivasi* regions. Perhaps it also sought to translate its wishes into reality by broadening the base of the movement to include non-*adivasi* laborers.

In order to avoid hastily assuming a causal connection between certain structural conditions and strategic choices, it is crucial to analyze the political logic that guides the actions of the CPI(M) and Shramik Sangathana. One way is to situate the two organizations in the context of similar political parties and movements cross-nationally. As we have seen, the Shramik Sangathana's achievements, weaknesses, and dilemmas strikingly resemble those of the new social movements in Western Europe and the United States that seek to prefigure a radically democratic approach. Similarly, the fact that social democratic parties in Western Europe have encountered such similar dilemmas to those of the CPI(M) suggests that there are tensions inherent in the attempt to achieve radical reform through parliamentary means.

The very fact that in the period under review the CPI(M) and Shramik Sangathana appear to be linked by a dialectic in which neither can afford to completely ignore the other suggests the dangers of viewing them as polar opposites that emerge from entirely distinctive socioeconomic conditions. If, as noted earlier, conditions in Dhulia district have nurtured grass-roots political movements, they have also given rise to the ongoing dialectic between grass-roots movements and the CPI(M), as indicated by the split in the Shramik Sangathana. Conversely, the CPI(M)'s approach to gender issues has clearly been influenced by the growth of the autonomous women's movement.

The questions that remain to be asked concern the relative importance of economic, social, and political influences upon agrarian mobilization in Maharashtra and West Bengal. Was the leadership of the Shramik Sangathana or an indigenous tradition of *adivasi* radicalism more important in determining the character of resistance in Dhulia district? Does the reformist character of the Bengali communist movement owe its existence more to the peculiarities of the Bengali caste and class systems or to the CPI(M)'s electoral preoccupations and democratic centralist organization?

I am less interested in establishing precise causality or hierarchies of causal influences than in exploring the texture of relationships between economic, social, and political realms. However, rather than rejecting the very enterprise of attempting to determine causality, I favor a more selective approach in which I reject certain forms of indeterminacy and accept others. In this respect my approach joins with others who reject determinist understandings but remain committed to analyzing relations between structure and politics.[1] For example, I believe that although agrarian militance cannot be consistently linked to agrarian capitalism, it is closely linked to large *adivasi* populations. Similarly, although I believe that political organizations exercise greater latitude than is often assumed, this latitude is much greater with respect to issues of gender inequality, which they have only begun to explore, than with respect to class inequality.

This study might have been more satisfying if it consistently assigned primary significance to one among the several influences that it examines. But approaches that systematically privilege the realm of production or the role of the state frequently oversimplify or underestimate the influences they discount. Often the very attempt to establish a single causal agent denies the dialectic between material and political influences. For example, the absence of dynamic, capitalist growth is as much a product as a cause of the growth of the communist movement in West Bengal. Similarly, *adivasi* radicalism in Dhulia district is both cause and effect of the Shramik Sangathana movement. At a broader level of analysis, it is difficult, though useful for heuristic purposes, to sustain the distinction between what I have termed structural conditions and political choices, for each deeply informs the other.

The Evaluative Dimension

This study attempts not just to analyze but also to evaluate the approaches of the CPI(M) and the Shramik Sangathana, and to evaluate them from the vantage point of their commitment to radically democratizing social relations. The objective is a complicated one in several respects, two of which will be addressed below. First, the requisite for social justice, seen from the perspective of women, subordinate classes, and *dalits* and *adivasis* substantially differ. Second, neither the story of the Shramik Sangathana nor that of the CPI(M) contains any straightforward political lessons, for each offers different understandings of success and failure.

With respect to the first question, this study moves between two axes: it often judges the CPI(M) and Shramik Sangathana from the vantage point of women, for their stance on gender subjects them to the most challenging test. For example, the failure of both organizations with respect to women's land rights exposes the inadequacy of their conceptions of agrarian reform. It also suggests many more shared weaknesses of the CPI(M) and Shramik Sangathana than would otherwise be apparent.

An effective strategy of social change must address gender inequality and in so doing may well have spillover effects in other domains. If the CPI(M)'s conservative conception of gender roles reflects and perpetuates the *bhadralok*'s hegemony within the party, a more radical stance on gender might lessen its elitism. However, to judge the CPI(M) and Shramik Sangathana exclusively in light of their approaches to gender inequality would overlook many of their achievements. Both the CPI(M) and the Shramik Sangathana have more effectively addressed class than gender inequality and the Shramik Sangathana has more effectively challenged caste than gender inequality.

Evaluating the CPI(M) and the Shramik Sangathana is also complicated because their trajectories have changed dramatically over time. But this seeming disadvantage also provides an opportunity. By studying these organizations over more than a decade, I became aware of strengths and weaknesses that had not previously been evident. In the early 1980s the Shramik Sangathana appeared to constitute a powerful model for radical change, whereas the CPI(M)'s reformism appeared to be leading the party toward decline. By contrast, several years later the Shramik Sangathana was in shambles, and the CPI(M) had distinguished itself as the only parliamentary communist party to gain reelection for a third term in West Bengal. When one surveys both periods, what emerge as the major achievements and shortcomings of the two strategies? In particular, why did the Shramik Sangathana's inspiring example dissolve, whereas the apparently unimaginative reformism of the CPI(M) endured?

In retrospect, it becomes understandable why the Shramik Sangathana could not have persisted in the organizational form it had assumed at its genesis. The life span of social movements is generally limited in seemingly contradictory ways. Social movements may disintegrate both when they fail to achieve their objectives and when they effectively do so. Both occurred in the case of the Shramik Sangathana: on the one hand, its revolutionary objectives were so grandiose and abstract that they created a vacuum that political parties successfully exploited. On the other hand, it was so successful in reducing the brutal exploitation of *adivasis* by dominant groups that *adivasi* youth felt little motivation to join an organization whose time they believed had passed.

Assessments of the Shramik Sangathana are further complicated if one considers its own criteria for success. To the extent that one of its major objectives was to create a decentralized, democratic people's movement, the fracturing of its formal organization might ironically be considered indicative of its success. After the split occurred, most of the activists who remained in the Shramik Sangathana were *adivasis*, so it more fully became a people's organization. More broadly, one might argue that the Shramik Sangathana's greatest achievement was that along with thousands of similar movements it contributed to the democratization of civil society.[2] Thus, as movements like the Shramik Sangathana disintegrate, they are reborn in the form of other citizen groups that represent the core of Indian democracy in an era in which its major institutions are in serious disrepair.

However, there is another standard by which to judge these organizations than their own (and even the view presented above is not shared by all the activists). The women's movement and ecology movements in India and elsewhere provide good examples of the possibilities for social movements to endure by periodically raising new issues, forming new alliances, and rethinking their strategies. Seen within this context, the Shramik Sangathana's demise appears to have been less preordained.

By contrast, the CPI(M)'s strengths have become more evident with the passage of time. As a parliamentary party rather than a movement organization, the CPI(M) has tended to eschew a confrontational strategy vis-à-vis the state and dominant classes within West Bengal, which has helped ensure its survival in office. Compared to the Shramik Sangathana's ambitious, idealistic goals, the CPI(M)'s cautious, pragmatic approach entailed some solid gains and fewer losses. For example, wage rates in West Bengal are higher and women more apt to receive nearly equal wages with men in Midnapur than in Dhulia district. Moreover, the CPI(M) has been far more effective than the Shramik Sangathana in protecting the rural poor from repression by "communal organizations" in complicity with the police.

But has the CPI(M)'s progressive abandonment of its earlier reformist zeal been any more inevitable than the Shramik Sangathana's organizational demise? To the contrary. The Left Front government has scarcely tested the limits of tolerance in West Bengal. Far from building upon its earlier achievements, it has not undertaken any major new agrarian reforms, although even its supporters find little to praise in its conduct of urban affairs.

Prospects for Radical Change in India

After analyzing two major leftist political movements in very different settings, one is tempted to conclude that the prospects for leftist organizing are grim indeed in India today. The CPI(M) has flourished by renouncing radical goals and women's liberation. The Shramik Sangathana remained more faithful to radical goals but failed dismally.

However, if both organizations failed, they also partially succeeded, and their strengths and weaknesses were complementary. The CPI(M) has demonstrated how the left might construct a successful political machine. Even if it has favored party supporters, the Left Front government has nonetheless achieved significant redistributive reform. The CPI(M)'s identification with Bengali "cultural nationalism" is also instructive. Given the weight of caste, religion, and regionalism in contemporary India, the CPI(M) has creatively made Bengali regional identity the basis for its reformist agenda without inciting the "communal" passions that political parties have unleashed elsewhere in India. The remaining challenge is for the CPI(M) to reject those aspects of Bengali cultural identity that embrace upper-class paternalism and male chauvinism.

The Shramik Sangathana's achievements are also instructive. It has demonstrated the possibility of appropriating radical, democratic, feminist values from *adivasis*, one of the most exploited groups in India today. It has thereby made manifest the much talked about notion of indigenous feminism. The Shramik Sangathana's major failing was that however noble its intentions and initial achievements, it was unable to develop the organizational capacity to sustain and extend *adivasi* militancy. It failed in part because of its disdain for formal procedures, organizational discipline, and hierarchy. But the Shramik Sangathana also failed because even in the early years it did not recognize and rectify its own departure from democratic methods. Herein lie possibilities for leftist organizations to learn from the Shramik Sangathana's mistakes.

Thus, this study can be read as suggesting that if a political strategy is to be radical, it must maintain a creative tension between "guided spontaneity" and organizational discipline, electoral participation and extraparliamentary mobilization, and pay attention to multiple forms of inequality in given historical settings. It can be read as an analysis of the imperative for left organizations to be democratic if they are to be radical. And who but women, uniquely located at the intersection of the home and the world, can better grasp the imperative to democratize the spheres of the family, production, and social life?

Notes

Chapter One

1. Observations about this demonstration are based on fieldwork in the Bankura district in the summer of 1979. Although this manuscript focuses on CPI(M) activities in the Midnapur district, I refer occasionally to Bankura district, where I did research in 1979–80. I discuss Bankura at greater length in earlier studies, including "Two Faces of Protest: Alternative Forms of Women's Mobilization in West Bengal and Maharashtra."

Research for this study was conducted in several phases. The first phase had its origins in doctoral research I undertook in 1979–80. During this period, I spent January to March in Maharashtra, April through October in West Bengal, and November to February in Maharashtra once again. The second phase of this research, conducted from January through May 1985, was doubly hindered, first by visa restrictions, which limited the scope of my research. Then, upon returning to New York in the fall of 1985, I experienced every scholar's nightmare: a carton containing all my notes disappeared. For a while it seemed that the book was not to be—and indeed I never recovered the fine-grained detail of the earlier research. However, I recaptured more than I would have imagined through the process of recollection and through correspondence with some of my informants in India. Some additional interviews were also conducted in West Bengal by Bela Bandhopadhayaya and Sreemati Chakrabarti and in Maharashtra by Manisha Desai in the spring of 1987.

2. In this study I use the term *adivasi* in preference to the more frequently used term *tribal*. The term *tribal* has been rightly criticized for its racist, evolutionary implications; its tendency to group together people thus defined, even though they live in different parts of the world; and its assumption that tribals are autochthonous, isolated groups that eschew slash-and-burn agriculture in favor of settled agricultural production. Research

that dispels these assumptions and shows that Indian "tribals" should not be identified with any one form of economic production, religious belief, or racial origin include S. C. Dube, "Introduction," in S. C. Dube, ed., *Tribal Heritage of India*, p. 2; N. K. Bose, *Tribal Life in India*, p. 4; and David Hardiman, *The Coming of the Devi: Adivasi Assertion in Western India*, pp. 11–15.

The term *adivasi*, which literally means "first settlers," suffers from some of the same misleading assumptions as the term *tribal*. (On this point see Gail Omvedt, "Are *Adivasis* Subaltern?" *Economic and Political Weekly* 23, no. 39 [Sept. 1988], pp. 2001–2.) Although it is often assumed to be indigenous, the term was coined by a Hindu social worker in the 1930s. Like *tribal*, the term *adivasi* lumps together diverse groups. However, *adivasi* is used by the Bhils to describe themselves and does not carry the pejorative connotations of the term *tribal*. As Hardiman notes, *adivasi* calls attention to a sense of collective identity that has emerged over the past century as a result of exploitation by outside groups.

3. I use the term *communal* in quotes because of its pejorative connotations in the Indian context. However, I continue to use the term because it is both clearer and more evocative to an Indian audience than the phrase *ethnic conflict*.

4. Throughout this study I tend to write about the CPI(M) and Shramik Sangathana in the present tense in order to convey a sense of immediacy about the struggles they have waged and the issues they have addressed.

5. For an elaboration of this argument, see Atul Kohli, "From Elite Activism to Democratic Consolidation: The Rise of Reform Communism in West Bengal."

6. Figures for 1977–78 are taken from the National Sample Survey (NSS) 32nd Round, *Sarvekshana*, vol. 4, nos. 3 and 4 (Jan.–April 1981), Table 16; and for 1983 from NSS 38th Round, *Sarvekshana*, vol. 9, no. 4 (April 1986), Table 1.

7. See Rosalind O'Hanlon, *Caste, Conflict, and Ideology: Mahatma Jotirao Phule and Low Caste Protest in Nineteenth-Century Western India*; Gail Omvedt, "Non-Brahmins and Communists in Bombay," *Economic and Political Weekly* 8, no. 16 (April 1973): 800–805, and "Jyotirao Phule and the Ideology of Social Revolution in India"; and Nalini Pandit, "Caste and Class in Maharashtra."

8. For a discussion of the CPI(M)'s role among agricultural laborers in Kerala, see Joseph Tharamangalam, *Agrarian Class Conflict: The Political Mobilization of Agricultural Laborers in Kuttanad, South India*.

9. Ashgar Ali Engineer argues that the intensity of "communalism" varies inversely with the strength of community identities (*Communalism and Communal Violence in India: An Analytic Approach to Hindu-Muslim Conflict* [Delhi: Ajanta Publishers, 1989], p. 7). This argument would help

explain why Bengali Hindus and Dhulia's *adivasis* display a powerful sense of community identity but very little ethnic chauvinism.

10. This argument is most eloquently made by Lloyd Rudolph and Susanne Hoeber Rudolph, *In Pursuit of Lakshmi: The Political Economy of the Indian State*.

11. See, for example, Godavari Parulekar, *Adivasi Revolt*, on *adivasis'* struggles against feudal domination in Thana district, Maharashtra, in the 1940s. Divergent sources concur on the antifeudal character of the Telengana movement (1948–51) in Hyderabad, from the classic work of P. Sundarayya, *Telengana People's Struggle and Its Lessons*, to revisionist pieces like Vasantha Kannabiran and K. Lalitha, "That Magic Time: Women in the Telengana People's Struggle," in *Recasting Women*, edited by Kumkum Sanghari and Sudesh Vaid.

On the relationship between the "green revolution" and peasant radicalism, see, for example, Francine Frankel, *India's Green Revolution*; Keith Griffin, *The Political Economy of Agrarian Change: An Essay on the Green Revolution*; and T. K. Oomen, "Green Revolution and Agrarian Conflict."

12. For debates on the respective roles of middle peasants and agricultural laborers in peasant movements, see Hamza Alavi, "Peasants and Revolution"; Marshall Bouton, *Agrarian Radicalism in South India*; D. N. Dhanagare, *Peasant Movements in India, 1920–1950*; and Kathleen Gough, "Indian Peasant Uprisings."

13. See, for example, Rajni Kothari, *Party Systems and Election Studies* (Bombay: Allied Publishers, 1967); W. H. Morris-Jones, *Government and Politics of India* (London: Hutchinson, 1964); and Myron Weiner, *Party Building in a New Nation* (Chicago: University of Chicago Press, 1967).

14. Ashgar Ali Engineer, *Communalism and Communal Violence in India*, p. 19; Rudolph and Rudolph, *In Pursuit of Lakshmi*, pp. 36–59.

15. Rajni Kothari has been especially emphatic about the linkages between political centralization and the emergence of grass-roots movements. See his "Grass-Roots Movements: The Search for Alternatives," "Towards Intervention," and "Will the State Wither Away?"

16. For a sampling of the literature on grass-roots movements, see my "Grass-Roots Movements and the State: Reflections on Radical Change in India"; Ramachandra Guha, *The Unquiet Woods: Ecological Change and Peasant Resistance in the Himalayas*; Rajni Kothari, *State against Democracy*; Vandana Shiva, *Staying Alive: Women, Ecology, and Survival in India*; and Thomas Weber, *Hugging the Trees: The Story of the Chipko Movement*.

A powerful, relatively recent social movement is that of agrarian producers, also referred to as the new agrarianism or the farmers' movement, in Karnataka, Uttar Pradesh, and Maharashtra, which has sought higher prices for agricultural products from the state. Because this demand only tangentially concerns the rural poor, farmers' movements have been dominated by middle and rich peasants. I discuss the genesis and significance of this movement in my "State Autonomy and Agrarian Transformation in India."

17. Dowry deaths refer to the practice of husbands and in-laws murdering new brides on the grounds that the dowry is insufficient, so that they can collect another dowry. For discussions of the phenomenon of dowry death, see Leslie Calman, *Women and Movement Politics in India*; Madhu Kishwar and Ruth Vanita, eds., *In Search of Answers*; and Maria Mies, *Patriarchy and Accumulation on a World Scale*. For more general treatments of the women's movement, see Gail Omvedt, *We Will Smash This Prison*; Vibhuti Patel, "Women's Liberation in India"; and Rama Joshi and Joanna Liddle, *Daughters of Independence: Gender, Class, and Caste in India*.

18. My questions have been influenced by those posed by Frances Fox Piven and Richard A. Cloward, *Poor Peoples' Movements: Why They Succeed, How They Fail*, and in the Indian context by Oomen's interest in the institutionalization of social movements. See T. K. Oomen, *From Mobilization to Institutionalization: The Dynamics of Agrarian Movement in Twentieth-Century Kerala*, and *Social Transformation in Rural India: Mobilization and State Intervention*.

19. There are some important exceptions to this generalization about the discipline. On the subject of agrarian peasant movements the outstanding example, and an important inspiration for my own work, is James Scott, notably *The Moral Economy of the Peasant* and *Weapons of the Weak*. Subaltern historiography of India includes: David Arnold, "Gramsci and Peasant Subalterneity in India"; Ranajit Guha, *Elementary Aspects of Peasant Insurgency in Colonial India*; Ranajit Guha, ed., *Subaltern Studies*, vols. I, II, III, and IV; and David Hardiman, *The Coming of the Devi*.

20. Among the most important exceptions are Madhu Kishwar and Gail Omvedt, whose prolific writings on rural women's resistance have broken new ground. Although Omvedt is impressed by the scope of women's consciousness and resistance, Kishwar is more skeptical.

21. See for, example, Lydia Sargent, ed., *Women and Revolution: A Discussion of the Unhappy Marriage of Marxism and Feminism*; Annette Kuhn and Ann Marie Wolpe, eds., *Feminism and Materialism: Women and Modes of Production*; and Michele Barrett, *Women's Oppression Today: The Marxist-Feminist Encounter*.

22. For a sampling of this wide-ranging literature, see Elizabeth Croll, *Feminism and Socialism in China*; Domitila Barrios de Chungara, *Let Me Speak! Testimony of a Woman of the Bolivian Mines*; Rigoberta Menchu, *I, Rigoberta Menchu: An Indian Woman in Guatemala*; Kay Ann Johnson, *Women, the Family, and Peasant Revolution in China*; Sonia Kruks, Rayna Rapp, and Marilyn Young, eds., *Promissory Notes: Women and the Transition to Socialism*; Margaret Randall, *Sandino's Daughters: Testimonies of*

Nicaraguan Women in Struggle, and *Women in Cuba Twenty Years Later*; Stephanie Urdang, *Fighting Two Colonialisms: Women in Guineau Bissau*, and *And Still They Dance: Women, War, and the Struggle for Change in Mozambique*.

23. This is not to say that the literature on agrarian communism is irrelevant to my study. Indeed, I am centrally concerned with the economic influences on communist mobilization described by Donald Zagoria in his seminal essay, "The Ecology of Peasant Communism in India" and with the regional moorings of communist parties as described by Marcus Franda, *Radical Politics in West Bengal*. However, within the Indian context, little attention has been devoted to political influences on the CPI(M); one important exception is Atul Kohli's *State and Poverty in India*.

24. See, for example, Jürgen Habermas, "New Social Movements"; Herbert Kitschelt, "New Social Movements in West Germany and the United States"; Laclau and Mouffe, *Hegemony and Socialist Strategy*; Melucci, "The Symbolic Challenge of Contemporary Movements"; and Touraine, *The Return of the Actor: Social Theory in Post-Industrial Society*.

25. Jo Freeman, "The Women's Liberation Movement: Its Origins, Structure, Activities, and Ideas," p. 551.

Chapter Two

1. Reference is made in this chapter to interviews conducted with bureaucrats, CPI(M) party officials, and Left Front government officials in Calcutta between January and March 1985. Unless otherwise specified, all interviews were conducted as part of this project.

Rather than citing each of these interviews separately, I list here the people interviewed in the order they appear in the chapter, along with the position they held at the time of the interview: Jyoti Basu, chief minister of West Bengal; Manoranjan Rai, president of the Centre for Industrial Trade Unions (CITU); Ashim Dasgupta, member of the West Bengal State Planning Advisory Board (1982–87) and subsequently finance minister (1987–92); Kanai Bhowmick, minister for minor irrigation (1982–87); Benoy Chowdhury, land and reforms minister (1982–87 and 1987–present); P. C. Bannerjee, secretary for land reforms; Nihar Bose, minister for cooperatives (1982–87); Biplab Dasgupta, director of the Comprehensive Area Development Program (CADP) and subsequently member of parliament (1989–91); Ajoy Sinha, special secretary to Jyoti Basu; D. Bandhopadhyaya, secretary for land reforms; Ashok Mitra, finance minister (1982–87); and Jatin Chakraborty, minister for public works (1982–87).

2. John D. Stephens, *The Transition from Capitalism to Socialism*; Gosta Esping-Andersen, *Politics against Markets*.

3. Adam Przeworski, "Social Democracy as a Historical Phenomenon,"

and Przeworski and John Sprague, *Paper Stones: A History of Electoral Socialism*; Claus Offe, *Disorganized Capitalism: Contemporary Transformations of Work and Politics*, and *Contradictions of the Welfare State*.

4. Leo Panitch, *Working-Class Politics in Crisis: Essays on Labour and the State*.

5. Ashok Rudra, "One Step Forward, Two Steps Backward," p. A61.

6. Atul Kohli, *The State and Poverty in India: The Politics of Reform*, p. 143.

7. On the tendency for the "two-stage theory" to become associated with reformist goals in the European context, see Carl Boggs, Jr., "Eurocommunism and the State Crisis of Legitimation"; and Sidney Tarrow, *Peasant Communism in Southern Italy*. Ronald Herring analyzes the dilemmas that parliamentary communists face in their stance on capitalist development in the Indian context in "Dilemmas of Agrarian Communism: Peasant Differentiation, Sectoral, and Village Politics."

8. On the challenges that European communist parties have faced in achieving radical reform at the local level, see Peter Lang, "The PCI at the Local Level: A Study of Strategic Performance"; Jerome Milch, "The PCF and Local Government: Continuity and Change"; Paolo Ceccareli, "Local Government Control and European Communist Parties"; Raffaella Nanetti and Robert Leonard, "Participatory Planning: The PCI's New Approach to Municipal Planning"; and Martin A. Schain, *French Communism and Local Power: Urban Politics and Political Change*.

9. Mary Fainsod Katzenstein and Carol McClurg Mueller, eds., *The Women's Movements of the United States and Western Europe*, explores the dilemmas that women's organizations experience in building coalitions with European communist parties.

10. Adam Przeworski, "Social Democracy as a Historical Phenomenon," pp. 30–31.

11. Bhabani Sen Gupta, *The CPI(M): Promises, Prospects, Problems*, p. 42.

12. Ibid., p. 76. According to Marcus Franda, the CPI(M) claimed to have distributed 200,000 acres of land under the second United Front government. Marcus Franda, "Radical Politics in West Bengal."

13. *Labour in West Bengal, 1983*, p. 11.

14. Ibid., p. 110.

15. As James Scott points out, although small holders may be more productive per unit of soil, they tend to market less and eat more. Thus, paradoxically, increased small-holder production may imply little gain in what is sold to consumers. Personal correspondence with James Scott, 24 September 1987.

16. Government of West Bengal, *Economic Review, 1984–1985*, p. 12.

17. Ashok Rudra, "Operation Barga," p. 40.

18. *Budget Statement by Benoy Krishna Chowdhury, Minister in Charge of Land and Land Reforms Department, West Bengal, 1985–1986*, pp. 2–3.

19. Kirsten Westergaard, "People's Participation, Local Government, and Rural Development: The Case of West Bengal, India," pp. 80–81.

A survey of fourteen villages in West Bengal found that only 20 percent of sharecroppers retained 75 percent of the crop whereas about 71 percent retained 50 percent of the crop. Registered sharecroppers were no more likely than unregistered sharecroppers to retain a larger share of the crop. Nripendra Bandhopadhyaya and Associates, *Evaluation of Land Reform Measures in West Bengal: A Report*, p. 47.

20. Ajit Kumar Ghosh, "Agrarian Reform in West Bengal: Objectives, Achievements, and Limitations," p. 24.

21. Bandhopadhyaya et al., *Evaluation of Land Reform Measures in West Bengal*, p. 14. The authors of this study note that the figures for the amount of land vested in West Bengal compared to other parts of India are somewhat inflated because they include land vested under the Estates Acquisition Act, which in other parts of India fell under the Zamindari Abolition Acts. Only the Land Reform Act in West Bengal is strictly comparable to ceiling laws in other parts of the country.

22. Under an act passed in 1978, the government also provided 184,000 people with titles to the small plots of land on which they lived. *Budget Statement by Benoy Krishna Chowdhury*, pp. 2–3.

23. Asim Dasgupta, *Rural Development Planning under the Left Front Government in West Bengal*, p. 8.

24. Bandhopadhyaya et al., *Evaluation of Land Reform Measures in West Bengal*, p. 9.

25. Boudhayan Chattopadhyaya, *Agrarian Structure, Tensions, Movements, and Peasant Organizations in West Bengal, 1936–1976*, vol. 1, part 2, *The Post-Independence Period*, p. 100.

26. In the *gram panchayat* elections, the CPI(M) won 60 percent and Congress (I) won 7 percent of the seats in 1978, whereas in 1983 Congress (I) won 27 percent and the CPI(M) 59 percent of the seats. In the *panchayat samiti* elections, the CPI(M) won 68 percent and Congress (I) won 5 percent of the seats in 1978, whereas the CPI(M) won 65 percent and Congress (I) won 26 percent of the seats in 1983. In the *zilla parishad* elections, the CPI(M) won 85 percent and Congress (I) 11 percent in 1978; in 1983, the CPI(M) won 82 percent and Congress (I) won 16 percent of the seats. However, these figures exaggerate the Congress party's gains: although many Congress candidates ran as Independents in the 1978 elections, they ran under their party banner in 1983. The Independent vote dropped from 25 percent to 6 percent in the *gram panchayat* elections and from 20 percent

to 4 percent in the *panchayat samiti* elections between 1978 and 1983. These figures were supplied by Surya Mishra, the chairperson of the *zilla parishad* for Midnapur district, on 15 March 1985.

27. Tarun Ganguly, "The Role of the Panchayats," *The Telegraph* (Calcutta), 22 May 1983, p. 9.

28. Montek S. Ahluwalia, "Rural Poverty in India," table 1b, p. 10.

29. Bhabani Sen Gupta, "Striving for Unity," *India Today* 1 (1–15 January 1981), p. 99.

30. The constitution permits the central government to declare "president's rule" in states in which it deems the elected state government unable to maintain law and order. Until legislative assembly elections are held, the central government rules that state from New Delhi.

31. *The Statesman* (Calcutta), 15 December 1984; *Business Standard* (Calcutta), 26 January 1987.

32. *Business Standard*, 28 March 1985.

33. "Politics of Food Supplies," p. 210.

34. Kohli, *The State and Poverty in India*, pp. 92–93.

35. This argument is developed by Amulya Ganguli, "The Outcome in Bengal: Why Congress-I Lost Its Way," *The Statesman* (Calcutta), 30 March 1987.

36. This is a portion of an article Hazra published in the Bengali daily *Bartaman*, on 13 January 1985. The CPI(M) suspended Hazra from the party upon his publication of this and another highly critical article. Hazra served five times as a member of the Legislative Assembly and once as a member of parliament.

37. Panitch makes a similar argument in *Working-Class Politics in Crisis*, p. 50.

38. *The Telegraph*, 2 December 1984. My field research suggests that in many cases, expulsions facilitated the weeding out of dissidents.

39. Communist Party of India (Marxist), *Documents of the Eleventh Congress of the CPI(M), Vijaywada, 26–31 January 1982*, pp. 243–45.

40. Another important achievement of the Left Front that is not directly relevant to the present discussion but should at least be noted in passing is the contribution it has made to national political developments. Despite the apparent powerlessness of state governments, Jytoi Basu and the CPI(M) more generally, in good part because of its role in West Bengal, have emerged as important players on the national political scene. As it completes its third term in office, the Left Front government also provides an important example to other opposition parties of the possibilities for the relatively stable, uncorrupted exercise of power at the state level.

41. Andrew Martin, "Is Democratic Control of Capitalism Possible? Some Notes towards an Answer," and *The Politics of Economic Policy in the United States*.

Chapter Three

1. Ronald Tiersky, *Ordinary Stalinism*, p. 47.

2. The term *Sanskritization*, which has become common parlance, was coined by M. N. Srinivas in 1982 in *Religion and Society among the Coorgs of South India*.

3. Most of the interviews cited in this chapter were conducted in Calcutta between January and March 1985; Chaya Bera and Sarala Maheshwari were interviewed during April and May 1987. I refer in this chapter to interviews with Renu Chakravarty, Bani Dasgupta, Bimala Maji, Vidhya Munshi, and Manikuntala Sen, all of whom were active in the early stages of the communist movement and joined the CPI after the split in 1964. Women leaders of the CPI(M) in West Bengal who were interviewed included: Aarti Dasgupta, the most prominent female trade unionist in CITU and member of the CPI(M)'s state secretariat; Chaya Bera, minister of relief (1982–87) and minister for health and family welfare (1987–present); Nirupama Chatterjee, member of the West Bengal state committee of the CPI(M) and minister of state and for social welfare (1982–87); Nando Rani Daal, president of the PBGMS in Midnapur district; Manjari Gupta, president of the All-India Democratic Women's Association; Shyamali Gupta, secretary of the PBGMS for West Bengal; Sarala Maheshwari, member of the central committee of the all-India CPI(M); Kanak Mukherjee, member of parliament and member of the central committee of the all-India CPI(M) and of its West Bengal state committee. Reference is also made to interviews with Prasad Rai, director of *panchayats*; A. K. Ghosh, then chairman of the West Bengal State Planning Advisory Board; Ashim Dasgupta; and Shambunath Mandi, minister for scheduled castes and scheduled tribes (1982–87).

4. Christina Gilmartin describes the early experience of Chinese communist women in a remarkably similar fashion. In contrast to the segregated lives that most women led in Chinese society, the communist subculture offered them a unique opportunity to remove themselves from patriarchal control. Thus, in the early years the dual commitment of these women to Marxism and feminism seemed quite compatible. Christina Gilmartin, "Early Women Communists in China."

5. As Temma Kaplan notes, women may be drawn to such activities as famine relief because of its connection to women's traditional concern with the preservation of life. Kaplan notes that female consciousness often contains progressive or even revolutionary potentialities. These possibilities were not realized in the Bengali context. Temma Kaplan, "Female Consciousness and Collective Action: The Case of Barcelona, 1910–1918."

6. Judith Adler Hellman, *Journeys among Women: Feminism in Five Italian Cities*, pp. 32–33.

7. Adrienne Cooper, "Sharecroppers and Landlords in Bengal, 1930–1950: The Dependency Web and Its Implications," pp. 248–49.

8. Renu Chakravarty, *Communists in Indian Women's Movement*, pp. 209–12.

9. In a study of Madras, Patricia Caplan shows how social welfare agencies not only perpetuate women's subordination but also contribute to the successful functioning of the capitalist state. Patricia Caplan, *Class and Gender in India: Women and Their Organizations in a South Indian City*.

10. Of the central government rural development schemes—the National Rural Employment Program, Rural Landless Employment Guarantee Program, Drought Prone Areas Program, and others—only one, the Development for Women and Children in the Rural Areas (DWCRA), focuses on women. So far the central government has released very limited funds for DWCRA and implemented the program in only fifty districts nationwide.

11. Communist Party of India (Marxist), *Documents of the Eleventh Congress of the CPI(M), Vijaywada, 26–31 January 1982*, p. 65.

12. In 1981 the CPI(M) created the national-level AIDWA, which has a membership today of 2.1 million women.

13. Amartya Sen and Sunil Sengupta, "Malnutrition of Rural Children and the Sex Bias."

14. This pattern contrasts with that of many socialist states in which women's political representation is much greater at the local than at the national level. However, it conforms to the all-India pattern, in which elite women of middle-class, upper-caste backgrounds have extensive opportunities to enter the national political arena and are readily accepted when they do so.

15. Chaya Bera, *Women and the Left Front Government*, p. 5.

16. As Kruks, Rapp, and Young point out, although communist movements and regimes have reinterpreted Marxism in the most far-reaching ways, their approach to issues concerning gender remains surprisingly unreformed. See Sonia Kruks, Rayna Rapp, and Marilyn Young, "Introduction," *Promissory Notes: Women in the Transition to Socialism*.

17. Judith Stacey, *Patriarchy and Socialist Revolution in China*, especially chapter 4.

18. Hellman, *Journeys among Women: Feminism in Five Italian Cities*, pp. 38–39.

19. Karen Beckwith, "Parties and Non-Party Associations: The Case of the Union of Italian Women and the Italian Communist Party" (unpublished paper).

20. The term *political space* is used by Judith Hellman in her discussion of the "red city" of Reggio, in which a small feminist collective lacked the "spazio politico" to survive. Hellman, *Journeys among Women*, p. 137.

Chapter Four

1. The influence of new social movements in Western Europe and the United States on the Third World is especially evident in the Latin American context. See, for example, the essays in the book edited by David Slater, *New Social Movements and the State in Latin America* (Amsterdam: CEDLA, 1985), including David Slater, "Social Movements and a Recasting of the Political"; Ernesto Laclau, "New Social Movements and the Plurality of the Social"; and Etienne Henry, "Urban Social Movements in Latin America."

2. My reference is to the consensus about the post-Marxist, postindustrial character of the "new" social movements; an exception to this generalization is Gunnar Olofsson, who questions how new and how significant contemporary social movements are. See Olofsson, "After the Working Class Movement? An Essay on What's 'New' and What's 'Social' in the New Social Movements." However, I do not mean to suggest that the social movement literature adopts a unified theoretical approach. Differences between the European and American perspectives are especially striking. These are discussed by Jean Cohen, "Strategy or Identity: New Theoretical Paradigms and Contemporary Social Movements," and several essays in the volume edited by Bert Klandermans, Hanspeter Krieser, and Sidney Tarrow, *From Structure to Action: Comparing Social Movement Research across Cultures*, vol. 1.

3. Such scholars include Carl Boggs, *Social Movements and Political Power*; Ernesto Laclau and Chantal Mouffe, *Hegemony and Socialist Strategy: Towards a Radical Democratic Politics*; and Alain Touraine, *The Return of the Actor: Social Theory in Post-Industrial Society*.

4. Sulabha Brahme and Ashok Upadhyaya, "A Critical Analysis of the Social Formation and Peasant Resistance in Maharashtra" (unpublished paper), p. 433.

5. In 1980 the GSS had fifty part-time unpaid youth committee members: twenty men and thirty women from forty villages. It had twelve full-time activists: eleven men and one woman—Chaya Suratvanti, Ambersingh's widow, who remained loyal to the GSS after the split. The GSS, which relies on government assistance, mainly performs charitable social work.

6. Brahme and Upadhyaya, "A Critical Analysis of the Social Formation," pp. 436–37. According to Brahme and Upadhyaya, the Sarvodaya found that Hindu cultivators had illegally appropriated ten thousand acres of land from tribals in fifty-seven villages in Shahada and Taloda *talukas*.

7. These were the Maharashtra Land Revenue Code and Tenancy Laws (Amendment) Act 1974 (Act No. 35 of 1974), which came into force on 6 July 1974, and the Maharashtra Restoration of Land to Scheduled Tribes Act 1974 (Act No. 14 of 1975), which came into force on 1 November 1975.

8. I refer in this chapter to interviews with the following Shramik Sangathana activists: Bhuribai, Hirkana, Vijay Kanhare, Dinanath Manohar, Pitabai, Saraswati, Nirmala Sathe, Kumar Shiralkar, Chander Singh, Vaharu Sonalkar, Sukmabai, Surtanbai, and Tagibai. I refer to them in the text by their first names for this is the way they were known in Dhulia district.

Activists from related organizations who were interviewed included: Chetna Gali of the Chatra Yuvak Sangarsh Vahini in Bodh Gaya district, Bihar; Gail Omvedt and Bharat Patankar, of the Shramik Mukti Daal in Sangli district; and, in Dhulia district, Sharad Patil of the Satya Shodhak Communist party, and Chaya Suratvanti of the Gram Swarajya Samiti.

9. In 1971 the government of Maharashtra appointed a committee headed by V. S. Page to study the employment conditions of agricultural laborers. In March 1974 the government decided to implement the committee's recommendations and thus to fix statutory minimum wages in Dhulia district for the first time. It increased minimum wages to 4.50 rupees per hour in October 1975. However, the government lacked both the ability and the will to ensure that employers paid minimum wages.

10. The best descriptions of the Prakashe demonstration and its aftermath are found in S. D. Kulkarni, "Caste and Class in a Tribal Movement"; and Maria Mies, "The Shahada Movement, a Peasant Movement in Maharashtra (India): Its Development and Perspectives."

11. Sharad Patil found that farmers who owned over 50 acres of land were completely unaffected by the drought and those owning twenty to thirty acres were barely affected. Middle peasants who owned ten to twenty acres, however, had to sell their livestock, sell or mortgage their land, and work on relief projects; half of them were practically starving. Sharad Patil, "Famine Conditions in Maharashtra: A Survey of Sakri Taluka."

12. Maria Mies, "The Shahada Movement, a Peasant Movement in Maharashtra (India): Its Development and Perspectives."

13. A great deal has been written about the Employment Guarantee Scheme in Maharashtra. See, for example, Norman Reynolds and Pushpa Sundar, "Maharashtra's Employment Guarantee Scheme: A Programme to Emulate?"; M. H. J., "Who Pays and Who Gains from EGS?"; and S. Bagchee, "Employment Guarantee Scheme in Maharashtra."

14. Sharad Patil, "Government's War on Adivasis," p. 1809.

15. The songs cited in this chapter and in the epigraph to chapter 8 were composed in the Bhil language, Bhilori, by Shramik Sangathana participants and are generally sung by Bhil women. They were translated for this study by Sujata Gotaskar, Bombay, October 1979.

16. The scheme, which Patil described in a letter to selected landlords and government officials, called for the employment of 1,200 watchmen, 100

"sergeants," and a number of armed "commanders" and "majors." The "Purshottam Sena" would involve a capital expenditure of 422,000 rupees and a recurring annual expenditure of 1.9 million rupees and would cover a total cultivated area of 474,000 acres. The coauthors of the letter included the chairman of the Satpuda Tapti Cooperative Sugar Factory, the president of the *panchayat samiti* of Shahada *taluka*, the chairman of the Dhulia District Central Cooperative Bank, and the chairman of the Maharashtra State Cooperative Bank. The scheme is discussed by Sandeep Pendse, "Repression against the Shramik Sangathana"; Brahme and Upadhyaya, "A Critical Analysis of the Social Formation," p. 446; and Darryl D'Monte, "Dhulia Peasant Movement Faces Stiff Resistance," *Times of India* (Bombay), July–August 1974.

17. In the 1979 elections, Vaharu received six thousand votes from the Taloda-Akkalkuwa constituency and Bhuribai three thousand votes from the Shahada constituency.

18. Bhuribai ran in a "scheduled tribe" constituency in Nandurbar *taluka*; she received 16,246 votes as against the 196,335 votes polled by Surupsingh Hira, the elected Congress party candidate.

19. Leslie Calman, *Protest in Democratic India: Authority's Response to Challenge*, conclusion.

20. This observation does not extend to the later stages of the Shramik Sangathana movement. Like political repression by the dominant classes, neglect by the state increased as the Shramik Sangathana weakened. The most shocking instance of state neglect occurred in 1987. As a result of what was first considered malnutrition and later diagnosed as sickle-cell anemia, over a hundred *adivasis* died between March and May in Akkalkuwa and Akrani *talukas*. The government provided no relief to the afflicted areas and appeared to be unaware of the outbreak of illness in its early stages.

21. See Alaka and Chetna, "When Women Get Land: A Report from Bodhgaya"; and Manimala, "Zameen Kenkar? Jote Onkar!" *Manushi* 14 (Jan.–Feb. 1983).

22. The best-known commentators on this question include James Scott, Eric Hobsbawm, and, in the Indian context, Ranajit Guha.

23. For evidence drawn from *adivasi* and *dalit* organizing in Bihar in the 1930s, see Stephen Henningham, "Autonomy and Organisation: Harijan and Adivasi Protest Movements."

24. Claus Offe, "New Social Movements: Challenging the Boundaries of Institutional Politics," p. 833.

25. I explore the dilemmas of grass-roots political organizations in India more fully in my "Grass-Roots Movements and the State: Reflections on Radical Change in India."

26. For discussions of both the promises and the shortcomings of a

decentralized, democratic approach, see Maren Lockwood Carden, "The Proliferation of a Social Movement: Ideology and Individual Incentive in the Contemporary Feminist Movement"; Craig Jenkins, "Resource Mobilization Theory and the Study of Social Movements"; and Frances Fox Piven and Richard A. Cloward, *Poor People's Movements: Why They Succeed, How They Fail.*

27. Jo Freeman, "The Women's Liberation Movement: Its Origins, Structure, Activities, and Ideas," p. 551.

28. The phrase was coined by Jo Freeman in *The Politics of Women's Liberation* (1975).

29. Many theorists are in agreement on this point. See, for example, Jürgen Habermas, "New Social Movements"; Herbert Kitschelt, "New Social Movements in West Germany and the United States"; Laclau and Mouffe, *Hegemony and Socialist Strategy*; Melucci, "The Symbolic Challenge"; and Touraine, *The Return of the Actor.*

30. Kitschelt, "New Social Movements in West Germany and the United States," p. 274.

31. A perceptive review essay by Allen Hunter criticizes Laclau and Mouffe along similar lines. Hunter, "Post-Marxism and the New Social Movements."

32. Touraine, *Return of the Actor*, p. 117.

33. Offe, "New Social Movements," p. 841.

34. This approach is most fully articulated by Arjun Appadurai and Carol Beckenridge, "Why Public Culture?" in *Public Culture* 1, no. 1 (Fall 1988): 5–9.

Chapter Five

1. Several scholars of the *purdah* system have commented on the underlying assumptions of women's vulnerability in a world fraught with danger. See, for example, Patricia Jeffery, *Frogs in a Well: Indian Women and Purdah*; and Hannah Papanek, "Purdah: Separate World and Symbolic Shelter."

2. See Peter Bertocci, "Social Stratification in Rural East Pakistan" (unpublished paper); and Ralph W. Nicholas, "Ecology and Village Structure in Deltaic West Bengal."

3. R. C. Majumdar, *History of Ancient Bengal*, pp. 25–27, 414–35.

4. A. F. Salahuddin Ahmed, *Social Ideas and Social Change in Bengal, 1818–1835*, p. 169.

5. The classic analysis of the formation of the Bengali *bhadralok* is John Broomfield, *Elite Conflict in a Plural Society*.

6. Among the diverse commentaries on the relatively fragmented, fluid character of caste in West Bengal are Nirmal Kumar Bose, "Some Aspects of

Caste in Bengal"; and Partha Chatterjee, *Bengal, 1920–1947*, and "Caste and Politics in West Bengal." The most exhaustive treatment of the complexity of West Bengal's caste structure remains Herbert H. Risley, *The Tribes and Castes of West Bengal: Ethnographic Glossary* (1891).

7. Tarashish Mukhopadhyaya, "The Caste Mobility Movement among the Mahishyas in Bengal" (unpublished thesis).

8. For a discussion of Sanskritization among the Mahatos, see Biman Kumar Das Gupta, "Caste Mobility among the Mahatos of South Manbhum," *Man in India* 42–43 (July–Sept. 1962): 228–36.

9. I am grateful to Atul Kohli for this insight.

10. For an exhaustive discussion of these issues, see Meredith Borthwick, *The Changing Role of Women in Bengal, 1849–1905*. Tapan Raychaudhuri emphasizes the continuity in attitudes toward women's sexuality, before and after the nineteenth-century social reform movement in Bengal, in "Norms of Family Life and Personal Morality among the Bengali Hindu Elite, 1600–1850." While noting the contradictory motives and consequences underlying social reform concerning women, Ghulam Murshid also stresses the limited commitment of the *bhadralok* to women's emancipation; see Murshid, *Reluctant Debutante: Response of Bengali Women to Modernization, 1849–1905*.

On a distinct but related note, Sumanta Banerjee notes that the consolidation of *bhadralok* identity entailed a growing abyss between elite and folk culture. The marginalization of the more sexually egalitarian traditions of the "lower orders" had important implications for women's public roles. Sumanta Banerjee, *The Parlour and the Streets: Elite and Popular Culture in Nineteenth-Century Calcutta*.

11. On the seclusion of Bengali Hindu women in the nineteenth century, see Meredith Borthwick, *The Changing Role of Women in Bengal, 1849–1905*; Usha Chakraborty, *Condition of Bengali Women around the Second Half of the Nineteenth Century*; and Margaret M. Urquhart, *Women of Bengal: A Study of the Hindu Pardanasins of Calcutta*.

12. However, the conclusion that Fruzzetti draws from women's externality to the male line is quite different from my own: Fruzzetti argues that women play a central role in determining blood and affinal ties in Bengali society by virtue of their lack of full incorporation into their husband's line. Lina M. Fruzzetti, *The Gift of a Virgin: Women, Marriage, and Ritual in Bengali Society*.

13. Ronald B. Inden and Ralph W. Nicholas, *Kinship in Bengali Culture*, p. 21.

14. Lina M. Fruzzetti and Akos Östör, *Kinship and Ritual in Bengal*.

15. Inden and Nicholas, *Kinship in Bengali Culture*, p. 23.

16. Susan Wadley, "Women and the Hindu Tradition." An opposing

perspective emphasizes the empowering aspects of the Hindu tradition for women. See, for example, Frédérique Apffel Marglin, *Wives of the God King: The Rituals of the Devadasis of Puri*; and Ann Grodzins Gold, *Fruitful Journeys: The Ways of Rajasthani Pilgrims.*

17. Margery Wolf, *Women and the Family in Rural Taiwan.* In a parallel fashion, Kay Johnson notes that older Chinese women, who acquired authority with age, resisted the communist family reforms; see Johnson, *Women, the Family, and Peasant Revolution in China.* For a discussion of the remarkably similar dependence of Bengali mothers on their sons, see Manisha Roy, *Bengali Women.*

18. Lynn E. Gatwood contrasts the *devi* tradition of powerful female divinity among the lower classes with "spouse-goddess" worship, entailing the domestication of the female deity among the upper classes. Lynn E. Gatwood, *Devi and the Spouse Goddess: Women, Sexuality, and Marriage in India.*

19. Parallels with the Latin American context are especially striking. Several scholars analyze the manner in which marianismo, the power women derive from their roles as mothers, has limited their access to political power on the same terms as men but encouraged them to project their maternal roles onto the political arena. See, for example, Elsa M. Chaney, *Supermadre: Women and Politics in Latin America*; Evelyn P. Stephens, "Marianismo: The Other Side of Machismo in Latin America"; and Julie M. Taylor, *Eva Peron: Myths of a Woman.*

20. Even though female "terrorists" used violent means, they were not thought to be violating the ethic of Bengali womanhood. Geraldine Forbes suggests that Hindu women's self-sacrifice may have been easily transposed from the family to the nation. See Geraldine Forbes, "Goddesses or Rebels: The Women Revolutionaries of Bengal."

21. Marathas were traditionally landlords and chiefs and the *kunbis,* cultivators. However, around 1911 the Marathas absorbed the *kunbis,* most likely as a result of competition between the Marathas and the Brahmins. Ravinder Kumar, *Western India in the Nineteenth Century,* chapter 1.

To appreciate the extent to which Marathas constitute the dominant status group and class in "typical" Maharashtrian villages, see Anthony T. Carter, *Elite Politics in Rural India*; Jayanta Lele, *Elite Pluralism and Class Rule: Political Development in Maharashtra*; and A. R. Kamat, "Politico-Economic Developments in Maharashtra: A Review of the Post-Independence Period."

22. Dr. Ambedkar, the renowned scheduled-caste leader, founded the Republican party to represent Mahar interests. The Dalit Panthers, an organization formed by Namdeo Dhasal (a Marxist) and Raja Dhule (a Buddhist) in 1975, have sustained *dalit* radicalism.

For a sampling of the literature on *dalit* radicalism in Maharashtra, see

Dhanajya Kheer, *Dr. Ambedkar: Life and Mission*; Owen Lynch, *The Politics of Untouchability*; Michael Moffat, *Untouchables in Contemporary India*; and Eleanor Zelliot, "Ambedkar and the Mahar Movement" (Ph.D. diss., University of Pennsylvania, 1969).

23. See, for example, Stephen Henningham, "Autonomy and Organisation: Harijan and Adivasi Protest Movements"; Ranajit Guha, *Elementary Aspects of Peasant Insurgency in Colonial India*; Swapan Dasgupta, "Adivasi Politics in Midnapur, 1760–1924"; and Tanika Sarkar, "Jitu Santal's Movement in Malda, 1924–1932: A Study in Tribal Protest."

24. K. D. Erskine, *Rajputana Gazetteers*, p. 228; and James Tod, *Annals and Antiquities of Rajasthan*.

25. Analyses of the complexities surrounding state policy toward *adivasis* include: Christoph von Fürer-Haimendorf, *Tribes of India: The Struggle for Survival*; S. D. Kulkarni, "Problems of Tribal Development in Maharashtra"; and K. S. Singh, "Transformation of Tribal Society: Integration vs. Assimilation."

26. P. V. Paranjape, "Kulaks and Adivasis: The Formation of Classes in Maharashtra," p. 7.

27. The finest, most in-depth study that exists on such a movement is David Hardiman's *The Coming of the Devi*. Although the Bhils in present-day Dhulia district did not actually participate in the Devi movement, their own social reform movements strikingly resemble it.

28. For an early analysis of the contrasting significance of dowry and bridewealth for women, see Jack Goody and S. J. Tambiah, *Bridewealth and Dowry*. In "Bridewealth and Dowry Revisited: The Position of Women in Sub-Saharan African and North India," Tambiah rethinks his earlier analysis in light of feminist criticism; in particular he concedes that dowry does not constitute a premortem inheritance, as he and Goody had earlier argued.

29. There are few studies of female deities in Maharashtra. One important exception, although its focus is primarily historical and on Hindus rather than *adivasis*, is D. D. Kosambi, *Myth and Reality: Studies in the Formation of Indian Culture*.

30. For an elaboration of the notion that Bengali culture emphasizes the hierarchically ordered nature of the universe, see Marvin Davis, *Rank and Rivalry: The Politics of Inequality in Rural West Bengal*. Christoph von Fürer-Haimendorf analyzes the reasons for the limited extent of individual free choice among Hindus in *South Asian Societies*, especially chapter 6.

Chapter Six

1. There has been a long and lively debate about the mode of production in Indian agriculture, much of which appeared in the pages of *Economic and*

Political Weekly and *Journal of Peasant Studies* in the early to mid-1970s, during the aftermath of the green revolution. The debate centers on such questions as: What would constitute the empirical basis for identifying agrarian capitalism? To what extent has it emerged in Indian agriculture? and, What are its international dimensions? The major limitation of the debate from the perspective of this study is its inadequate attention to the linkages between the mode of production and agrarian protest.

Early contributions to the debate include: Hamza Alavi, "India and the Colonial Mode of Production"; Jairus Banaji, "For a Theory of Colonial Modes of Production"; Paresh Chattopadhyaya, "On the Question of the Mode of Production in Indian Agriculture: A Preliminary Note"; Harry Cleaver, "Internationalization of Capital and Mode of Production in Agriculture"; André Gunder Frank, "On 'Feudal' Modes, Models, and Methods of Escaping Capitalist Reality"; Utsa Patnaik, "Capitalist Development in Agriculture"; and Ashok Rudra, "In Search of the Capitalist Farmer."

Scholars took up the debate once again in the 1980s—again in a series of articles published in the *Economic and Political Weekly* and the *Journal of Peasant Studies*—but with greater self-consciousness about the use of Marxist categories and with greater attention to class formation and alignments. See, for example, Hamza Alavi, "Structure of Colonial Formations"; Amit Bhaduri, *The Economic Structure of Backward Agriculture*; Amit Bhaduri, Hussain Zillur Rahman, and Ann-Lisbet Arn, "Persistence and Polarisation: A Study in the Dynamics of Agrarian Contradiction"; T. J. Byers, "Mode of Production and Non-European Pre-Colonial Societies"; and Ashok Rudra, "Pre-Capitalist Modes of Production in Non-European Societies."

An altogether different debate, which is less theoretically and more empirically grounded, concerns the relationship between the green revolution and agrarian radicalism. Participants in this debate include: Francine Frankel, *India's Green Revolution*; Keith Griffin, *The Political Economy of Agrarian Change: An Essay on the Green Revolution*; P. C. Joshi, "Agrarian Social Structure and Social Change"; and T. K. Oomen, "Green Revolution and Agrarian Conflict."

2. A highly influential body of scholarship asserts that middle peasants have played the leading roles in agrarian radicalism, particularly with the commercialization of agriculture. See, above all, Hamza Alavi, "Peasants and Revolution"; and Eric Wolf, *Peasant Wars of the Twentieth Century*. Their argument has been refuted by numerous scholars in the Indian context, including Kathleen E. Gough, "Indian Peasant Uprisings"; and D. N. Dhanagare, *Peasant Movements in India, 1920–1950*. Other works contending that agricultural wage laborers have been the prime source of rural militancy in India include: Marshall Bouton, *Agrarian Radicalism in South*

India; K. P. Kannan, *Of Rural Proletarian Struggles: Mobilisation and Organization of Rural Workers in Southwest India*; and Joseph Tharamangalam, *Agrarian Class Conflict: The Political Mobilization of Agricultural Laborers in Kuttanad, South India*.

3. See Joan P. Mencher, "Kerala and Madras: A Comparative Study of Ecology and Social Structure"; André Beteille, *Studies in Agrarian Social Structure*; Alan R. Beals, *Village Life in South India*; Donald W. Attwood, "Capital and Transformation of Agrarian Class Systems: Sugar Production in India"; and David Ludden, "Productive Power in Agriculture: A Survey of Work on the Local History of British India," in *Agrarian Power and Productivity in South Asia*, ed. Meghnad Desai, Susanne Hoeber Rudolph, and Ashok Rudra.

4. Burton Stein, *Peasant, Society, and State in Medieval South India*; and David Ludden, "Economic Development and Social Change in Indian Agriculture: A Historical Perspective."

5. For correctives to Ludden's perspective, see Amiya K. Bagchi, "Reflections on Patterns of Regional Growth in India during British Rule"; and B. B. Chaudhuri, "Agricultural Production in Bengal, 1850–1900: Coexistence of Decline and Growth."

6. Ravinder Kumar, "The Rise of Rich Peasants in Western India."

7. One evidence of British responsibility for transforming class relations concerns the experience of Akkalkuwa *taluka*. Whereas the British seized control of Shahada, Taloda, and Nandurbar by the first quarter of the nineteenth century and ushered cultivating castes into these regions, they did not colonize Akkalkuwa until a century later. When cultivating castes subsequently migrated to Akkalkuwa, *adivasis* had already established a more viable small-holder economy than in the regions that the British had colonized earlier. Although Akkalkuwa was endowed with the same natural resources as these other *talukas*, it experienced less capitalist development and little agrarian mobilization. Paranjape, "Kulaks and Adivasis: The Formation of Classes in Maharashtra," p. 14.

8. J. F. Richards and Michelle B. McAlpin, "Cotton Cultivating and Land Clearing in the Bombay Deccan and Karnataka: 1818–1920," in *Global Deforestation and the Nineteenth-Century World Economy*, edited by Richard P. Tucker and J. F. Richards, p. 89.

9. *Gazetteer of the Bombay Presidency*, pp. 330, 409, and 417. Note that Shahada, Taloda, and Nandurbar are the three *talukas* in Dhulia district in which the Shramik Sangathana movement is most active.

10. P. V. Paranjape, "Kulaks and Adivasis: The Formation of Classes in Maharashtra," p. 12.

11. Ibid., p. 216.

12. Jan Breman similarly comments that the *hali* system in southern Gujarat, which bears a resemblance to *saldar* in Dhulia district, should not be mistaken for a feudal relationship. He notes that it has been quite common for "unfree" labor to persist for some period following the intensification of agricultural production. Jan Breman, *Of Peasants, Migrants, and Paupers*. However, as he emphasizes in his earlier book, the persistence of attached labor deters class mobilization among the rural poor. Jan Breman, *Patronage and Exploitation: Changing Agrarian Relations in South Gujarat, India*.

13. Sulabha Brahme and Ashok Upadhyaya, "A Critical Analysis of the Social Formation and Peasant Resistance in Maharashtra" (unpublished manuscript), p. 406.

14. Sulabha Brahme and Ashok Upadhyaya, "Study of Economic Conditions of Agricultural Labour in Dhulia District, Maharashtra" (unpublished manuscript), p. 117.

15. Maharashtra is the third largest sugar producer in India; within Maharashtra, 72 percent of the land under sugarcane is located in the western part of the state. See Attwood, "Capital and Transformation of Agrarian Class Systems," p. 40. As Donald Attwood and B. S. Baviskar have shown, the key to high levels of sugar production in Maharashtra lies in the functioning of sugar cooperatives. See, for example, Donald W. Attwood, "Social and Political Preconditions for Successful Cooperatives: The Cooperative Sugar Factories of Western India"; D. W. Attwood and B. S. Baviskar, "Why Do Some Cooperatives Work But Not Others? A Comparative Analysis of Sugar Cooperatives in India"; B. S. Baviskar, *The Politics of Development: Sugar Cooperatives in Rural Maharashtra*; and B. S. Baviskar and D. W. Attwood, "Rural Cooperatives in India: A Comparative Analysis of Their Economic Survival and Social Impact."

As critics have pointed out, Attwood and Baviskar do not sufficiently consider the significance of class inequality in either the formation or the functioning of sugar cooperatives. See Jim Matson, "Class Struggles in Cooperative Development: The Subordination of Labor in the Cooperative Sugar Industry of Maharashtra, India"; and Gail Omvedt, "Wishing Away Class Politics."

16. John Harris similarly argues that capitalist transformation does not eradicate relations based on caste and kinship in *Capitalism and Peasant Farming: Agrarian Structure and Ideology in Northern Tamil Nadu*.

17. Paranjape, "Kulaks and Adivasis," p. 13.

18. Rajat K. Ray, "The Crisis of Bengal Agriculture, 1870–1927—The Dynamics of Immobility."

19. Ibid., p. 248.

20. Ibid., p. 250.

21. Other factors contributed to agrarian stagnation in the colonial pe-

riod; the government scarcely invested in the agrarian sector (14.6 percent by the early twentieth century) and the capital intensive import-export sector it created had negligible multiplier effects. Because British fiscal and monetary policies constrained the growth of per capita consumption, farmers were forced to export rice at well below market prices in order to survive. Rajat Ray and Ratna Ray, "The Dynamics of Continuity in Rural Bengal under the British Imperium: A Study of Quasi-Stable Equilibrium in Underdeveloped Societies in a Changing World," pp. 103–4.

22. Atul Kohli, "From Elite Activism to Democratic Consolidation," p. 401.

23. *Zamindars* were predominantly Brahmins whereas the *jotedars* were drawn from respectable agricultural castes. With the expansion of international trade in the second half of the nineteenth century, *jotedars* gained new access to credit and commodity markets. This led to increasing conflict between the *jotedars* and the *zamindars* over claims to the surplus. Although *zamindars* frequently demanded increased rents, *jotedars* resisted these demands and attempted to involve the colonial state on their side. Rajat Ray and Ratna Ray, "*Zamindars* and *Jotedars*: A Study of Rural Politics in Bengal"; and Willem Van Schendel and Aminul Haque Faraizi, *Rural Labourers in Bengal, 1880–1980*, p. 29.

24. Rajat and Ratna Ray point out that Congress fared best in regions in which it allied with the *jotedars*; thus, for example, although it gained significant support from the Mahishyas in eastern Midnapur, it failed to create a mass base in western Bengal, where it allied with Hindu *zamindars* against the Muslim *jotedars*. Rajat Ray and Ratna Ray, "*Zamindars* and *Jotedars:* A Study of Rural Politics in Bengal," p. 102.

25. Kohli, "From Elite Activism to Democratic Consolidation," pp. 375–76.

26. Biplab Dasgupta, "Agricultural Labour under Colonial, Semi-Capitalist, and Capitalist Conditions: A Case Study of West Bengal," *Economic and Political Weekly* 19, no. 39 (29 Sept. 1984), p. A133.

27. Van Schendel and Faraizi, *Rural Labourers in Bengal*, p. 21.

28. James K. Boyce, *Agrarian Impasse in Bengal: Agricultural Growth in Bangladesh and West Bengal, 1949–1980*, p. 259. Boyce notes that West Bengal's agrarian structure contains two kinds of inefficiencies: the first arises from the lower land productivity associated with sharecropping and wage labor than that associated with owner cultivation. The second has to do with the absence of irrigational facilities; although water is the leading agricultural input, only two-fifths of the gross cropped area was irrigated in West Bengal by the 1970s.

29. Boyce, *Agrarian Impasse in Bengal*, p. 3. Also see Montek S. Ahluwalia, "Rural Poverty and Agricultural Performance in India," on the population below the poverty line in West Bengal.

30. Boyce, *Agrarian Impasse in Bengal*, p. 46.
31. Ibid., pp. 44–45.
32. Van Schendel and Faraizi, *Rural Labourers in Bengal*, p. 123.
33. Ibid, p. 62.
34. Ibid., p. 97.
35. Gail Omvedt first developed this argument in "Women and Rural Revolt in India" but still upholds its basic premises seven years later in "Women in Popular Movements: India and Thailand during the Decade for Women" (unpublished report).
36. Studies point to systematic underestimation of women's work because of census enumerators' exclusion of certain kinds of work, biases against recognizing women's availability for work, and questionable distinctions between primary and secondary forms of employment. See, for example, Bina Agarwal, "Work Participation of Rural Women in the Third World: Some Data and Conceptual Biases"; Leela Gulati, "Occupational Distribution of Working Women: An Interstate Comparison"; Gita Sen, "Women's Work and Women Agricultural Labourers: A Study of the Indian Census" (unpublished paper); and Pushpa Sundar, "Characteristics of Female Employment: Implications of Research and Policy."

In West Bengal, Pranab Bardhan estimates—on the basis of 1972–73 National Sample Survey (NSS) data—that about 28 percent of adult women who are usually in the labor force seasonally withdraw into domestic work when opportunities for gainful employment are slack. When Bardhan asked women who were classified as housewives whether they would work for wages if work was available, 30 percent answered affirmatively. Bardhan suggests that women who withdraw from the labor force should automatically be considered unemployed as a result of the absence of job opportunities: "Some Employment and Unemployment Characteristics of Rural Women: An Analysis of NSS Data for West Bengal, 1972–1973," pp. 36–37.

37. *Census of India (1961), Series 10, Maharashtra*, pp. 150–51; *Census of India (1981), Series 12, Maharashtra*, pp. 172–75, 208–11; *Census of India (1961), Vol. 16, West Bengal*, pp. 523, 178–79, 182–83; and *Census of India (1981), Series 23, West Bengal*, pp. 180–83, 264–67.

Notwithstanding the problems discussed earlier, the census provides the most exhaustive information on women's labor-force participation through time and below the state level. Furthermore, 1961 and 1981 census data are more comparable than are figures from other years because the 1981 census reverted to the liberal definition of worker that had been employed twenty years earlier; by contrast, the 1971 census distinguished between "main work" and "secondary work" and tended to relegate women's work to the latter category. Furthermore, Gita Sen estimates that in 1971 the undercounting was greater for cultivators than agricultural laborers and less for

West Bengal and Maharashtra than for some other states. Sen, "Women's Work and Women Agricultural Labourers" (unpublished paper).

38. Kumaresh Chakravarty and G. C. Tiwari, "Regional Variations in Women's Employment: A Case Study of Five Villages in Three Indian States" (unpublished paper), p. 47.

39. Barbara Harris, "Paddy Milling: Problems in Policy and the Choice of Technology," p. 294.

40. Figures for 1977–78 are taken from National Sample Survey (NSS), 32d Round, *Sarvekshana*, vol. 4, nos. 3 and 4 (Jan.–April 1981), table 16; for 1983 from NSS, 38th Round, *Sarvekshana*, vol. 9, no. 4 (April 1986), table 1.

41. For documentation, see Jenneke Arens and Jos van Beurden, *Jhagarpur: Poor Peasants and Women in a Village in Bangladesh*; and Leela Gulati, "Profile of a Female Agricultural Laborer."

42. Johnson, *Women, the Family, and Peasant Revolution in China*, pp. 231–32 and passim.

43. Agarwal, "Women, Poverty, and Agricultural Growth in India," pp. 170–75; Barbara Harris, "The Intrafamily Distribution of Hunger in South Asia" (unpublished paper); and Amartya Sen and Sunil Sengupta, "Malnutrition of Rural Children and the Sex Bias."

44. Chakravarty and Tiwari, "Regional Variations in Women's Employment," p. 46.

45. National Sample Survey, 32d Round, Survey of Employment and Unemployment, 1977–78, report series no. 298, tables 10 and 13.

46. The differential ratio of male to female wages increased from 1.66 to 1.76 in West Bengal and declined from 2.49 to 2.11 in Maharashtra between 1964–65 and 1974–75. Bina Agarwal, "Women, Poverty, and Agricultural Growth in India," p. 209.

It is difficult to explain differences in male-female wage disparities among Indian states. The states' levels of economic development, the proportion of female agricultural laborers, and state government policies do not appear to play a very significant role in many cases. In West Bengal, for example, the relatively small disparity in male-female wages does not reflect the Left Front government's influence since this information was gathered in 1977–78. Even the figures on wage rates for various tasks that women perform, such as transplanting, weeding, and harvesting, suggest no relationship between the ratio of women and the ratio of wages they receive in West Bengal.

47. One of the first and most important contributions to this subject is Ursula Sharma's *Women, Work, and Property in North-West India*. Sharma insists that women's performance of agricultural work is only one determinant among many of women's social power. Rights in land, which are

transmitted through a male inheritance system, are far more significant. Given male control over female labor power, women's labor-force participation does not confer independence upon them.

48. Borthwick reports that among the wealthiest families, *stridhan* could take the form of immovable property. Because upper-class women were in *purdah*, they appointed male agents to manage their estates, without losing control over their land. Many women became affluent enough to purchase *zamindari* land with their *stridhan*. Borthwick reports that in 1836 more than half of the principal *zamindars* in Rajshahi were women. Borthwick, *The Changing Role of Women in Bengal*, p. 21.

49. Bina Agarwal notes that some of the other ways in which women continue to be disadvantaged include: (1) children of predeceased daughters do not figure among class-one heirs; (2) upon divorce the wife has no claim to the property that her husband has acquired during their marriage; (3) a man's unrestricted right to will away property provides an important means by which women can be disinherited. Bina Agarwal, "Who Sows? Who Reaps? Women and Land Rights in India," p. 540.

50. *Towards Equality: Report of the Committee on the Status of Women in India*, p. 137.

51. This finding is suggested by personal observation in Midnapur district and confirmed in the context of Bangladesh by Mead Cain, Syeda Rokeya Khanam, and Shamsun Nahar, "Class Patriarchy and Women's Work in Bangladesh," p. 433.

52. On the average, Klass notes, villagers' prefer to marry their daughters some five to ten miles from their natal villages. Morton Klass, "Marriage Rules in Bengal," *American Anthropologist* 68 (1966): 960–61.

53. K. S. Singh, "Tribal Women and Their Land Rights: A Preliminary Report" (unpublished paper), p. 2.

54. Christoph von Fürer-Haimendorf, *Tribes of India: The Struggle for Survival*, pp. 164–65.

55. Y. V. S. Nath, *The Bhils of Ratanmal: An Analysis of the Social Structure of a Western Indian Community*, p. 86.

56. See S. L. Doshi, *Bhils: Between Societal Awareness and Cultural Synthesis*.

57. Gail Omvedt, "Adivasi Women and Personal Law," p. 22.

58. On this point, see Bina Agarwal, "Tribal Matriliny in Transition" (unpublished paper), esp. pp. 93–95; and Kishwar, "Challenging the Denial of Land Rights to Women," p. 5, on the impact of capitalist development on Ho women in Bihar.

59. Agarwal, "Who Sows, Who Reaps?"

60. Kishwar reports the same phenomenon concerning Ho women in Bihar in "Challenging the Denial of Land Rights to Women."

61. This argument is developed by K. S. Singh, "Tribal Women and Their Land Rights: A Preliminary Report" (unpublished paper), pp. 13–14.

62. See, for example, K. C. Alexander, "Emergence of Peasant Organisations in South India"; Marshall Bouton, *Agrarian Radicalism in South India*; Joseph Tharamangalam, *Agrarian Class Conflict: The Political Mobilization of Agricultural Laborers in Kuttanad, South India*; and Donald Zagoria, "The Ecology of Peasant Communism in India."

63. National Sample Survey, 38th Round (1983), reported in NSS report no. 341 (June 1987), table 3.1.

Chapter Seven

1. V. I. Lenin, "Preliminary Draft Theses on the Agrarian Question."

2. The point is elaborated by Peter J. Bertocci, "Social Organization and Agricultural Development in Bangladesh," p. 31; and by André Beteille, *Studies in Agrarian Social Structure*, pp. 199–200.

3. Thus, the foremost scholars of rural class relations employ the criteria of landownership while recognizing its limitations. See, for example, Lloyd I. Rudolph and Susanne Hoeber Rudolph, *In Pursuit of Lakshmi: The Political Economy of the Indian State*, p. 336; Utsa Patnaik, "Class Differentiation within the Peasantry," pp. A82–83; and Venkatesh Athreya, Gustav Boklin, Goran Djurfelt, and Steffan Lindberg, "Identification of Agrarian Classes: A Methodological Essay with Empirical Material from South India," pp. 147–48.

4. For a further elaboration of this question, see Athreya et al., "Identification of Agrarian Classes," p. 157; and Pranab Bardhan, "Agrarian Class Formation in India," p. 75.

5. Reflecting the former tendency, Ashok Rudra identifies only two classes in Indian agriculture, "big landowners" and "agricultural laborers." Rudra argues that these polar categories are "theoretically correct" because they are politically useful. Ashok Rudra, "Class Relations in Indian Agriculture—I," pp. 916–23. By contrast, Athreya et. al. identify nine finely graded social classes, including, for example, "lower middle, middle, and upper middle peasants," in "Identification of Agrarian Classes," p. 186 and passim.

6. I do not differentiate between "capitalist rich peasants" and "feudal or semifeudal landlords," for these distinctions are not germane to my study. The Marxist understanding, which CPI(M) and Shramik Sangathana leaders accept, differentiates them as follows: rich peasants work on their own land whereas landlords only supervise cultivation. More important, "capitalist rich peasants" derive their major profits from wage labor, whereas "feudal" or "semifeudal" landlords derive most of their profits from land rent.

Nor have I included within my sample people whose principal income derives from nonagricultural work, although many of the people I interviewed supplemented their income through such pursuits. Nonagriculturalists constituted an extremely small proportion of the population of all of the villages I studied.

7. The first agricultural labor enquiry used time-disposition criteria as the basis for identifying agricultural laborers. But this criteria proved to be flawed, for the amount of time spent on performing wage labor was partly dependent on economic conditions in the region.

8. Swapan Dasgupta, "Adivasi Politics in Midnapur, 1760–1924."

9. *Peoples' Democracy*, 16 July 1978, p. 2.

10. Despite extensive scholarly interest in West Bengal, few studies explore the dynamic of social relationships in the rural context. Most such studies are anthropological: Lina Fruzzetti and Akos Östör, *Kinship and Ritual in Bengal*; Ramakrishna Mukherjee, *Six Villages of Bengal*; and Ronald P. Rohner and Manjusri Chaki-Sircar, *Women and Children in a Bengali Village*.

11. Paanagar, Anjalinagar, and Lodhanagar are pseudonyms, derived from certain noteworthy features of each village: Paanagar is the village in which *paan*, or betel leaves, are grown; Anjalinagar is the village in which Anjali Das was formerly *gram panchayat pradhan*; and Lodhanagar is inhabited by the Lodhas.

12. I refer in this chapter to interviews conducted in Midnapur between January and March 1985 with Sibsadhan Bhattacharya, the head of the block-level *panchayat samiti*; Maujam Hussein, CPI(M) MLA from Debra; Surya Mishra, the head of the Midnapur district *zilla parishad*; Bishwanath Mukherjee, the secretary of the CPI for West Bengal; and Sukumar Sengupta, the chairman of the CPI(M) in Midnapur district. In addition, in order to protect their identity, I refer to the following people by pseudonym: Dhiren Chattopadhyaya, the former director of the Rural Development Program (also a pseudonym); Gita Hui from Anjalinagar village and Anjali Das, former head of the *gram panchayat* that includes Anjalinagar; Hitesh and Renu, activists from Lodhanagar village; and Santosh Jena and Radhanath Quila, each of whom served at different times as *pradhans* of the *gram panchayat* that included Paanagar. In a few cases, such as that of Dhiren Chattopadhyaya, the informants requested anonymity.

13. Tamluk police station covers an area of about ninety square miles and includes 185 inhabited villages and a total rural population of 164,976. The average population of each village is 892. *District Census Handbook: Midnapur*, 1961, vol. 1, p. 46.

Information about the population of Paanagar, as of other villages in Midnapur and Dhulia district, are taken from the District Census Handbooks for Dhulia and Midnapur districts, 1971. The figures have been altered by less than 5 percent in all cases to preserve the anonymity of the villages.

14. Many families own weaving looms and contract their services to intermediaries, who pay them fifty to a hundred rupees a month. Middlemen also supply women with tobacco and leaves, with which they roll an average of a thousand *biri* cigarettes daily, earning about 4.50 rupees. Other sources of income include basket weaving, spinning, and dairy production. Many families are also involved in business and trade in the town of Tamluk.

15. In 1980, male agricultural laborers earned four rupees, a main meal, and a lighter meal (tiffin), and female laborers three rupees daily.

16. Sixty-seven percent of the male population in Paanagar compared to 40 percent in Midnapur are literate. Literacy rates among women are much lower, though still higher than the district average. Sixteen percent of women in Paanagar compared to 11 percent of rural women in Midnapur are literate. *District Census Handbook: Midnapur*, 1971, vol. 2, p. 300.

17. The results of the 1977 Legislative Assembly elections reflect the heterogeneity of political influences in Tamluk. The CPI, CPI(M), Janata, and Congress parties each won a single seat and Independents four seats.

18. Ralph W. Nicholas, "Village Factions and Political Parties in Rural West Bengal," p. 20, and "Structure of Politics in the Villages of Southern Asia."

19. By 1979 "Operation Barga" had registered 19 sharecroppers in Paanagar and 741 sharecroppers in Tamluk subdivision. By 1979 only a third of an acre of land had been vested in Paanagar village; in Tamluk police station, 174 acres had been vested under the Estates Acquisitions Act, and only 4 acres under the Land Reforms Act. In Tamluk subdivision, 26,636 acres had been vested under the Estates Acquisitions Act and 672 acres under the Land Reforms Act; of this, a total of 8,935 acres had been distributed in Tamluk subdivision. The amount of land vested and distributed is even lower in Tamluk p.s. than in the subdivision as a whole. These figures were supplied by the subdivisional land reforms officer, Tamluk, May 1979.

20. Debra p.s. contains 453 villages and covers an area of 130 square miles. On the average 225 people inhabit each village. *District Census Handbook: Midnapur*, 1961, vol. 1, p. 46.

21. The limited extent of agricultural mechanization in the village can be seen from the fact that in 1979 the total number of implements in the village included about three hundred *desi* (indigenous—that is, cattle-drawn) plows, nine threshers, twelve sprayers, and two dusters. In Debra p.s. there were only three tractors, seven power tillers, twenty-five iron plows, and forty threshers.

22. The main form of employment in the lean season is government road construction through the Food for Work and Rural Works Programs. About

eighty men and women in the village are engaged in household industry, manufacturing, trade, commerce, and other services.

23. Wealthier landowners can borrow money from the United Bank of India, the Agricultural Credit Society, and the Land Development Cooperative Bank, which charge between 9 and 14 percent interest annually. Poor peasants can borrow from the CADP. Anjalinagar is one of the sixty-one villages in Debra in which the CADP is active. This largely publicly financed rural development organization builds tube wells, supplies seeds, fertilizers, and pesticides, and provides technical guidance and loans.

24. By 1979 a total of 3,458 acres of agricultural land (of which 492 were unsuitable for cultivation) had been vested in Debra. The second United Front government vested 400 acres of land. However, it only acquired 200 acres and distributed 54 acres because hundreds of landlords filed court cases to prevent the land from being distributed. Since 1977 the CPI(M) has only vested and distributed 16 acres of land in block eleven, which includes Anjalinagar village.

In Anjalinagar, 11 acres have been distributed under the Land Reforms Act and 89 acres under the Estates Acquisition Act (including 67 acres of agricultural land, 5 acres of nonagricultural land, and 16 acres of other land). Of the 89 acres, only 6 acres have been vested and distributed since 1977. These figures were provided by the junior land reforms officer in Balichak, Debra, June 1979.

25. In the harvesting season of 1979, male laborers earned 4 rupees and a kilo of rice daily; female laborers earned 50 paise less. In the agriculture lean season, male laborers earned 1.50 rupees and one kilo of rice and women 50 paise less daily.

The *kisan sabha* estimated that at these wages, employers earned a profit of 14 to 18 rupees a day on each adult worker.

26. On the correlation between strikes and agricultural wage rates in West Bengal, see Pranab Bardhan and Ashok Rudra, "Terms and Conditions of Labour Contracts in Agriculture: Results of a Survey in West Bengal in 1979," p. 96.

27. Jhargram covers a radius of 202 square miles and contains 490 villages. The villages, which contain a population of about 172 persons each, are more thinly populated than the villages in eastern Midnapur. *District Census Handbook: Midnapur*, vol. 1, p. 48.

28. Gour Chandra Bagchi and Sukumar Sinha, *Bhumi Dhan Sol Village Survey Monograph*, p. 29.

29. Laborers migrate to the plains twice a year, in July-August and December-January. About thirty-four Lodha families reported having migrated to the plains for employment in 1978.

Laborers are hired on a contract and a daily basis in the harvesting season. In 1979 the wage rates averaged three kilos of rice plus two meals a day for men and three rupees plus one meal for women. Since a kilo of rice cost a little over one rupee at the time, men's daily earnings slightly exceeded those of women. By 1987 the harvesting season wage was eight rupees plus three kilos of rice for men and eight rupees for women. At that time, rice cost 1.80 rupees per kilo under the "tribal" development scheme subsidized by the government and 3.50 rupees per kilo on the open market.

30. The government provides employment under the Food for Work Program for six weeks in the year at the wage rate of two rupees plus two kilos of rice or three rupees plus two kilos of wheat.

31. Between 1975 and 1979, the Rural Development Program (RDP) loaned out a total of thirty-eight thousand rupees to poor peasants and agricultural laborers at 8 percent interest annually; by June 1979 they had repaid thirty-five thousand rupees. Very little other institutional credit is available to the Lodhas.

The dearth of employment opportunities has led to high levels of indebtedness. The rural poor are unable to obtain loans from banks and cooperatives. Instead they must borrow from moneylenders, who charge an average of 25 percent interest per month. Although it is difficult to obtain precise figures on rural indebtedness, Dhiren Chattopadhyaya surveyed 1,700 families in twenty-five villages (including Lodhanagar) between 1975 and 1978. He found that the average family borrowed 595 rupees a year from moneylenders at 300 percent annual interest and 30 rupees from other sources at 13 percent interest. He estimated that on the average 520 rupees of the loan was used for "distress" purposes (including illness, drought, court cases, and food scarcity), 95 rupees for social occasions (primarily marriages and religious festivals), and 10 rupees for productive purposes (such as investments in the land).

32. P. K. Bhowmick, *The Lodhas of West Bengal: A Socio-Economic Study*, p. 280.

33. Bhowmick notes that between 1916, when the crime register was started, and 1952, when the Criminal Tribes Act was revoked, 591 Lodhas, or 30 percent of all male adult Lodhas, were registered and considered habitual criminals. Bhowmick, *The Lodhas of West Bengal*, p. 267.

34. Ibid., p. 268. Bhowmick defines dacoity as: "A crime in which an organized attempt is made to forcibly occupy the movable properties of others, sometimes resulting in the murder of those resisting such attempts." Although large gangs commit dacoities, four people or fewer commit robberies, which may be "on a highway, in a market place, in a residence, or a shop." Thus, in comparison to robbery, dacoity involves larger numbers of people, more damage to property and persons, and greater premeditation.

35. Dhiren Chattopadhyaya was influenced by Paulo Freire's approach, which is explicated in *Pedagogy of the Oppressed* (trans. Myra Bergman Ranos; New York: Seabury Press, 1970).

36. In Debra, the CADP provided loans to 112 women whose yearly income was up to 3,500 rupees annually; the interest rate for these loans averaged 12 percent. The central government has made loans of up to 3,400 rupees per person for *adivasi* and *dalit* women in Jhargram; so far only 8 women in the subdivision have received such loans.

37. This is not to suggest that most villagers favored joint titles to the land. The responses of villagers who were questioned about this significantly differed according to caste and landowning patterns: agricultural laborers and poor peasants from *adivasi* and *dalit* backgrounds were most favorably predisposed to joint titles to the land; Hindu cultivators favored male landownership. There were also significant differences between villages: Paanagar was most opposed to joint titles whereas Lodhanagar was most favorably predisposed.

38. *Census of India (1961), Series 10, Maharashtra*, pp. 150–51; *Census of India (1961), Vol. 16, West Bengal*, pp. 523, 128–29, 182–83; *Census of India (1981), Series 12, Maharashtra*, pp. 172–75, 208–11; *Census of India (1981), Series 23, West Bengal*, pp. 183, 264–67.

39. Hitesh Sanyal, "Congress Movements in the Villages of Eastern Midnapur, 1921–1931," Calcutta: Centre for Studies in Social Sciences, 1985.

40. Sanjib Baruah emphasizes the deep-rooted structural constraints upon further land reform in West Bengal in "The End of the Road in Land Reform? Limits to Redistribution in West Bengal, India."

Chapter Eight

1. Interviews were conducted between January and March 1985 with the following Shramik Sangathana activists, all of whom are referred to by pseudonym: Chander, Gulab, Prakash, and Ravi.

2. Dhulia District Gazetteer, p. 197, which draws its information from the census figures available in the *District Census Handbook: Dhulia* for 1961. The average population per village is about 835 in Dhulia district, 371 in Taloda, 790 in Shahada, and 895 in Nandurbar.

3. Ibid., p. 272.

4. Ibid., p. 256.

5. I have changed the names of the villages and omitted precise information about their location. I have linked the pseudonyms to the villages' levels of economic development. Thus Udaspur is the most Underdeveloped, Madhyampur is in the Middle, and Daulatpur is the most Developed of the three villages I studied.

6. Laborers are all employed on a daily basis. The workday averages nine hours for men and seven hours for women. In 1980 the daily wage rate for men was 4 rupees for plowing and 3 rupees for sowing. Women received 3

rupees daily for harvesting and weeding. In the lean season men earned about 3 rupees and women 1.75 to 2 rupees daily.

7. Barrington Moore, Jr., *Social Origins of Dictatorship and Democracy*, p. 422.

8. *The Navashakti*, 18 September 1978 (translated from Marathi).

9. McKim Marriott, "The Feast of Love." For a rich analysis of the symbolism of ritual systems in the south-central African context, see Victor Turner, *The Forest of Symbols: Aspects of Ndembu Ritual*.

10. Ibid., p. 206.

11. Ibid., p. 212.

12. Judith Van Allen, "'Aba Riots' or Igbo 'Women's War'? Ideology, Stratification, and the Invisibility of Women," pp. 61–62.

13. Marriage constitutes the overwhelming reason for interrural migration. In 1961, 71 percent of men compared to 49 percent of women were born in the place where they were enumerated in the census. *Dhulia District Gazetteer*, 1974, p. 199. The figures are again drawn from the 1961 census.

Chapter Nine

1. See, for example, Cerny and Unger's discussions of the dialectic between structure and agency in Philip G. Cerny, *The Changing Architecture of Politics: Structure, Agency, and the Future of the State*; and Roberto Mangabeira Unger, *False Necessity: Anti-Necessitarian Social Theory in the Service of Radical Democracy*, part 1 of *Politics: A Work in Constructive Social Theory*.

2. My argument is inspired by Tarrow's analysis of how protest revitalized Italian democracy in the late 1960s and early 1970s. Sidney Tarrow, *Democracy and Despair: Protest and Politics in Italy, 1965–1975*.

Glossary

arti (arati)	Ceremony in which a lighted lamp is moved in circular fashion around an idol.
abhadra	(Bengali) Common people.
adivasi	Lit., original inhabitant; refers to pre-Aryan tribal peoples.
anradhan	(Bengali) Community grain bank.
antahpur	(Bengali) Lit., inner place; inner sanctum of the home.
bangsa	(Bengali) Lit., line; family line.
bhadralok	English-educated Bengalis of upper-caste and upper-class backgrounds.
bhadramahila	Mothers, daughters, and wives of the *bhadralok*.
bhajan	Devotional song.
bhakti	Devotion.
block	Unit of administrative organization below the subdivisional level within the district.
boro	(Bengali) Bigger.
bratas	Vows that give religious authority and sanctity to Bengali women's lives.
crore	Ten million.
dadan	(Bengali) A loan taken from cultivators against commitment of future labor.

dalit	Lit., oppressed; untouchables, officially designated scheduled castes, formerly called Harijans by Mahatma Gandhi.
dayabhaga	The form of Hindu inheritance law that traditionally prevailed in Bengal.
dharni chasi	Rich peasant.
district	Primary administrative subdivision of a state.
dokhinpara	(Bengali) Southern residential section of a village.
ekta parishad	(Marathi) Unity conference.
garib chasi	Poor peasant.
goonda	Thug.
gotra	(Hindi) Clan.
gram panchayat	Village-level *panchayat*. See also *panchayat*.
gram pradhan	Chief councillor of the *gram panchayat*.
Holi	The Indian spring festival, celebrated when winter crops are harvested and characterized by festivities of riotous abandon, notably spraying friends, family, and passersby with colored liquids and powders.
jotedar	(Bengal) Landlord.
jowar	(Marathi) Millet.
kharif	(Marathi) Autumn season; autumn crops.
khet mazdoor	Lit., field worker; agricultural laborer.
kisan sabha	(Bengali) Peasant organization.
lakh	One hundred thousand.
madhyam chasi	(Marathi) Middle peasant. See also *majhari chasi*.
mahila samiti	(Bengali) Women's organization.
mohwa	A forest tree of north India, known for its edible, nutritious flowers as well as for its oil, wood, and bark.
majhari chasi	(Bengali) Middle peasant.

maldar	(Maharashtra) Landlord.
malik	(Bengali) Master.
mangalsutra	Necklace made of gold and black beads that married women wear.
morcha	Demonstration.
paan	A digestive, chewed after meals, made from betel leaves into which betel nut and other spices, sometimes including tobacco, are rolled.
panch	Committee of elders informally organized at the village level, from which women were traditionally excluded.
panchayat	Lit., council of five; traditional form of rural self-government, given official standing in 1958.
panchayat samiti	Lit., council committee; block-level *panchayat* consisting of representatives from the *gram panchayats*.
putta	Land title.
peshwa	(Marathi) Minister.
pranam	(Bengali) Lit., salutation; a bow of obeisance.
purdah	Lit., curtain; the practice of female seclusion.
rabi	(Marathi) Spring season; crops grown in the spring.
rakta	(Bengali) Blood.
sal	(Bengali) Large, spreading timber tree found in West Bengal.
saldar	(Marathi) Annual contract laborer.
samadhi	(Marathi) Society.
Sanskritization	Upward caste mobility through emulation of Brahminic customs; the term was coined by the Indian sociologist M. N. Srinivas in 1982.
sarpanch	Chief councillor of the village-level *panchayat* in Maharashtra.

Savaras	Mythical forest-dwelling community in Hindu epic literature; Lodha *adivasis* consider Savaras their ancestors.
scheduled castes	See *dalits*.
sneha	(Bengali) Protective, parental love.
solo ana	(Bengali) Village council.
subapati	Chief councillor of the block-level *panchayat samiti*.
subhadipati	Chief councillor of the district-level *zilla parishad* in West Bengal.
subdivision	Primary administrative division of a district.
Sudra	Member of the lowest of the four major Hindu castes, traditionally employed as laborers and servants.
talati	Individual who maintains village accounts and land records.
taluka	(Marathi) Subdistrict. See also *tehsil*.
tarun mandal	(Marathi) Youth organization.
tehsil	(Marathi) Subdistrict.
tehsildar	(Marathi) Subdistrict-level official.
thana	(Bengali) A police station; unit of a subdivision.
unni	(Bengali) Honorific form of second-person pronoun.
uttarpara	(Bengali) The northern residential section of a village.
zamindar	A revenue collector under the Mughals; the British made *zamindars* into landlords in 1793.
zilla parishad	District-level *panchayat* (or council), consisting of representatives from the *panchayat samitis*.

Selected Bibliography

Abbreviations

EPW	Economic and Political Weekly
IESHR	Indian Economic and Social History Review
JPS	Journal of Peasant Studies

Government Documents

Agriculture and Co-operation Department. *Report of the Committee on Relief from Rural and Urban Indebtedness*. V. S. Page, Chairman. Bombay, October 1975.

Agriculture and Co-operation Department. *Report of the Committee on Problems of Illicit Moneylending and Bonded Labour*. V. S. Page, Chairman. Bombay, October 1977.

Bagchi, Gour Chandra, and Sukumar Sinha. *Bhumi Dhan Sol Village Survey Monograph*. Census of India. Vol. 16, part 6. 1964.

Bannerji, Amiya Kumar, ed. *West Bengal District Gazetteer: Bankura*. Calcutta: State Editor, 1968.

Budget Statement by Benoy Krishna Chowdhury, Minister in Charge of Land and Land Reforms Department, West Bengal, 1985–1986. Calcutta: West Bengal Government Press, 1985.

Calcutta Metropolitan Planning Organization. *Unemployment and Employment in West Bengal*. Calcutta: State Editor, March 1972.

Census of India (1961). Series 10, Maharashtra. General Economic Tables. R. B. Chari, Director of Census Operations, Maharashtra.

Census of India (1961). Vol. 16, West Bengal. General Economic Tables. J. Datta Gupta, Director of Census Operations, West Bengal.

Census of India (1971). Series 22, West Bengal. Part 10-B. District Census Handbook, Midnapur. Directorate of Census Operations, West Bengal.

Census of India (1981). Series 12, Maharashtra. General Economic Tables. P. P. Mahana, Indian Administrative Service, Director of Census Operations, Maharashtra.

Census of India (1981). Series 23, West Bengal. General Economic Tables. S. N. Ghosh, Indian Administrative Service, Director of Census Operations, West Bengal.

Chakrabarty, B., and P. Roy. *Twenty Villages of West Bengal: A Socio-Economic Study on Intercommunity Differences.* Calcutta: Scheduled Castes and Tribes Welfare Department, Government of West Bengal, 1972.

Das, Amal Kumar, Sunil Kumar Basu, Manas Kamal Chaudhuri, Ramendranath Saha, and Nelai Chandra Khan. *Scheduled Tribes and Scheduled Castes of West Bengal: Programmes, Facts, and Figures.* Calcutta: Government of West Bengal, 1978.

Dasgupta, Asim. *Rural Development Planning under the Left Front Government in West Bengal.* Calcutta: Information and Cultural Affairs Department, Government of West Bengal, 1981.

Department of Statistics, Ministry of Planning. *National Sample Survey, 32d Round.* Survey of Employment and Unemployment, Report Series no. 298, tables 10 and 13, 1977–78.

Department of Statistics, Ministry of Planning. *National Sample Survey, 32d Round. Sarvekshana,* vol. 4, nos. 3 and 4, April 1981.

Department of Statistics, Ministry of Planning. *National Sample Survey, 38th Round. Sarvekshana,* vol. 9, no. 4, April 1986.

Development of Social Welfare. *Draft Sixth Five-Year Tribal Sub-Plan, 1978–1983.* Bombay.

Dhulia District Gazetteer. Bombay: Maharashtra State Gazetteer, 1974.

Directorate of Economics and Statistics. *Statistical Abstract of Maharashtra State for 1974–1975.* Bombay, 1978.

District Census Handbook: Dhulia. Directorate of Census Operations, Census 1961. Series 10, Maharashtra.

District Census Handbook: Dhulia. Directorate of Census Operations, Census 1971. Series 11, Maharashtra.

District Census Handbook: Dhulia. Directorate of Census Operations, Census 1981. Series 12, Maharashtra.

District Census Handbook: Midnapore. Directorate of Census Operations, Census 1961. Vol. 16, West Bengal.

District Census Handbook: Midnapore. Directorate of Census Operations, Census 1971. Vol. 2, West Bengal.

District Census Handbook: Midnapore. Directorate of Census Operations, Census 1981. Series 23, West Bengal.

Gazetteer of the Bombay Presidency. Vol. 12. Khandesh, 1880.

Gazetteer of India, Maharashtra State, Dhulia District (revised edition). Bombay, 1974.

Government of West Bengal, *Economic Review, 1984–1985*. Calcutta: West Bengal Government Press, 1985.

Karve, Iravati. *Maharashtra: Land and Its People*. Maharashtra State Gazetteer, General Series. Bombay, 1968.

Labour in West Bengal, 1983. Calcutta: Department of Labour, Government of West Bengal, Sree Saraswaty Press, 1983.

Land and Land Revenue Department. *Land Reforms in West Bengal: A Statistical Report*. Calcutta: West Bengal Government Press, 1979.

Risley, Herbert H. *The Tribes and Castes of Bengal: Ethnographic Glossary*. 2 vols. Calcutta: Bengal Secretariat Press, 1891.

Towards Equality: Report of the Committee on the Status of Women in India. Government of India, Ministry of Education and Social Welfare. New Delhi, December 1975.

Tribal Research and Training Institute. "Statistics on Scheduled Tribes." *Tribal Research Bulletin*, March 1979.

Unpublished Works

Agarwal, Bina. "Tribal Matriliny in Transition." Unpublished paper, June 1988.

Bandhopadhyaya, Nripendra, and Associates. *Evaluation of Land Reform Measures in West Bengal: A Report*. Bangkok: The Asian Employment Program ILO/ARTEP, June 1985.

Bertocci, Peter. "Social Stratification in Rural East Pakistan." Paper presented at the seminar on "Systems of Rank," University of Chicago, 1971, and National Seminar on Pakistan, April 1971.

Brahme, Sulabha, and Ashok Upadhyaya. "A Critical Analysis of the Social Formation and Peasant Resistance in Maharashtra." Poona: Shankar Brahme Samajvijyana Granthalaya, November 1979.

———. "Study of Economic Conditions of Agricultural Labour in Dhulia District, Maharashtra." Poona: Shankar Brahme Samajvijyana Granthalaya, 1975.

Chakravarty, Kumaresh, and G. C. Tiwari. "Regional Variations in Women's Employment: A Case Study of Five Villages in Three Indian States." New Delhi: Indian Council of Social Science Research, 1978.

Chattopadhyaya, Boudhayan. *Agrarian Structure, Tensions, Movements, and Peasant Organizations in West Bengal, 1936–1976*. Vol. 1, part 2, *The Post-Independence Period*. Calcutta: CRESIDA, 1983.

Das Gupta, Ranajit, and Nripendra Bandhopadhyaya. "Causes of Stagnation in West Bengal Agriculture: A Discursive Review." Problems of the

Economy and Planning in West Bengal, Proceedings of a symposium, Center for Studies in Social Sciences. Calcutta, 24–25 February 1974.

Ghosh, Ajit Kumar. "Agrarian Reform in West Bengal: Objectives, Achievements, and Limitations." Geneva: ILO World Employment Program Working Paper, May 1980.

Gram Swarajya Samiti, "Shahada Chalwal." Shahada, 1974.

Gupta, Amit. "Protest, Participation, and Egalitarian Trends: A Study of Women's Mobilization for Change." Paper presented at the All-India Sociological Conference, University of Jabalpur, 28–30 December 1979.

Harris, Barbara. "The Intrafamily Distribution of Hunger in South Asia." Paper for WIDER Project on Hunger and Poverty. Seminar on Food Strategies, Helsinki, July 1986.

Kanhare, Sujata, and Mira Savara. "A Case Study on the Organizing of Landless Tribal Women in Maharashtra, India." Sponsored by the Asian and Pacific Center for Women and Development, June 1980.

Krishnamurthy, K. G. "Tribal Women in India: A Study." Sponsored by the Indian Council of Social Science Research. New Delhi, December 1976.

Mukhopadhyaya, Tarashish. "The Caste Mobility Movement among the Mahishyas in Bengal." M.A. thesis, University of Michigan, 1968.

———. "Religion and Society in Eight Villages of Eastern Midnapur, West Bengal." Ph.D. diss., Calcutta University, 1975.

Omvedt, Gail. "Effects of Agricultural Development on the Status of Women." Paper prepared for ILO, Madras, 6–11 April 1981.

———. "Women in Popular Movements: India and Thailand during the Decade for Women." Report prepared for the UNRISD popular participation program, June 1985.

Sen, Gita. "Women's Work and Women Agricultural Labourers: A Study of the Indian Census." Center for Development Studies, Working Paper no. 159, Trivandrum, February 1983.

Shramik Sangathana. "A New Attempt at Organized Assault on the Adivasis of Shahada and Taloda." Shahada, July 1978.

———. "On the Shahada Movement." 1975. In the files of Bombay Urban Industrial League for Development [BUILD] Documentation Centre, Bombay.

———. "Our Stand." Shahada, July 1977.

———. "Review of Three Years." Shahada, April 1976.

———. Untitled pamphlet regarding private army being raised by landlords of Dhulia, 1974. In the files of BUILD Documentation Centre, Bombay.

Singh, K. S. "Tribal Women and Their Land Rights: A Preliminary Report." Paper presented at the National Seminar on Women and Access to Land and Other Productive Resources, Delhi University, New Delhi, 11–13 January 1988.

Westergaard, Kirsten. "People's Participation, Local Government, and Rural Development: The Case of West Bengal, India." Research Report no. 8, Center for Development Research, Copenhagen, March 1986.

Zelliot, Eleanor. "Ambedkar and the Mahar Movement." Ph.D. diss., University of Pennsylvania, 1969.

Secondary Sources

Abdullah, Tahrunessa A., and Sondra A. Zeidenstein. *Village Women in Bangladesh: Prospects for Change*. New York: Pergamon Press, 1982.

Agarwal, Bina. "Work Participation of Rural Women in the Third World: Some Data and Conceptual Biases." *EPW* 20, nos. 51–52, (21–28 Dec. 1985): A155–A164.

———. "Who Sows? Who Reaps? Women and Land Rights in India." *JPS* 15, no. 4 (July 1988): 531–81.

———. "Women, Poverty, and Agricultural Growth in India." *JPS* 13, no. 4 (July 1986): 165–220.

"Agricultural Workers in Action: The Story of the Shramik Sangathana." *How* (June 1978): 24–31.

Ahluwalia, Montek S. "Rural Poverty and Agricultural Performance in India." *Journal of Development Studies* 14, no. 3 (April 1978): 298–323.

———. "Rural Poverty in India." World Bank Staff Working Papers no. 279, 1978.

Ahmed, A. F. Salahuddin. *Social Ideas and Social Change in Bengal, 1818–1835*. Leiden: Brill, 1965.

Alaka and Chetna. "When Women Get Land: A Report from Bodhgaya." *Manushi* 7, no. 40 (May–June 1987): 25–26.

Alavi, Hamza. "India and the Colonial Mode of Production." *EPW* 10, nos. 34–35 (Aug. 1975): 1235–62.

———. "Peasants and Revolution." In *The Socialist Register*, edited by Ralph Miliband and Ralph Seville. London: Merlin Press, 1965.

Alexander, K. C. "Emergence of Peasant Organisations in South India." *EPW* 15, no. 26 (28 June 1980): A72–A84.

———. "Peasant Classes and Primordial Loyalties." *JPS* 1 (Oct. 1973): 22–63.

Arens, Jenneke, and Jos van Beurden. *Jhagarpur: Poor Peasants and Women in a Village in Bangladesh*. Calcutta: Orient Longman, 1980.

Arnold, David. "Gramsci and Peasant Subalterneity in India," *JPS* 2, no. 41 (July 1984): 155–57.

Arrighi, Giovanni, Terence K. Hopkins, and Immanuel Wallerstein. "Dilemmas of Anti-Systemic Movements." *Social Research* 53, no. 1 (Spring 1986): 185–206.

Athreya, Venkatesh, Gustav Boklin, Goran Djurfelt, and Steffan Lindberg.

"Identification of Agrarian Classes: A Methodological Essay with Empirical Material from South India." *JPS* 14, no. 2 (Jan. 1987): 147–90.

Attwood, Donald W. "Capital and Transformation of Agrarian Class Systems: Sugar Production in India." In *Agrarian Power and Productivity in South Asia*, edited by Meghnad Desai, Susanne Hoeber Rudolph, and Ashok Rudra. Berkeley: University of California Press, 1984.

———. "Social and Political Preconditions for Successful Cooperatives: The Cooperative Sugar Factories of Western India." In *Who Shares? Cooperatives and Rural Development*, edited by D. W. Attwood and B. S. Baviskar. Delhi: Oxford University Press, 1988.

Attwood, Donald W., and B. S. Baviskar. "Why Do Some Cooperatives Work But Not Others? A Comparative Analysis of Sugar Cooperatives in India." *EPW* 22, no. 26 (27 June 1987): A38–A56.

Atyachar Virodh Samiti. "The Marathwada Riots: A Report." *EPW* 14, no. 19 (12 May 1979): 845–51.

Aya, Rod. "Popular Intervention in Revolutionary Situations." In *State Making and Social Movements: Essays in Theory and History*, edited by Charles Bright and Susan Harding. Ann Arbor: University of Michigan Press, 1984.

Bagchee, S. "Employment Guarantee Scheme in Maharashtra." *EPW* 19, no. 37 (15 Sept. 1984): 1633–38.

Bagchi, Amiya K. "Reflections on Patterns of Regional Growth in India during British Rule." *Bengal Past and Present* 95, no. 180 (Jan.–June 1976): 247–89.

Bagchi, Jashodhara. "Representing Motherhood: Ideology of Motherhood in Colonial Bengal." *EPW* 25, no. 43 (20–27 Oct. 1990): WS65–WS72.

Bailey, F. A. " 'Tribe' and 'Caste' in India." *Contributions to Indian Sociology* 2, no. 5 (Oct. 1961): 7–19.

Banaji, Jairus. "For a Theory of Colonial Modes of Production." *EPW* 7, no. 52 (23 Dec. 1972): 2498–2502.

Bandhopadhyaya, Nripendra. "Causes of Sharp Increase in Agricultural Labourers, 1961–1971." *EPW* 12, no. 53 (31 Dec. 1977): A111–A126.

Banerjee, Sumanta. *The Parlour and the Streets: Elite and Popular Culture in Nineteenth-Century Calcutta*. Calcutta: Seagull Books, 1989.

Bardhan, Kalpana. "Factors Affecting Wage Rates for Agricultural Labour." *EPW* 8, no. 26 (June 1973): A56–A64.

Bardhan, Pranab. "Agrarian Class Formation in India." *JPS* 10, no. 1 (Oct. 1982): 73–94.

———. *Land, Labor, and Rural Poverty: Essays in Development Economics*. New York: Columbia University Press, 1984.

———. "Some Employment and Unemployment Characteristics of Rural Women: An Analysis of NSS Data for West Bengal." *EPW* 8, no. 12 (25 March 1978): A21–A27.

———. "Terms and Conditions of Labour Contracts in Agriculture: Results of a Survey in West Bengal in 1979." *Oxford Bulletin of Economics and Statistics* 43, no. 1 (1981): 89–111.

———. "Terms and Conditions of Sharecropping Contracts: An Analysis of Village Survey Data in India." *Journal of Development Studies* 16, no. 3 (1980): 287–302.

Bardhan, Pranab, and Ashok Rudra. *Agrarian Relations in West Bengal: Results of Two Surveys*. Bombay: Somaiya Publishers, 1983.

———. "Interlinkage of Land, Labour, and Credit Relations: An Analysis of Village Survey Data in East India." *EPW* 13 (Feb. 1978): 367–84.

Barrett, Michelle. *Women's Oppression Today: The Marxist-Feminist Encounter*. London: Verso, 1988.

Barrios de Chungara, Domitila (with Moema Viezzer). *Let Me Speak! Testimony of a Woman of the Bolivian Mines*. Translated by Victoria Ortiz. New York: Monthly Review Press: 1978.

Baruah, Sanjib. "The End of the Road in Land Reform? Limits to Redistribution in West Bengal, India." *Development and Change* 21 (1990): 119–40.

———. "Turmoil on the Left: The Soviet Reforms and Indian Communists." *Socialism and Democracy* 8 (Spring–Summer 1989): 11–43.

Basu, Amrita. "Democratic Centralism in the Home and the World: Women and the Communist Movement in West Bengal." In *Promissory Notes: Women in the Transition to Socialism*, edited by Sonia Kruks, Rayna Rapp, and Marilyn Young. New York: Monthly Review Press, 1989.

———. "Grass-Roots Movements and the State: Reflections on Radical Change in India." *Theory and Society* 16 (1987): 647–74.

———. "State Autonomy and Agrarian Transformation in India." *Comparative Politics* 22 , no. 4 (July 1990): 483–500.

———. "Transcending Commonality: The Challenge of Difference in The Indian Women's Movement." *The Barnard Occasional Papers on Women's Issues* 2, no. 3, 1987.

———. "Two Faces of Protest: Alternative Forms of Women's Mobilization in West Bengal and Maharashtra." In *The Extended Family: Women and Political Participation in India and Pakistan*, edited by Gail Minault. New Delhi: Chanakya Publications, 1981.

Baviskar, B. S. *The Politics of Development: Sugar Cooperatives in Rural Maharashtra*. Delhi: Oxford University Press, 1980.

Baviskar, B. S., and D. W. Attwood. "Rural Cooperatives in India: A Comparative Analysis of Their Economic Survival and Social Impact." *Contributions to Indian Sociology* 18, no. 1 (Jan.–June 1984): 85–107.

Beals, Alan R. *Village Life in South India*. Chicago: Aldine, 1974.

Beneria, Lourdes, and Gita Sen. "Accumulation, Reproduction, and Women's Role in Economic Development: Boserup Revisited." *Signs* 7, no. 2 (Winter 1981): 279–98.

Bera, Chaya. *Women and the Left Front Government*. Calcutta: National Book Agency, 1990.

Bertocci, Peter J. "Social Organization and Agricultural Development in Bangladesh." In *Rural Development in Bangladesh and Pakistan*, edited by Robert D. Stevens, Hamza Alavi, and Peter J. Bertocci. Honolulu: University of Hawaii Press, 1976.

Beteille, André. *Studies in Agrarian Social Structure*. New Delhi: Oxford University Press, 1974.

Bhaduri, Amit, Hussain Zillur Rahman, and Ann-Lisbet Arn. "Persistence and Polarisation: A Study in the Dynamics of Agrarian Contradiction." *JPS* 13, no. 3 (April 1986): 82–89.

Bhardwaj, Gopal. "Socio-Political Movements among the Tribes of India." In *Tribal Heritage of India: Ethnicity, Identity and Interaction*, vol. 1, edited by S. C. Dube. New Delhi: Vikas Publishing House, 1977.

"The Bhil Movement in Dhulia." *EPW* 7, nos. 5–7 (Feb. 1972): 205, 207.

Bhowmick, P. K. *The Lodhas of West Bengal: A Socio-Economic Study*. Calcutta: Punthi Pustak, 1963.

———. *Occupational Mobility and Caste Structure in Bengal*. Calcutta: Indian Publications, 1969.

———. *Socio-Cultural Profile of Frontier Bengal*. Calcutta: Punthi Pusthak, 1976.

Biswas, Arabinda, and Nripendra Bandhopadhyaya. "Problems of Labour Enterprise in West Bengal Agriculture." *Social Scientist* 6, nos. 6–7 (Jan.–Feb. 1978): 25–39.

Boggs, Carl, Jr. "Eurocommunism and the State Crisis of Legitimation." *Berkeley Journal of Sociology* 23 (1978–79): 35–81.

———. *Social Movements and Political Power*. Philadelphia: Temple University Press, 1987.

Borthwick, Meredith. *The Changing Role of Women in Bengal, 1849–1905*. Princeton: Princeton University Press, 1984.

Bose, Buddhadeb. "Agrarian Programme of Left Front Government in West Bengal." *EPW* 16, no. 50 (12 Dec. 1981): 2053–60.

Bose, Nirmal Kumar. "Some Aspects of Caste in Bengal." *Journal of American Folklore* 71 (July–Sept. 1958): 397–412.

———. *Tribal Life in India*. New Delhi: National Book Trust of India, 1971.

Boserup, Esther. *Women's Role in Economic Development*. New York: St. Martin's Press, 1970.

Bouton, Marshall. *Agrarian Radicalism in South India*. Princeton: Princeton University Press, 1986.

Boyce, James K. *Agrarian Impasse in Bengal: Agricultural Growth in Bangladesh and West Bengal, 1949–1980*. Delhi: Oxford University Press, 1987.

Brass, Paul R. "Political Parties of the Radical Left in South Asian Politics."

In *Radical Politics in South Asia*, edited by Paul R. Brass and Marcus F. Franda. Cambridge, Mass.: MIT Press, 1973.

Breman, Jan. *Patronage and Exploitation: Changing Agrarian Relations in South Gujarat, India*. Berkeley: University of California Press, 1974.

———. *Of Peasants, Migrants, and Paupers*. Delhi: Oxford University Press, 1985.

Broomfield, John. *Elite Conflict in a Plural Society*. Berkeley: University of California Press, 1968.

Burman, Roy B. "Challenges and Responses in Tribal India." In *Social Movements in India*, edited by M. S. A. Rao. New Delhi: Manohar Publishers, 1979.

Byers, T. J. "The Dialectic of India's Green Revolution." *South Asian Review* 5 (Jan. 1972): 99–116.

———. "Mode of Production and Non-European Pre-Colonial Societies." *JPS* 12, nos. 2–3 (Jan.–April 1985): 1–18.

Cain, Mead, Syeda Rokeya Khanam, and Shamsun Nahar. "Class, Patriarchy and Women's Work in Bangladesh." *Population and Development Review* 5, no. 3 (Sept. 1979): 405–38.

Calman, Leslie. *Protest in Democratic India: Authority's Response to Challenge*. Boulder: Westview Press, 1985.

———. *Toward Empowerment: Women and Movement Politics in India*. Forthcoming.

Caplan, Patricia. *Class and Gender in India: Women and Their Organizations in a South Indian City*. London: Tavistock Publications, 1985.

Carden, Maren Lockwood. "The Proliferation of a Social Movement: Ideology and Individual Incentive in the Contemporary Feminist Movement." *Research in Social Movements, Conflicts, and Change* 1 (1978): 179–96.

Carter, Anthony T. *Elite Politics in Rural India*. Cambridge: Cambridge University Press, 1974.

Ceccareli, Paolo. "Local Government Control and European Communist Parties." In *Political Power and Social Theory*, vol. 3, edited by Maurice Zeitlin. Greenwich, Conn.: Jai Press, 1982.

Cerny, Philip G. *The Changing Architecture of Politics: Structure, Agency and the Future of the State*. London: Sage Publications, 1990.

Chakraborty, Usha. *Condition of Bengali Women around the Second Half of the Nineteenth Century*. Calcutta: Bardhan Press, 1963.

Chakravarty, Renu. *Communists in Indian Women's Movement, 1940–1950*. New Delhi: People's Publishing House, 1980.

Chaney, Elsa M. *Supermadre: Women and Politics in Latin America*. Austin: University of Texas Press, 1979.

Charlesworth, Neil. "The 'Middle Peasant Thesis' and the Roots of Rural Agitation in India, 1914–1947." *JPS* 7, no. 3 (April 1980): 259–80.

Chatterjee, Atreyi. "Landless Agricultural Women Workers: A Statistical Profile." *Indian Farming* 25 (Nov. 1975): 31–33.

Chatterjee, Partha. "Caste and Politics in West Bengal." In *Land, Caste, and Politics in Indian States*, edited by Gail Omvedt. Delhi: Smt. Pushpa, Authors' Guild Publications, 1982.

———. *Bengal, 1920–1947*. Calcutta: K. P. Bagchi, 1984.

Chattopadhyaya, Gouranjan. *Ranjana: A Village in West Bengal*. Calcutta: Bookland Private Limited, 1963.

Chattopadhyaya, Paresh. "On the Question of the Mode of Production in Indian Agriculture: A Preliminary Note." *EPW* 7, no. 13 (25 March 1972): A39–A46.

Chaudhuri, B. B. "Agricultural Production in Bengal, 1850–1900: Coexistence of Decline and Growth." *Bengal Past and Present* 88 (July–Dec. 1969): 152–206.

Choudhury, Roy P. "Land Reforms: Promise and Fulfillment." *EPW* 15, no. 51 (20 December 1980): 2171–73.

Chowdhuri, Satyabrata. *Leftist Movements in India*. Calcutta: Rabindra Bharati University, 1976.

Cleaver, Harry. "Internationalization of Capital and Mode of Production in Agriculture." *EPW* 11, no. 13 (27 March 1976): A2–A16.

Cohen, Jean. "Strategy or Identity: New Theoretical Paradigms and Contemporary Social Movements." *Social Research* 52, no. 4 (Winter 1985): 663–716.

Communist Party of India (Marxist). *Documents of the Eleventh Congress of the CPI(M), Vijaywada, January 26–31, 1982*. New Delhi: Desraj Chadha, 1982.

Connell, John, Biplab Dasgupta, Roy Lashley, and Michael Lipton. *Migration from Rural Areas: The Evidence from Village Studies*. Delhi: Oxford University Press, 1976.

Cooper, Adrienne. "Sharecroppers and Landlords in Bengal, 1930–1950: The Dependency Web and Its Implications." *JPS* 10, nos. 2–3 (Jan.–April 1983): 227–55.

———. "When Peasant Women Arose." *Manushi* (July–Aug. 1979): 47–50.

Croll, Elisabeth. *Feminism and Socialism in China*. London: Routledge and Kegan Paul, 1978.

Dandekar, V. M. "Integration of Women in Economic Development." *EPW* 17, no. 44 (30 Oct. 1983): 1782–86.

Das, Narendra Nath. *History of Midnapur, Part II*. Calcutta: Midnapur Sanskriti Parishad, 1962.

Dasgupta, Biplab. "A Typology of Village Socio-Economic Systems from Indian Studies." *EPW* 10, nos. 33–35 (Aug. 1975): 1395–1414.

———. *Village Society and Labour Use*. New Delhi: Oxford University Press, 1977.
———. *Village Studies in the Third World*. New Delhi: Hindustan Publishing Co., 1978.
Dasgupta, Swapan. "Adivasi Politics in Midnapur, 1760–1924." In *Subaltern Studies IV: Writings on South Asian History and Society*, edited by Ranajit Guha. Delhi: Oxford University Press, 1985.
Davin, Delia. *Woman-Work: Women and the Party in Revolutionary China*. New York: Oxford University Press, 1976.
Davis, Marvin. "A Philosophy of Hindu Rank from Rural West Bengal." *Journal of Asian Studies* 36, no. 1 (Nov. 1976): 5–24.
———. *Rank and Rivalry: The Politics of Inequality in Rural West Bengal*. Cambridge: Cambridge University Press, 1983.
De, Nitish R. "India's Agrarian Situation: Some Aspects of the Changing Context." In *Agrarian Relations in India*, edited by Arvind H. Das and V. Nilakant. New Delhi: Manohar Books, 1979.
Deal, Douglas. "Peasant Revolts and Resistance in the Modern World: A Comparative View." *Journal of Contemporary Asia* 5, no. 4 (1975): 414–43.
Deere, Carmen Diana. "Rural Women's Subsistence Production in the Capitalist Periphery." *Review of Radical Political Economics* 8, no. 1 (Spring 1976): 9–17.
Desai, A. R., ed. *Peasant Struggles in India*. Delhi: Oxford University Press, 1979.
Dhanagare, D. N. *Peasant Movements in India, 1920–1950*. Delhi: Oxford University Press, 1983.
Doshi, Shambu Lal. *Bhils: Between Societal Awareness and Cultural Synthesis*. New Delhi: Sterling Publishers, 1971.
Dube, S. C., ed. *Tribal Heritage of India*. Vol. 1, *Ethnicity, Identity, and Interaction*. New Delhi: Vikas Publishing House, 1977.
Dutt, Nripendra K. *Origins and Growth of Caste in India*. Vol. 2. Calcutta: Firma K. L. Mukhapadhyay, 1965.
Erskine, K. D. *Rajputana Gazetteers*. Vol. 11A. Ajmer: Scottish Mission Industries, 1908.
Esping-Andersen, Gosta. *Politics against Markets*. Princeton: Princeton University Press, 1985.
Forbes, Geraldine. "Goddesses or Rebels: The Women Revolutionaries of Bengal." In *Bengal in the Nineteenth and Twentieth Centuries*, edited by John R. McLane, Jr. Ann Arbor: University of Michigan Press, 1975.
———. "Votes for Women: The Demand for Women's Franchise in India." In *Symbols of Power: Studies on the Political Status of Women in India*, vol. 1, edited by Vina Mazumdar. Bombay: Allied Publishers, 1979.

Franda, Marcus F. *Political Development and Political Decay in Bengal.* Calcutta: Firma K. L. Mukhopadhyay, 1971.

———. *Radical Politics in West Bengal.* Cambridge, Mass.: MIT Press, 1971.

———. "Radical Politics in West Bengal." In *Radical Politics in South Asia,* edited by Paul R. Brass and Marcus F. Franda. Cambridge, Mass.: MIT Press, 1973.

Frank, André Gunder. "On 'Feudal' Modes, Models, and Methods of Escaping Capitalist Reality." *EPW* 8, no. 1 (6 Jan. 1973): 36–37.

Frankel, Francine. *India's Green Revolution.* Princeton: Princeton University Press, 1971.

———. *India's Political Economy, 1947–1977: The Gradual Revolution.* Princeton: Princeton University Press, 1978.

Freeman, Jo. *The Politics of Women's Liberation.* New York: McKay, 1975.

———. "The Women's Liberation Movement: Its Origins, Structure, Activities, and Ideas." In *Women: A Feminist Perspective,* edited by Jo Freeman. Mountain View, Calif.: Mayfield Publishing Co., 1974.

Fruzzetti, Lina M. *The Gift of a Virgin: Women, Marriage, and Ritual in Bengali Society.* New Brunswick, N. J.: Rutgers University Press, 1982.

———. "Seed and Earth: A Cultural Analysis of Kinship in a Bengali Town." *Contributions to Indian Sociology* 10, no. 1 (Jan.–June 1976): 97–133.

Fruzzetti, Lina M., and Akos Östör. *Kinship and Ritual in Bengal.* New Delhi: South Asian Publishers, 1984.

Fruzzetti, Lina, Akos Östör, and Steve Barnett. "The Cultural Construction of the Person in Bengal and Tamil Nadu." *Contributions to Indian Sociology* 10, no. 1 (Jan.–June 1976): 157–82.

Fuchs, Stephen. *Rebellious Prophets: A Study of Messianic Movements in Indian Religions.* Bombay: Asia Publishing House, 1965.

Ganguly, Bangendu. "Profile of Women in West Bengal." In *Symbols of Power: Studies on the Political Status of Women in India,* vol. 1, edited by Vina Mazumdar. Bombay: Allied Publishers, 1979.

Gatwood, Lynn E. *Devi and the Spouse Goddess: Women, Sexuality, and Marriage in India.* Riverdale, Md.: The Riverdale Company, 1985.

Gerlach, L. P., and V. H. Hines. *People, Power, Change: Movements of Social Transformation.* Indianapolis: Bobbs-Merrill, 1970.

Ghose, Sankar. *Political Ideas and Movements in India.* Bombay: Allied Publishers, 1975.

Ghosh, Shankar. *The Disinherited State: A Study of West Bengal, 1967–70.* Bombay: Orient Longman, 1971.

Gilmartin, Christina. "Early Women Communists in China." In *Promissory Notes: Women in the Transition to Socialism,* edited by Sonia Kruks, Rayna Rapp, and Marilyn Young. New York: Monthly Review Press, 1989.

Gold, Ann Grodzins. *Fruitful Journeys: The Ways of Rajasthani Pilgrims*. Berkeley: University of California Press, 1988.

Goody, Jack, and S. J. Tambiah. *Bridewealth and Dowry*. Cambridge: Cambridge University Press, 1973.

Gornick, Vivian. *The Romance of American Communism*. New York: Basic Books, 1977.

Gough, Kathleen. "Indian Peasant Uprisings." *EPW* 9, nos. 32–34 (Aug. 1974): 1391–1412.

———. "Peasant Resistance and Revolt in South India." *Pacific Affairs* 41, no. 4 (Winter 1968–69): 526–44.

Griffin, Keith. *The Political Economy of Agrarian Change: An Essay on the Green Revolution*. Cambridge: Harvard University Press, 1974.

Guha, Ramachandra. *The Unquiet Woods: Ecological Change and Peasant Resistance in the Himalayas*. Delhi: Oxford University Press, 1989.

Guha, Ranajit. *Elementary Aspects of Peasant Insurgency in Colonial India*. Delhi: Oxford University Press, 1983.

———. "The Prose of Counter-Insurgency." In *Subaltern Studies III: Writings on South Asian History and Society*, edited by Ranajit Guha. Delhi: Oxford University Press, 1983.

Gulati, Leela. "Female Work Participation: A Study of Inter-State Differences." *EPW* 10, nos. 1–2 (11 Jan. 1975): 35–42.

———. "Occupational Distribution of Working Women: An Interstate Comparison." *EPW* 10, no. 43 (25 Oct. 1975): 1692–1704.

Gupta, Bhabani Sen. *Communism in Indian Politics*. New York: Columbia University Press, 1972.

———. *The CPI(M): Promises, Prospects, Problems*. New Delhi: Young Asia Publications, 1979.

Habermas, Jürgen. "New Social Movements." *Telos* 49 (Fall 1981): 33–37.

Hardiman, David. *The Coming of the Devi: Adivasi Assertion in Western India*. Delhi: Oxford University Press, 1987.

———. "The Crisis of the Lesser Patidars: Peasant Agitations in Gujarat, District Gajosat, 1917–1934." In *Congress and the Raj: Facets of Indian Struggle, 1917–1947*, edited by D. A. Low. London: Heinemann, 1977.

Harris, Barbara. "Paddy Milling: Problems in Policy and the Choice of Technology." In *Green Revolution? Technology and Change in Rice-growing Areas of Tamil Nadu and Sri Lanka*, edited by B. H. Farmer. London: Macmillan Press, 1977.

Harris, John. *Capitalism and Peasant Farming: Agrarian Structure and Ideology in Northern Tamil Nadu*. Bombay: Oxford University Press, 1982.

Hauswirth, Frieda. *Purdah: The Status of Indian Women*. New York: Vanguard Press, 1932.

Hellman, Judith Adler. *Journeys among Women: Feminism in Five Italian Cities*. New York: Oxford University Press, 1987.

Henningham, Stephen. "Autonomy and Organisation: Harijan and Adivasi Protest Movements." *EPW* 16, no. 27 (4 July 1981): 1153–56.

Herring, Ronald. "Dilemmas of Agrarian Communism: Peasant Differentiation, Sectoral, and Village Politics." *Third World Quarterly* 11, no. 1 (Jan. 1989): 89–115.

———. *Land to the Tiller: The Political Economy of Agrarian Reform in South Asia*. New Haven: Yale University Press, 1983.

Hobsbawm, Eric J. *Primitive Rebels*. New York: W. W. Norton, 1959.

Hunter, Allen. "Post-Marxism and the New Social Movements." *Theory and Society* 17 (1988): 885–900.

Inden, Ronald B., and Ralph W. Nicholas. *Kinship in Bengali Culture*. Chicago: University of Chicago Press, 1977.

———. *Marriage and Rank in Bengali Culture: A History of Caste and Clan in Middle Period Bengal*. Berkeley: University of California Press, 1976.

Islam, M. Mufakharul. *Bengal Agriculture, 1920–1946: A Quantitative Study*. Cambridge: Cambridge University Press, 1978.

M. H. J., "Who Pays and Who Gains From EGS?" *EPW* 17, no. 31 (31 July 1982): 1226–28.

Jacobson, Doranne, and Susan S. Wadley. *Women in India: Two Perspectives*. Columbia, Mo.: South Asia Books, 1977.

Jain, Devaki. "The Household Trap: Report on a Field Survey of Female Activity Patterns." In *The Tyranny of the Household: Investigative Essays on Women's Work*, edited by Devaki Jain and Nirmala Banerjee. Delhi: Shakti Books, 1985.

Jannuzi, Tomasson F., and James T. Peach. *The Agrarian Structure of Bangladesh: An Impediment to Development*. Boulder: Westview Press, 1980.

Jay, Edward. "Revitalization Movements in Tribal India." In *Aspects of Religion in Indian Society*, edited by L. P. Vidyarthi. Meerut: Kedar Nath and Ram Nath, 1962.

Jeffery, Patricia. *Frogs in a Well: Indian Women and Purdah*. London: Zed Press, 1979.

Jenkins, Craig. "Resource Mobilization Theory and the Study of Social Movements." *American Review of Sociology* 9 (1983): 527–53.

Johnson, Kay Ann. *Women, the Family, and Peasant Revolution in China*. Chicago: University of Chicago Press, 1983.

Joshi, P. C. "Agrarian Social Structure and Social Change." *Sankhya: The Indian Journal of Statistics* 21, series B, (Dec. 1969): 29–39.

Joshi, Rama, and Joanna Liddle. *Daughters of Independence: Gender, Class, and Caste in India*. London: Zed Books, 1986.

Kamat, A. R. "Politico-Economic Developments in Maharashtra: A Review of the Post-Independence Period." *EPW* 15, no. 40 (4 Oct. 1980): 1669–78.

Kannabiran, Vasantha, and K. Lalitha. "That Magic Time: The Women in the Telengana People's Struggle." In *Recasting Women*, edited by Kumkum Sanghari and Sudesh Vaid. New Delhi: Kali for Women, 1989.

Kannan, K. P. *Of Rural Proletarian Struggles: Mobilisation and Organisation of Rural Workers in Southwest India*. Delhi: Oxford University Press, 1988.

Kaplan, Temma. "Female Consciousness and Collective Action: The Case of Barcelona, 1910–1918." *Signs* 7, no. 31 (Spring 1982): 545–66.

Katzenstein, Mary Fainsod, and Carol McClurg Mueller, eds. *The Women's Movement of the United States and Western Europe*. Philadelphia: Temple University Press, 1987.

Kemp, Susan. "How Women's Work is Perceived: Hunger or Humiliation?" In *The Changing Division of Labor in South Asia*, edited by James Warner Bjorkman. Riverdale, Md.: The Riverdale Company Publishers, 1986.

Kheer, Dhanajya. *Dr. Ambedkar: Life and Mission*. Bombay: Popular Prakashan, 1974.

Kinsley, David R. *Hindu Goddesses: Visions of the Divine Feminine in the Hindu Religious Tradition*. Berkeley: University of California Press, 1988.

Kishwar, Madhu. "Challenging the Denial of Land Rights to Women." *Manushi* 3, no. 1 (Nov.–Dec. 1982): 2–10.

———. "Nature of Women's Mobilisation in Rural India: An Exploratory Essay." *EPW* 23, nos. 52 and 53 (Dec. 1988): 2754–63.

Kishwar, Madhu, and Ruth Vanita. *In Search of Answers*. London: Zed Press, 1984.

Kitschelt, Herbert. "New Social Movements in West Germany and the United States." *Political Power and Social Theory* 5 (1985): 273–324.

Klandermans, Bert, Hanspeter Krieser, and Sidney Tarrow. *From Structure to Action: Comparing Social Movement Research across Cultures*. Greenwich, Conn.: JAI Press, 1988.

Klass, Morton. *Caste: The Emergence of the South Asian Social System*. Philadelphia: Institute for the Study of Human Issues, 1980.

Kochanek, Stanley. "Regulation and Liberalization Theology in India." *Asian Survey* 25, no. 12 (Dec. 1986): 1284–1308.

Kohli, Atul. "From Elite Activism to Democratic Consolidation: The Rise of Reform Communism in West Bengal." In *Dominance and State Power in India: Decline of a Social Order*, vol. 2, edited by Francine Frankel and M. S. A. Rao. Delhi: Oxford University Press, 1990.

———. "Politics of Economic Liberalization in India." *World Development* 17 (March 1989): 305–28.

———. *The State and Poverty in India: The Politics of Reform*. Cambridge: Cambridge University Press, 1987.

Konar, Harekrishna. *Agrarian Problems of India*. Calcutta: Ganashakti Publishers, 1977.

Kosambi, D. D. *Myth and Reality: Studies in the Formation of Indian Culture*. Bombay: Popular Prakashan, 1962.

Kothari, Rajni. "Grass-Roots Movements: The Search for Alternatives." *Illustrated Weekly*, 29 April 1984.

———. *State against Democracy: The Search for Humane Government*. New Delhi: Ajanta, 1988.

———. "Towards Intervention." *Seminar*, no. 269, annual number (January 1982): 22–27.

———. "Will the State Wither Away?" *Illustrated Weekly*, 8 July 1984.

Krishnamurthy, Sunanda. "Wage Differentials in Agriculture by Caste, Sex, and Operations." *EPW* 23, no. 50 (10 Dec. 1988): 2651–57.

Kruks, Sonia, Rayna Rapp, and Marilyn Young, eds. *Promissory Notes: Women in the Transition to Socialism*. New York: Monthly Review Press, 1989.

Kuhn, Annette, and Ann Marie Wolpe, eds. *Feminism and Materialism: Women and Modes of Production*. London: Routlege and Kegan Paul, 1978.

Kulkarni, S. D. "Adivasi Sub-Plan: A Mid-Term Appraisal." *EPW* 12, no. 3 (15 January 1977): 43–45.

———. "Alienation of Adivasis' Lands: Government Not Serious." *EPW* 9, no. 35 (31 August 1974): 1469–71.

———. "Caste and Class in a Tribal Movement." *Indian Cultural Quarterly* 34, no. 3 (1979): 22–30.

———. "Encroachments on Forest Lands: The Experience of Maharashtra." *EPW* 14, no. 45 (10 November 1979): 1846–49.

———. "Land Problems of the Adivasis." *New Quest* 10 (July–Aug. 1978): 286–90.

———. "Law and the Adivasis: Story of the Peasants of Akkalkuwa." *EPW* 10, nos. 25–26 (21–28 June 1975): 973–76.

———. "Over a Century of Tyranny." *EPW* 9, no. 10 (9 March 1974): 389–92.

———. "Problems of Tribal Development in Maharashtra." *EPW* 15, no. 38 (20 September 1980): 1598–1600.

Kumar, Ravinder. "The Rise of Rich Peasants in Western India." In *Soundings in Modern South Asian History*, edited by D. A. Low. Berkeley: University of California Press, 1968.

———. *Western India in the Nineteenth Century: A Study in the Social History of Maharashtra*. London: Routledge and Kegan Paul, 1968.

Kynch, Jocelyn, and Amartya Sen. "Indian Women: Well-Being and Survival." *Cambridge Journal of Economics* 7, nos. 3–4 (Sept.–Dec. 1983): 363–80.

Laclau, Ernesto, and Chantal Mouffe. *Hegemony and Socialist Strategy: Towards a Radical Democratic Politics*. London: Verso, 1985.

Lang, Peter. "The PCI at the Local Level: A Study of Strategic Performance." In *Communism in Italy and France*, edited by D. L. M. Blackmer and S. Tarrow. Princeton: Princeton University Press, 1975.

Lannoy, Richard. *The Speaking Tree*. London: Oxford University Press, 1971.

Laushey, David. *Bengal Terrorism and the Marxist Left: Aspects of Regional Nationalism in India, 1904–1942*. Calcutta: Firma Mukhopadhyay, 1975.

Lele, Jayanta. *Elite Pluralism and Class Rule: Political Development in Maharashtra*. Bombay: Popular Prakashan, 1982.

Lenin, V. I. "Preliminary Draft Theses on the Agrarian Question." In *Collected Works*, vol. 31. Moscow: Progress Publishers, 1966.

Lieten, Kristoffer. "Caste and Class in Politics." *EPW* 14, nos. 7–8 (Feb. 1979): 313–26.

Limaye, Balmohan. "Adivasis in Maharashtra and Their Movements." *Magova* (May 1974): 25–33. Translated from the Marathi. In the files of BUILD Documentation Centre, Bombay.

Ludden, David. "Economic Development and Social Change in Indian Agriculture: A Historical Perspective." In *Power and Poverty, Development and Development Projects in the Third World*, edited by J. Galaty and T. Bruneau. Boulder: Westview Press, 1988.

———. "Productive Power in Agriculture: A Survey of Work on the Local History of British India." In *Agrarian Power and Productivity in South Asia*, edited by Meghnad Desai, Susanne Hoeber Rudolph, and Ashok Rudra. Berkeley: University of California Press, 1984.

Lynch, Owen. *The Politics of Untouchability*. New York: Columbia University Press, 1976.

McCarthy, Florence E. "Bengali Village Women as Mediators of Social Change." *Human Organization* 36, no. 4 (Winter 1977): 363–70.

Majumdar, R. C. *History of Ancient Bengal*. Calcutta: Bharadwaj and Company, 1971.

Marglin, Frédérique Apffel. *Wives of the God King: The Rituals of the Devadasis of Puri*. Delhi: Oxford University Press, 1985.

Marriott, McKim. "The Feast of Love." In *Krishna: Myths, Rites, and Attitudes*, edited by Milton Singer. Chicago: University of Chicago Press, 1968.

Martin, Andrew. "Is Democratic Control of Capitalism Possible? Some Notes towards an Answer." In *Stress and Contradiction in Modern Capitalism*, edited by L. Lindberg et al. Lexington, Mass.: D. C. Heath, 1975.

———. *The Politics of Economic Policy in the United States*. Beverly Hills, Calif.: Sage, 1973.

Matson, Jim. "Class Struggles in Cooperative Development: The Subordination of Labor in the Cooperative Sugar Industry of Maharashtra, India." *Bulletin of Concerned Asian Scholars* 15, no. 3 (July–Aug. 1983): 18–29.

Melucci, Alberto. "The Symbolic Challenge of Contemporary Movements." *Social Research* 52, no. 4 (Winter 1985): 789–816.

Mencher, Joan P. "Change Agents and Villagers: Their Relations and the Role of Class Values." *EPW* 5, nos. 29–31 (July 1970): 1187–97.

———. "Kerala and Madras: A Comparative Study of Ecology and Social Structure." *Ethnology* 5, no. 2 (April 1966): 135–71.

———, ed. *Social Anthropology of Peasantry*. Bombay: Somaiya Publications, 1983.

Menchu, Rigoberta. *I, Rigoberta Menchu: An Indian Woman in Guatemala*. Introduction by Elisabeth Burgos-Debray. Trans. Ann Wright. London: Verso, 1984.

Michels, Robert. *Political Parties: A Sociological Study of the Oligarchical Tendencies of Modern Democracy*. New York: The Free Press, 1962.

Mies, Maria. "Capitalist Development and Subsistence Reproduction: Rural Women in India." *Bulletin of Concerned Asian Scholars* 12, no. 1 (Jan.–March 1980): 2–14.

———. *Patriarchy and Accumulation on a World Scale*. London: Zed Press, 1986.

———. "The Shahada Movement, a Peasant Movement in Maharashtra (India): Its Development and Perspectives." *JPS* 3, no. 4 (July 1976): 472–82.

Migdal, John. *Peasants, Politics, and Revolution: Pressures towards Political and Social Change in the Third World*. Berkeley: University of California Press, 1979.

Milch, Jerome. "The PCF and Local Government: Continuity and Change." In *Communism in Italy and France*, edited by D. L. M. Blackmer and S. Tarrow. Princeton: Princeton University Press, 1975.

Minault, Gail, ed. *The Extended Family: Women and Political Participation in India and Pakistan*. New Delhi: Chanakya Publishers, 1981.

Moffat, Michael. "Untouchables and the Caste System: A Tamil Case Study." *Contributions to Indian Sociology* 9, no. 1 (1975): 111–22.

———. *Untouchables in Contemporary India*. Tucson: University of Arizona Press, 1972.

Molyneux, Maxine. "Socialist Societies: Progress towards Women's Emancipation?" *Monthly Review* 34 (July–Aug. 1982): 56–100.

Moore, Barrington, Jr. *Social Origins of Dictatorship and Democracy: Lord and Peasant in the Making of the Modern World*. Boston: Beacon Press, 1966.

Mukherjee, Kanak. *International Women's Year and Ourselves*. Calcutta: Ekshate, 1976.

Mukherjee, Ramakrishna. *The Dynamics of a Rural Society*. Berlin: Akademie-Verlag, 1957.

———. *Six Villages of Bengal*. Bombay: Popular Prakashan, 1971.

———. *West Bengal Family Structures, 1946–1966*. New Delhi: Macmillan, 1976.

Mukhopadhyaya, Asim. "Operation Bargadar." *EPW* 14, no. 37 (15 Sept. 1979): 1566–67.

Mukhopadhyaya, Rajatsubhra. "The Structure of Stratification in a West Bengal Village." *Bulletin of the Cultural Research Institute* 13, nos. 3–4 (1979): 64–71.

Mukhopadhyay, Tarasish. "The Jajmani Relationship in Rural West Bengal." In *Bengal East and West*, edited by Alexander Lipsky. Michigan: South Asia Occasional Paper no. 13 (1969): 139–49.

Murshid, Ghulam. *Reluctant Debutante: Response of Bengali Women to Modernization, 1849–1905*. Rajshahi: Sahitya Samsad, Rajshahi University, 1983.

Naik, T. B. *The Bhils: A Study*. Delhi: Bharatiya Adimjat Sevak Sangh, 1957.

Nanetti, Raffaella, and Robert Leonard. "Participatory Planning: The PCI's New Approach to Municipal Planning." *European Journal of Political Research* 7, no. 1 (March 1979): 49–65.

Nath, Kamla. "Women in the Working Force in India." *EPW* 3, no. 31 (3 Aug. 1968): 1205–13.

Nath, Y. V. S. *The Bhils of Ratanmal: An Analysis of the Social Structure of a Western Indian Community*. Baroda: Maharaja Sayajirao University of Baroda, 1960.

Newaj, Kheda, and Ashok Rudra. "Agrarian Transformation in a District of West Bengal." *EPW* 10, no. 13 (March 1975): A22–A23.

Nicholas, Ralph W. "Ecology and Village Structure in Deltaic West Bengal." *The Economic Weekly* 15 (July 1963): 1185–96.

———. "Structure of Politics in the Villages of Southern Asia." In *Structure and Change in Indian Society*, edited by Milton Singer and Bernard S. Cohn. Chicago: Aldine Publishers, 1968.

———. "Village Factions and Political Parties in Rural West Bengal." *Journal of Commonwealth Political Studies* 2 (1963): 17–32.

Nossiter, T. J. *Communism in Kerala: A Study in Political Adaptation*. Berkeley: University of California Press, 1982.

O'Hanlon, Rosalind. *Caste, Conflict, and Ideology: Mahatma Jotirao Phule and Low Caste Protest in Nineteenth-Century Western India*. Cambridge: Cambridge University Press, 1985.

Oberschall, Anthony. *Social Conflicts and Social Movements*. Englewood Cliffs, N.J.: Prentice Hall, 1973.

Offe, Claus. "New Social Movements: Challenging the Boundaries of Institutional Politics." *Social Research* 52, no. 4 (Winter 1985): 817–68.

———. *Contradictions of the Welfare State*. Cambridge, Mass.: MIT Press, 1984.

———. *Disorganized Capitalism: Contemporary Transformations of Work and Politics*. Cambridge, Mass.: MIT Press, 1985.
Olofsson, Gunner. "After the Working Class Movement? An Essay on What's 'New' and What's 'Social' in the New Social Movements." *Acta Sociologica* 31, no. 1 (1988): 15–34.
Omvedt, Gail. "Adivasis, Culture, and Modes of Production in India." *Bulletin of Concerned Asian Scholars* 12, no. 1 (Jan.–March 1980): 15–22.
———. "Adivasi Women and Personal Law." *Manushi* 3, no. 4 (Aug.–Sept. 1983): 20–22.
———. "Capitalist Agriculture and Rural Classes in India." *EPW* 16 (Dec. 1981): A136–A159.
———. "Jyotirao Phule and the Ideology of Social Revolution in India." *EPW* 6, no. 37 (11 Sept. 1971): 1969–78.
———. "Revolution and the Rural Proletariat in Contemporary Western India." *Journal of Contemporary Asia* 13, no. 3 (1973): 261–76.
———. *We Will Smash This Prison!* London: Zed Press, 1980.
———. "Wishing Away Class Politics." *EPW* 16, no. 7 (Feb. 1981): 235.
———. "Women and Rural Revolt in India." *JPS* 5, no. 3 (April 1978): 370–413.
———, ed. *Land, Caste, and Politics in Indian States*. Delhi: Smt. Pushpa, Authors' Guild Publications, 1982.
Oomen, T. K. *From Mobilization to Institutionalization: The Dynamics of Agrarian Movement in Twentieth-Century Kerala*. Bombay: Popular Prakashan, 1985.
———. "Green Revolution and Agrarian Conflict." *EPW* 6 (June 1971): A99–A103.
———. *Social Transformation in Rural India: Mobilization and State Intervention*. Delhi: Vikas Publishing House, 1984.
Orenstein, Henry. *Gaon: Conflict and Cohesion in an Indian Village*. Princeton: Princeton University Press, 1965.
Pandit, Nalini. "Caste and Class in Maharashtra." *EPW* 14, nos. 7–8 (Feb. 1979): 425–39.
Panitch, Leo. *Working-Class Politics in Crisis: Essays on Labour and the State*. London: Verso Books, 1986.
Papanek, Hannah. "Purdah: Separate World and Symbolic Shelter." In *Separate Worlds: Studies of Purdah in South Asia*, edited by Gail Minault and Hannah Papanek. New Delhi: Chanakya Publishers, 1982.
Paranjape, P. V. "Kulaks and Adivasis: The Formation of Classes in Maharashtra." *Bulletin of Concerned Asian Scholars* 13, no. 1 (Jan.–March 1981): 3–21.
Parulekar, Godavari. *Adivasi Revolt*. Calcutta: National Book Agency, Private Limited, 1975.

Patel, M. L. *Changing Land Problems of Tribal India*. Bhopal: Progress Publishers, 1974.

Patel, Vibhuti. "Women's Liberation in India." *New Left Review*, no. 153 (Sept.–Oct. 1985): 75–86.

Patil, Sharad. "Dialectics of Caste and Class Conflicts." *EPW* 14, nos. 7–8 (Feb. 1979): 287–97.

———. "Famine Conditions in Maharashtra: A Survey of Sakri Taluka." *EPW* 30, no. 3 (July 1973): 1316–17.

———. "Forest Development or Adivasi Oppression in Maharashtra?" *Social Scientist* 3, no. 3 (Oct. 1974): 51–56.

———. "Government's War on Adivasis." *EPW* 9, no. 43 (26 October 1974): 1808–10.

Patnaik, Utsa. "Capitalist Development in Agriculture." *EPW* 6, no. 39 (25 Sept. 1971): A123–A130.

———. "Class Differentiation within the Peasantry." *EPW* 11, no. 39 (Sept. 25, 1976): A82–A83.

Pendse, Sandeep. "Repression against the Shramik Sangathana." *Magova* (June 1972): 9–12. Translated from the Marathi. In the files of BUILD Documentation Centre, Bombay.

"Physical Attack on Adivasis: Slander Campaign against Shramik Sangathana." *How* (Sept. 1978): 1–2.

Piven, Frances. "The Social Structuring of Protest." *Politics and Society* 6, no. 3 (1976): 297–326.

Piven, Frances Fox, and Richard A. Cloward. "Hidden Protest: The Channelling of Female Innovation and Resistance." *Signs* 4, no. 4 (Summer 1979): 651–69.

———. *Poor People's Movements: Why They Succeed, How They Fail*. New York: Vintage Books, 1977.

Portes, Alejandro, and John Walton. *Urban Latin America: The Political Conditions from Above and Below*. Austin: University of Texas Press, 1962.

Pouchepadass, Jacques. "Peasant Classes in Twentieth-Century Agrarian Movements in India." In *Peasants in History: Essays in Honour of Daniel Thorner*, edited by E. J. Hobsbawm et al. New Delhi: Oxford University Press, 1980.

Przeworski, Adam. "Social Democracy as a Historical Phenomenon." *New Left Review* 122 (Aug.–Sept. 1980): 27–57.

Przeworski, Adam, and John Sprague. *Paper Stones: A History of Electoral Socialism*. Chicago: University of Chicago Press, 1985.

Raghavaiah, V. *Tribal Revolts*. Nellore, Andhra Pradesh: Rashtra Adimajati Sevak Sangh, 1971.

Raghavian, V. R. "Background of Tribal Struggles in India." In *Peasant*

Struggles in India, edited by A. R. Desai. Bombay: Oxford University Press, 1979.
Ranadive, B. T. "Caste, Class, and Property Relations." *EPW* 14 (Feb. 1979): 337–49.
Randall, Margaret. *Sandino's Daughters: Testimonies of Nicaraguan Women in Struggle*. Edited by Linda Yanz. Vancouver and Toronto: New Star Books, 1981.
———. *Women in Cuba Twenty Years Later*. New York: Smyrna Press, 1981.
Ranga, N. G. *Kisans and Communists*. Bombay: Pratibha Publishers, 1949.
Rasul, M. A. *A History of the All-India Kisan Sabha*. Calcutta: National Book Agency, 1974.
Ray, Rajat K. "The Crisis of Bengal Agriculture, 1870–1927—The Dynamics of Immobility." *IESHR* 10, no. 3 (Sept. 1973): 244–79.
———. "*Zamindars* and *Jotedars:* A Study of Rural Politics in Bengal." *Modern Asian Studies* 9, no. 1 (1975): 81–102.
Ray, Rajat K., and Ratna Ray. "The Dynamics of Continuity in Rural Bengal under the British Imperium: A Study of Quasi-Stable Equilibrium in Underdeveloped Societies in a Changing World." *IESHR* 10 no. 2 (June 1973): 103–28.
Raychaudhuri, Tapan. "Norms of Family Life and Personal Morality among the Bengali Hindu Elite, 1600–1850." In *Aspects of Bengali History and Society*, edited by Rachel Van M. Baumer. Honolulu: University Press of Hawaii, 1975.
Rege, Mangesh. "Shahada: January 30 to May 1." *Magova* (June 1972): 4–5. Translated from the Marathi. In the files of BUILD Documentation Centre, Bombay.
"Report of the Seminar on Women and Development, 28–29 January 1979." *Voice of the Oppressed*. Calcutta: Saimcudo, 1979.
Reynolds, Norman, and Pushpa Sundar. "Maharashtra's Employment Guarantee Scheme: A Programme to Emulate?" *EPW* 12, no. 29 (July 1977): 1149–58.
Richards, J. F. and Michelle B. McAlpin. "Cotton Cultivating and Land Clearing in the Bombay Deccan and Karnatak: 1818–1920." In *Global Deforestation and the Nineteenth-Century World Economy*, edited by Richard P. Tucker and J. F. Richards. Durham, N.C.: Duke University Press, Policy Studies, 1983.
Rohner, Ronald P., and Manjusri Chaki-Sircar. *Women and Children in a Bengali Village*. Hanover, N.H.: University Press of New England, 1988.
Rosen, George. *Peasant Society in a Changing Economy: Comparative Development in Southeast Asia and India*. Urbana: University of Illinois Press, 1975.

Rowbotham, Sheila, Lynne Segal, and Hilary Wainwright. *Beyond the Fragments: Feminism and the Making of Socialism*. Boston: Alyson Press, 1981.

Roy, Manisha. *Bengali Women*. Chicago: University of Chicago Press, 1975.

Roy, Ranajit. *The Agony of West Bengal: A Study of Union-State Relations*. Calcutta: New Age Publishers, 1971.

Rubin, Barnett. "Economic Liberalization and the Indian State." *Third World Quarterly*, 7, no. 4 (Oct. 1985): 942–57.

Rudolph, Lloyd, and Susanne Hoeber Rudolph. *In Search of Lakshmi: The Political Economy of the Indian State*. Chicago: University of Chicago Press, 1987.

Rudra, Ashok. "Class Relations in Indian Agriculture—I." *EPW* 13, no. 22 (3 June 1978): 916–23.

———. "In Search of the Capitalist Farmer." *EPW* 5, no. 26 (27 June 1970): A85–A87.

———. "Left Front Government." *EPW* 12, no. 36 (3 Sept. 1977): 1563–65.

———. "One Step Forward, Two Steps Backward." *EPW* 15, nos. 25–26 (20–27 June 1981): A61–A68.

———. "Operation Barga." *Paschim Banger Bargadar*. Calcutta: Kathasilpa, 1981. Translated from the Bengali.

Rudra, Ashok, and Pranab Bardhan. *Agrarian Relations in West Bengal: Results of Two Surveys*. New Delhi: Somaiya Publications, 1983.

Sacchidananda. "Social Structure, Status and Mobility Patterns: The Case of Tribal Women." *Man in India* 58 (Jan.–March 1978): 1–12.

Sargent, Lydia, ed., *Women and Revolution: A Discussion of the Unhappy Marriage of Marxism and Feminism*. Boston: South End Press, 1981.

Sarkar, Sumit. "The Conditions and Nature of Subaltern Militancy." In *Subaltern Studies III: Writings on South Asian History and Society*, edited by Ranajit Guha. Delhi: Oxford University Press, 1984.

Sarkar, Susobhan. *Bengal Renaissance and Other Essays*. New Delhi: People's Publishing House, 1970.

Sarkar, Tanika. "Jitu Santal's Movement in Malda, 1924–1932: A Study in Tribal Protest." In *Subaltern Studies IV: Writings on South Asian History and Society*, edited by Ranajit Guha. Delhi: Oxford University Press, 1985.

Sawant, D., and Ritu Dewan. "Rural Female Labor and Economic Development." *EPW* 14, no. 26 (30 June 1979): 1091–98.

Schain, Martin A. *French Communism and Local Power: Urban Politics and Political Change*. London: Frances Pinter, 1985.

Scott, James. "Hegemony and the Peasantry." *Politics and Society* 7, no. 3 (1977): 267–96.

———. *The Moral Economy of the Peasant*. New Haven: Yale University Press, 1976.

———. "Revolution in the Revolution: Peasants and Commissars." *Theory and Society* 7, nos. 1–2 (1979): 97–134.
———. *Weapons of the Weak*. New Haven: Yale University Press, 1986.
Sen, Amartya. *Resources, Values, and Development*. Cambridge: Harvard University Press, 1984.
Sen, Amartya, and Sunil Sengupta. "Malnutrition of Rural Children and the Sex Bias." *EPW* 18, nos. 19–21 (May 1983): 855–64.
Sen, Bhowani. *Evolution of Agrarian Relations in India*. New Delhi: People's Publishing House, 1962.
Sen, Sunil. *Agrarian Struggle in Bengal, 1946–1947*. New Delhi: People's Publishing House, 1972.
Sengupta, S. "Confusion over Land Reforms: West Bengal Experience." *EPW* 5, no. 26 (June 1970): 1003–4.
Sengupta, Shankar. *A Study of Women in Bengal*. Calcutta: Indian Publications, 1970.
Sharma, Ursula. *Women, Work, and Property in North-West India*. London: Tavistock, 1980.
Shiva, Vandana. *Staying Alive: Women, Ecology, and Survival in India*. London: Zed Press, 1988.
Singh, K. Suresh. "Transformation of Tribal Society: Integration vs. Assimilation." *EPW* 17, no. 34 (21 Aug. 1982): 1376–88.
———, ed. *Tribal Situation in India*. Simla: Indian Institute of Advanced Studies, 1972.
Srinivas, M. N. *Religion and Society among the Coorgs of South India*. London: Asia Publishing House, 1982.
Stacey, Judith. "China's Socialist Revolution, Peasant Families and the Uses of the Past." *Theory and Society* 9, no. 2 (1980): 269–81.
———. *Patriarchy and Socialist Revolution in China*. Berkeley: University of California Press, 1983.
Stein, Burton. *Peasant, Society, and State in Medieval South India*. Delhi: Oxford University Press, 1980.
Stephens, Evelyn P. "Marianismo: The Other Side of Machismo in Latin America." In *Female and Male in Latin America*, edited by Ann Pescatello. Pittsburgh: University of Pittsburgh Press, 1973.
Stephens, John D. *The Transition from Capitalism to Socialism*. Urbana: University of Illinois Press, 1986.
Sundar, Pushpa. "Characteristics of Female Employment: Implications of Research and Policy." *EPW* 16, no. 19 (9 May 1981): 863–71.
Sundarayya, P. *Telengana People's Struggle and Its Lessons*. Calcutta: CPI(M) Publications, 1972.
Swamy, Dalip S. "Differentiation of Peasantry in India." *EPW* 11, no. 50 (11 December 1976): 1933–39.

Tambiah, Stanley. "Bridewealth and Dowry Revisited: The Position of Women in Sub-Saharan Africa and North India," *Current Anthroplogy* 30, no. 4 (Oct. 1989): 413–35.

Tarrow, Sidney. *Democracy and Despair: Protest and Politics in Italy, 1965–1975*. Oxford: Clarendon Press, 1989.

———. *Peasant Communism in Southern Italy*. New York: Yale University Press, 1976.

Taylor, Julie M. *Eva Peron: Myths of a Woman*. Chicago: University of Chicago Press, 1979.

Thapar, Romesh, ed. *Tribe, Caste, and Religion in India*. Delhi: Macmillan, 1977.

Tharamangalam, Joseph. *Agrarian Class Conflict: The Political Mobilization of Agricultural Laborers in Kuttanad, South India*. Vancouver: University of British Columbia Press, 1981.

Thorner, Alice, and Daniel Thorner. *Land and Labour in India*. Bombay: Asia Publishing House, 1962.

Tiersky, Ronald. *Ordinary Stalinism*. London: Allen and Unwin, 1985.

Tilly, Charles. "Social Movements and National Politics." In *State Making and Social Movements: Essays in Theory and History*, edited by Charles Bright and Susan Harding. Ann Arbor: University of Michigan Press, 1984.

Tod, James. *Annals and Antiquities of Rajasthan*. London: Routledge and Kegan Paul, 1970.

Touraine, Alain. *The Return of the Actor: Social Theory in Post-Industrial Society*. Minneapolis: University of Minnesota Press, 1988.

Trivedi, Harsh. *Scheduled Caste Women: Studies in Exploitation*. New Delhi: Concept Publishers, 1976.

Tucker, Richard P., and J. F. Richards. *Global Deforestation and the Nineteenth-Century World Economy*. Durham, N.C.: Duke University Press, 1983.

Turner, Victor. *The Forest of Symbols: Aspects of Ndembu Ritual*. Ithaca: Cornell University Press, 1967.

Unger, Roberto Mangabeira. *False Necessity: Anti-Necessitarian Social Theory in the Service of Radical Democracy*. Part 1 of *Politics: A Work in Constructive Social Theory*. Cambridge: Cambridge University Press, 1987.

Upadhyaya, Ashok. "Class Struggle in Rural Maharashtra: Towards a New Perspective." *JPS* 7, no. 2 (Jan. 1980): 212–34.

Urdang, Stephanie. *And They Still Dance: Women, War, and the Struggle for Change in Mozambique*. New York: Monthly Review Press, 1989.

———. *Fighting Two Colonialisms: Women in Guineau Bissau*. New York: Monthly Review Press, 1979.

Urquhart, Margaret M. *Women of Bengal: A Study of the Hindu Pardanasins of Calcutta*. Calcutta: N.p., 1927.

Van Allen, Judith. "'Aba Riots' or Igbo 'Women's War'?: Ideology, Stratification, and the Invisibility of Women." In *Women in Africa*, edited by Nancy Hafkin and Elizabeth Bay. Stanford: Stanford University Press, 1976.

Van M. Baumer, Rachel, ed. *Aspects of Bengali History and Society*. Honolulu: University of Hawaii Press, 1975.

Van Schendel, Willem. *Peasant Mobility: The Odds of Life in Rural Bangladesh*. New Delhi: Manohar Books, 1982.

Van Schendel, Willem, and Aminul Haque Faraizi. *Rural Labourers in Bengal, 1880–1980*. Rotterdam: Erasmus University, Comparative Asian Studies Program, no. 12, 1984.

Von Fürer-Haimendorf, Christoph. *South Asian Societies*. London: East-West Publications, 1967.

———. *Tribes of India: The Struggle for Survival*. Delhi: Oxford University Press, 1982.

Vyas, V. S. *Agricultural Labour in Four Indian States*. Gujarat: Sardar Vallabhai Vidyapath, 1966.

Wade, Robert. *Village Republics: Economic Conditions for Collective Action in South India*. New York: Cambridge University Press, 1988.

Wadley, Susan. "Women and the Hindu Tradition." *Signs* 3, no. 1 (Autumn 1977): 113–25.

Weber, Thomas. *Hugging the Trees: The Story of the Chipko Movement*. New Delhi: Penguin Books, 1989.

Weiner, Myron. *The Politics of Scarcity, Public Pressure, and Political Response in India*. Chicago: University of Chicago Press, 1962.

West Bengal Committee, Communist Party of India (Marxist). *Significant Six Years of the Left Front Government of West Bengal*. Calcutta: Ganashakti Printers, 1983.

Winters, Jacqueline. "Land in Women's Names—An Experiment in Thanjavur." *Manushi* 44 (Jan.–Feb. 1988): 10.

Wolf, Eric R. *Peasant Wars of the Twentieth Century*. New York: Harper and Row, 1969.

Wolf, Margery. *Women and the Family in Rural Taiwan*. Stanford: Stanford University Press, 1972.

Zagoria, Donald S. "Communism in Asia." *Commentary* 39, no. 2 (Feb. 1965): 53–58.

———. "The Ecology of Peasant Communism in India." *American Political Science Review* 65 (1971): 144–58.

Index

Compositor: Keystone Typesetting, Inc.
Text: Aldus
Display: Aldus
Printer: Edwards Brothers, Inc.
Binder: Edwards Brothers, Inc.